iOS 15 Application Development for Beginners

Learn Swift Programming and Build iPhone Apps with SwiftUI and Xcode 13

Arpit Kulsreshtha

www.bpbonline.com

FIRST EDITION 2022

Copyright © BPB Publications, India

ISBN: 978-93-55511-102

To View Complete
BPB Publications Catalogue
Scan the QR Code:

Dedicated to

Anita Kulsreshtha and *Late Yogesh Kulsreshtha*
*My Parents, Thank You For Continued
Support and Encouragements*

About the Author

Arpit Kulsreshtha has eight Years of experience in Mobile Application Development, Team Lead, and Project Management with a strong focus on Data Structure, Software Architecture, Machine Learning and Artificial Intelligence while working on iOS, Android, Symbian, macOS, tvOS, watchOS apps with Swift, Objective-C, J2ME, C#, Dart, Xamarin, React Native and Flutter technologies.

He has experience in developing Mobile apps for different domains like Business, E - Commerce, Education, Finance, Health & Fitness, Lifestyle, Entertainment, and Medical etc. A Professional with deep knowledge of software architecture, analysis, application integration and development. He is a technical enthusiast, blogger, and avid traveller. Other than reading and writing technical concepts and blogs, he loves to spend time on Quora and other writing groups.

About the Reviewer

Dheeraj Takyar: I am an extrovert person by nature. I have started my career as a ios application developer. Currently I am working as a hybrid application developer over react native and have a 10 years of experience. I like to learn and adopt new things.

Acknowledgement

There are plenty of people who have helped to bring this book to light, I want to thank you for the continued and ongoing support they have given me during the writing of this book

First and foremost, I want to thank my wife, Akanksha Khare, for being a package of inspiration and courage for motivating my writings. Dear Family, Ankit Kulshrestha, Pallavi Raj, Mukesh Khare, Sandhya Khare, Aadya Kulshrestha, Aayush Khare, and Sarthak Khare, thank you for being awesome and part of my life. To all individuals I have had the opportunity to lead, be led by, or work with their mentorship and leadership, I want to say thank you for being a part of my professional journey and learning which plays a vital role in the foundation of this book.

I would like to thank Dheeraj Takyar and Ravi Tailor for their wonderful support and guidance and help during the writing of this book.

Finally, I would like to thank Mr Nrip Jain and the BPB Publications team for giving me this opportunity to write my first book for them.

Preface

Apple iOS app development is a platform to develop mobile applications with Swift language for iPhone, iPad, and iPod devices. Apple recently released its new series of iPhone with version 13 with its new iOS 15 which have updates of new APIs in Core location, SwiftUI, Share Play, and Machine Learning. For years, Apple has used Xcode as their development tool and IDE which includes the iOS SDK, tools, compilers and frameworks that require you to design, develop, and write code for your iOS apps.

In this book, we explained how to set up and install an iOS app development environment and tools which will help you to learn and practice Swift language and further you can use Swift and SwiftUI for iOS apps. We have explained iOS frameworks, such as Core Location and MapKit for GPS with map-enabled applications, AVFoundation Framework for Camera and Media enabled applications, Core Data for local database implementation and Core ML framework for Machine Learning and Artificial Intelligent based applications on iOS platform.

We have also covered the mobile application architecture and patterns which will help you to write code with reusable and clean components that will increase the readability of the overall project. Once, you will be enabled to complete iOS app development then learning to publish and manage apps on the Apple store will help you to make your apps live on the Apple platform.

The primary goal of this book is to provide all necessary information and concepts with hands-on code to make you a complete iOS app developer from where you can learn advanced concepts of the Apple platform to increase your knowledge base. We focus on the essentials and cover the material from basic to advanced manner for you. Over the 15 chapters in this book, you will learn the following:

Chapter 1 Introduces the Apple development IDE with step by step installation and setup of tools while learning about the playground that will enable you to practice Swift code with instant and quick results.

Chapter 2 We discussed the Swift Fundamentals that includes Types, Constants and Variables in Swift, Operators, String and Characters, Collection Types, Control Flow, Conditional Statements, Control Transfer, Functions and Closures. This chapter gives you the initial and strong foundation of Swift language.

Chapter 3 We discussed further Object-oriented concepts in Swift such as Implementation of Classes and Structure. In depth explanation of the role of Properties in Swift classes with the type of methods. We also evaluated the Inheritance, Initialization and deinitialization of classes.

Chapter 4 Introduced protocol-oriented programming that includes the use of protocols and Extensions to add new programming features to classes without changing their actual code. We explained the role and benefits of Error handling in Swift too.

Chapter 5 Explained the UI interface design and development with StoryBoard and UIKit framework that will enable you to learn different UI components, such as tab bar, table view, collection view etc as well as make that design compatible and responsive for every iOS device which supports the latest development SDK.

Chapter 6 Discussed the SwiftUI framework which is a declarative UI framework where you do not need to play with UI interface design and develop the UI with declarative code that takes less time compared to UIKit interface design development.

Chapter 7 Discussed the local database operations with SQLite as well as with Core Data framework which use Object-relational mapping to map data to app business logic in an object-oriented manner and simplify overall experience compared to direct SQLite handling.

Chapter 8 Every iOS app has its container to handle files and cache in iOS. We discussed the App file Manager that makes you develop such a solution via which you will be able to manage file handling properly.

Chapter 9 Discussed the app gestures recognizer provided by Apple as well as the implementation of Custom app gestures.

Chapter 10 Explained the current GPS location tracking with MapKit to track the geographic location of the user and show other location references on the map to visualize in real time.

Chapter 11 AVFoundation framework explained in the light of using multimedia features of camera and photo gallery to use photos and videos in iOS apps.

Chapter 12 Discussed the Artificial Intelligence and Machine Learning techniques such as Computer vision and NLP model training with Create ML framework and those models in the app with Core ML 2 Framework.

Chapter 13 Discussed the communication of iOS apps with server-side components to sync the data with Apple networking classes as well as the Alamofire framework.

Chapter 14 Discussed the App patterns and code Architecture to make your development work more efficient and clean that will enable you to write high end architectural code with reusability and better readability.

Chapter 15 Explained the step by step process to make your complete and bug-free iOS app live on the Apple app store which requires learning App store management as well as understanding App store Review guidelines to better handle rejections.

Code Bundle and Coloured Images

Please follow the link to download the
Code Bundle and the *Coloured Images* of the book:

https://rebrand.ly/17b9bf

The code bundle for the book is also hosted on GitHub at **https://github.com/ bpbpublications/iOS-15-Application-Development-for-Beginners**. In case there's an update to the code, it will be updated on the existing GitHub repository.

We have code bundles from our rich catalogue of books and videos available at **https://github.com/bpbpublications**. Check them out!

Errata

We take immense pride in our work at BPB Publications and follow best practices to ensure the accuracy of our content to provide with an indulging reading experience to our subscribers. Our readers are our mirrors, and we use their inputs to reflect and improve upon human errors, if any, that may have occurred during the publishing processes involved. To let us maintain the quality and help us reach out to any readers who might be having difficulties due to any unforeseen errors, please write to us at :

errata@bpbonline.com

Your support, suggestions and feedbacks are highly appreciated by the BPB Publications' Family.

Piracy

If you come across any illegal copies of our works in any form on the internet, we would be grateful if you would provide us with the location address or website name. Please contact us at **business@bpbonline.com** with a link to the material.

If you are interested in becoming an author

If there is a topic that you have expertise in, and you are interested in either writing or contributing to a book, please visit **www.bpbonline.com**. We have worked with thousands of developers and tech professionals, just like you, to help them share their insights with the global tech community. You can make a general application, apply for a specific hot topic that we are recruiting an author for, or submit your own idea.

Reviews

Please leave a review. Once you have read and used this book, why not leave a review on the site that you purchased it from? Potential readers can then see and use your unbiased opinion to make purchase decisions. We at BPB can understand what you think about our products, and our authors can see your feedback on their book. Thank you!

For more information about BPB, please visit **www.bpbonline.com**.

Table of Contents

1. Getting Started with Xcode 1
    Introduction 1
    Structure 1
    Objectives 2
    Xcode IDE 2
    Download and install Xcode 2
    Xcode user interface 6
        Xcode search navigator 6
        Xcode issue navigator 7
    Configuring Xcode project 7
        Default project setup 8
        Creating and adding new file 9
        Build Storyboard UI 10
        Assistant editor 10
        Utility area 10
    Run and build Xcode iOS project 10
        Simulator 11
        Run app on device 12
    Code with Xcode Playground 13
    Xcode Organizer 15
    Conclusion 15
    Multiple choice questions 16
        Answers 17

2. Swift Fundamentals 19
    Introduction 19
    Structure 19
    Objectives 20
    Swift features 20
    Types, constant, and variable 20
    Swift operators 22

Assignment operator..22

Arithmetic operator 22

Compound assignment operator 22

Comparison operator..23

Ternary conditional operator 23

Nil: Coalescing operator 24

Range operator...25

    Closed range operator...25

    Half open range operator..25

    One sided range...26

Logical operator 26

Logical NOT operator...26

    Logical AND operator...27

    Logical OR operator 27

Strings and characters 28

    String literals...28

        Empty strings..29

        String mutability..29

    Characters 30

        Concating Strings and Characters......................................30

        String interpolation..30

Collection types...31

    Mutability of Collections 31

    Arrays 31

    Sets...32

    Dictionaries..33

Control flow 34

    The for-in loops 34

    The while loops...35

        While 35

        Repeat:while 35

Conditional statements 36

    if:else 36

    Switch 37

Control transfer statements...37

Continue *38*

Break *38*

Fallthrough *39*

Early exit *39*

Functions 39

Defining and calling functions *40*

Parameters and return values *40*

Nested functions *41*

Closures 41

Trailing closures *42*

Autoclosures *43*

Conclusion 43

Multiple choice questions 44

Answers *45*

3. Classes, Struct, and Enumerations **47**

Introduction 47

Structure 47

Objectives 48

Enumerations 48

Recursive enumeration *49*

Structures and classes 49

Comparison of classes and structure *49*

Reference type classes *50*

Identity operator *50*

Properties 51

Stored properties *51*

Computed properties *51*

Read-only computed property *51*

Property observers *52*

Property wrappers *53*

Global and local variables *54*

Type properties *54*

Querying and setting type property *55*

Methods 56
    Instance methods 56
    Type methods 56
Inheritance 57
    Base class 57
    Subclassing 57
    Overriding 58
Initialization 59
    Initializers 59
        Customizing initialization 60
    Deinitialization 60
Conclusion 61
Multiple choice questions 61
    Answers 62

4. Protocols, Extensions, and Error Handling 63
Introduction 63
Structure 63
Objectives 64
Optional chaining 64
    Importance of optional chaining 64
Error handling 65
    Throwing errors 65
        Handling errors 65
Type casting 67
    Checking Types 68
        Downcasting 68
        Casting for Any and AnyObject 69
    Nested Types 69
Extensions 69
    Computed properties 70
    Initializers 70
    Methods 71
    Subscripts 71

Protocols 72

    Property requirement 72

    Method requirement 72

    Initializer requirements 73

        Protocols as Types 74

        Delegations 74

    Protocols inheritance 75

        Class only Protocols 75

Generics 75

    Type parameters 76

    Naming type parameters 76

    Extending a generic type 76

Conclusion 77

Multiple choice questions 77

    Answers 78

5. **TabBar, TableView, and CollectionView** 79

Introduction 79

Structure 79

Objectives 79

Interface builder 80

    Storyboard 80

        View controller scene 81

        Respond to the app-based life-cycle events 85

UI components 88

    Exploring window 89

        How to add the UI control on Storyboard View Controller? 89

        Connect UI element to Swift code 90

        UIControl 90

        UIButton 91

        UILabel 91

        UITextField 92

        UITextView 92

        UISwitch 93

        UIStepper 93

UISegmentController 94

UIPageControl 94

UIProgressView 94

UIPickerView 94

UIDatePicker 94

UIImageView 95

UITabBar 95

UITableView 96

UICollectionView 98

UINavigationController 101

UINavigationBar 102

Conclusion 102

Multiple choice questions 102

Answers 103

6. **User Interface Design with SwiftUI** 105

Introduction 105

Structure 105

Objectives 106

SwiftUI feature 106

Declarative framework 107

View protocol 107

Getting started with SwiftUI 108

SwiftUI elements 109

Previews in Xcode 109

Combining views using stacks 109

Grids with ScrollView 111

Container views 113

Working with Form and Navigation in SwiftUI 116

SwiftUI drawing and animations 118

Drawing custom shapes with path 120

Drawing curved shapes in SwiftUI 121

Animation views 123

Architecture views 124

Presentation views 127

Conclusion 130

Multiple choice questions 130

Answers 131

7. DataBase with SQLite and Core Data 133

Introduction 133

Structure 134

Objectives 134

UserDefaults 134

Property list 135

Reading a plist with Swift 136

Writing data to plist 137

SQLite 138

Working with SQLite in Swift 138

Creating and connecting to database 139

Creating a table 139

Inserting data 141

Reading and retrieving data 142

Deleting data 144

CoreData 145

Difference between SQLite and CoreData 146

CoreData create schema 146

Inserting data 149

Retrieving data 150

Deleting data 151

Conclusion 152

Multiple choice questions 152

Answers 153

8. File Handling in iOS 155

Introduction 155

Structure 155

Objectives 156

File systems in iOS 156

App bundle container 157

Data container *157*

    Document directory...*157*

    Library – application support directory *158*

    Library – cache *158*

    Temp directory *159*

iCloud container *159*

App file manager *159*

  AppFileStatusChecking protocol *159*

Conclusion *173*

Multiple choice questions...*173*

  Answers *174*

9. App Gesture Recognizers in iOS **175**

Introduction..*175*

Structure..*175*

Objectives..*176*

Standard gestures *176*

  Handling UIKit gesture...*176*

    Tap Gesture Recognizer...*178*

    Pinch Gesture Recognizer *179*

    Swipe Gesture Recognizer..*180*

    Pan Gesture Recognizer *181*

    Long Press Gesture Recognizer...*183*

    Rotation Gesture Recognizer...*185*

    Hover Gesture Recognizer..*186*

Implementing a custom gesture recognizer...*187*

  Gesture recognizer state machine *187*

  Handling cancellation...*187*

  Implementing a Discrete Gesture Recognizer *188*

    Touch events *189*

3D touch interactions *192*

  UIPreviewInteraction *192*

Conclusion..*193*

Multiple choice questions...*193*

  Answers *194*

10. **Core Location with MapKit**...195

    Introduction...195

    Structure..195

    Objectives..196

    CLLocationManager..196

        Add location permissions..196

            When in use..196

            Always use 197

    App Location Manager...197

        Setup Location Manager...197

            Activity type..198

            Distance filter 198

            Desired accuracy 198

            Pause location updates 198

            Allow background location...199

            Check location enabled...200

            Start and stop location tracking..201

            Get current user location...202

            Location Manager Delegates 203

            Significant location change 204

    Show current location on map...204

        Location with Google maps...204

        Location with Apple Maps...205

        Convert location into place mark address...206

        Convert a place address to location coordinates 207

            Types of Core Location Errors 208

        Monitoring the user's proximity to geographic regions...............................209

            Handle region notifications 209

    Conclusion..210

    Multiple choice questions...210

        Answers 211

11. **Camera and Photo Library**...213

    Introduction...213

    Structure..213

Objectives..214

App media permissions...214

   Add option to choose camera and gallery 215

      Allow editing...217

      Source types..218

UIIMagePickerController 218

   Working with movies and live photos...219

   UIVideoEditorController 219

Live Photos 221

Implement camera features...221

   Configure a capture session 221

   Setting up a capture session 221

   Display a camera preview 222

   Rear and front facing cameras switching 222

   Capture a photo..223

Conclusion 225

Multiple choice questions..225

   Answers 226

12. Machine Learning with Core ML......................................**227**

Introduction..227

Structure...227

Objectives...228

CoreML...228

   Core ML converters 228

      Save a CoreML model package 229

      Updating a model file to model package 229

   Create ML 230

   MLImageClassifier..231

   MLTextClassifier..231

   MLActionClassifier 232

   MLSoundClassifier..232

   MLActivityClassifier...232

   Improve model's accuracy..232

Vision framework 233

Object detection in still images...233

    Create vision request 234

    Detection results...235

    Best way to use vision framework 235

Natural language framework 235

    Identification of language in text...236

        Tokenizing text 236

        Parts of speech tagging..237

        Named entity recognition...238

Speech framework 239

    Permissions to use speech recognition...239

        Live audio speech recognition...240

Sound analysis 241

    Audio file sound classification 241

Conclusion 242

Multiple choice questions..243

    Answers 244

13. Networking in iOS Apps...**245**

Introduction...245

Structure...245

Objective...246

REST architecture..246

    Information content type 246

    HTTP structure 246

        Request methods..247

        HTTP headers...248

        HTTP body 249

Connection reachability 249

Alamofire 252

    API encoding 252

    URL encoding 253

        Alamofire headers 253

        Alamofire request..253

        Alamofire response handling 254

Alamofire image 254

   Image downloader 255

   Alamofire Network Activity Indicator 256

URLSession 256

  Operation queue 257

   Add operation in operation queue 257

  Types of URL sessions 258

  URLSessionConfiguration 258

   Types of URL session tasks 259

   URLSession delegate 259

   App transport security 261

Conclusion 261

Multiple choice questions 261

  Answers 262

14. Mobile App Patterns and Architectures 263

Introduction 263

Structure 263

Objective 264

Design patterns in iOS 264

  Creational patterns 264

   Prototype pattern 265

   Factory pattern 266

   Abstract Factory pattern 267

   Builder pattern 268

   Singleton Design pattern 269

  Structural patterns 270

   Facade Design 270

 Adapter 272

   Bridge 274

   Decorator 275

  Behavioral patterns 277

   Template pattern 277

   State pattern 279

   Observer pattern 281

   Mediator pattern 282

Iterator pattern 284

Mobile app architecture case studies 285

    CASE - 1 285

        Case 1: Solution discussion 285

    CASE - 2 286

        Case 2: Solution discussion 286

Mobile app architectures 286

    Data layer 288

    Business layer 288

    Presentation layer 288

    Types of mobile app architectures 288

        Model View Controller 289

        Model View Presenter 290

        Model View View-Model 290

        VIPER Clean architecture 291

Redux architecture in iOS 292

    ReSwift in iOS 292

Conclusion 294

Multiple choice questions 295

    Answers 296

15. Publish iOS App on the App Store 297

Introduction 297

Structure 297

Objectives 298

Prepare app for App Store Upload 298

    Prepare build for App Store 300

        Create distribution certificate 300

        Register an app identifier 302

        Create distribution profile 302

        Create app build for App Store 303

Prepare App Store connect for app submission 304

    Users and access 306

    My Apps 307

        Update a new version of app 309

TestFlight...*309*

Internal and external tester groups *310*

   Invite testers *310*

   Test information *312*

   Beta app feedback..*312*

XCode Cloud *313*

Manage Apple review rejections *314*

   iOS human interface design guidelines......................................*314*

   Avoid common app rejection...*315*

      Not enough features *315*

      Incomplete information *315*

      Requesting permissions...*316*

      Crashes and bugs...*316*

      Broken links and placeholder contents *316*

Conclusion *316*

Multiple choice questions...*317*

   Answers *318*

Index **319-329**

CHAPTER 1
Getting Started with Xcode

Introduction

After a big success in Mac computers, Apple shifted their focus to consumer electronic products such as iPod, iPhone, iPad etc. Apple introduced their new products with the success and advancements of iOS (Apple's OS for their consumer electronic products). With the iPhone achieving an even bigger success, in 2008, Apple introduced the App Store for third party apps, which began a new era of app developments. As the consumers started moving from the Mac machines to mobiles, the application development opened a new platform for the business to acquire more consumers that can use apps on the go while they are walking, traveling etc. Apple already had an IDE Xcode which was used by the developers for Mac application development. They have now made upgrades to it and accommodated the iOS app development in the same Xcode. In this chapter, we will start our application development with Xcode and build our first simple sample application which will look like a blank app in a simulator while testing.

Structure

In this chapter, we will cover the following topics:
- Xcode IDE
- Download and Install Xcode

- Xcode User Interface
- Configuring Xcode Project
- Run and Build Xcode iOS Project
- Code with Xcode Playground
- Xcode Organizer

Objectives

After studying this chapter, you will be able to use Xcode IDE for app development, use a simulator to test the developed applications, and create an iOS Project in Xcode IDE.

Xcode IDE

Xcode is an Integrated Development Environment (IDE) which contains the software development tools developed by the Apple Company for developing the applications and software for MacOS, iPhone, iPad, iPod Touch, iWatch, and Apple TV.

Xcode includes the Xcode IDE, Swift, SwiftUI and C/ C++/ Objective-C compilers, Instruments analysis tool, simulators, the latest SDKs, and other hundreds of powerful features. Swift is a programming language that is fast, safe, and modern. SwiftUI is a declarative UI language used for the interactive app user interface.

Technical requirements

To fulfil the learning requirements and coding goals of this book, we will require the following:

- An Apple system such as Mac mini, Macbook, iMac, etc, with MacOS 10.16Big Sur OS version.
- An Apple ID (if you don't have one, this chapter will help you to create an Apple ID).
- Apple iOS device (optional) (if you have one, you can run the apps on the device; otherwise Xcode Simulator will be enough to check how your apps work).

We will start downloading the Xcode IDE for developing iOS applications from the Mac App Store.

Download and install Xcode

Before starting the development of the iOS apps, we need to download and install Xcode; the following are the steps to perform the Xcode installation:

1. Open the Mac App Store.

2. Search for the keyword **Xcode** and press the return key.

3. In **Search Results**, Xcode version 13.0 will appear, click on **Get and Install**.

4. Now, a box will appear which will ask for an Apple ID; if you already have an Apple ID, fill in the mentioned field and it will ask for a password for your Apple account. Refer to *figure 1.1* as follows:

Figure 1.1: Account information

If you don't have Apple ID, you must create a new Apple ID with the help of the following Apple support article:

https://support.apple.com/en-in/HT204316

5. The latest version of Xcode is 13 which includes Swift 5.5, SDKs for iOS 15, iPadOS 15, tvOS 15, watchOS 8, and MacOS Big Sur.

5. Open the Xcode from the App Store. This will install some supported SDK software for some time and will open the Xcode Welcome page, shown in *figure 1.2* as follows:

Figure 1.2: Xcode Welcome Window

No recent projects will be seen if you are launching it for the first time. Click on **Create a new Xcode project** to set up a new project for iOS apps development.

7. Now, you will see a set of new options to choose from, shown in *figure 1.3* as follows:

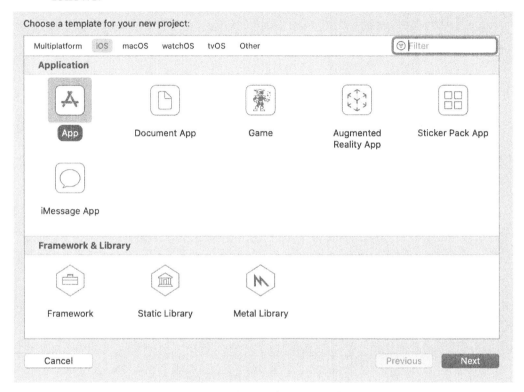

Figure 1.3: *Select Application Platform*

To make an app for iPhone and iPad, select the option as iOS. Similarly, select watchOS, tvOS MacOS, and multi-platform for iWatch, Apple TV, Mac apps, and hybrid apps respectively. Then select **App** and click on **Next**.

8. The next screen will have some fields to fill up regarding the setting up of the project, such as product name, team, organization name, organization identifier, language, and user interface. Let's understand what possible values these fields could have and how it would impact the project, which is going to be created, as follows:

- **Product Name**: This will be the name of your App which will be entered in the text field of the project name.

- **Team**: Apple Developer account of Team for the project. We will discuss this in detail in *Chapter 15: Publish Apps on the App Store*.

- **Organization Name**: The name of your company that owns the development of this project. You can just put your name for now while you learn.

- **Organization Identifier**: This identifier is created with the conjunction of company name. For now, enter **com.organizationname**.

- **Bundle Identifier**: This field is not allowed for you to edit. It's automatically created by combining an organization name with an organization identifier. This identifier is used to identify the apps uniquely on the Apple App Store. Refer to *figure 1.4* as follows:

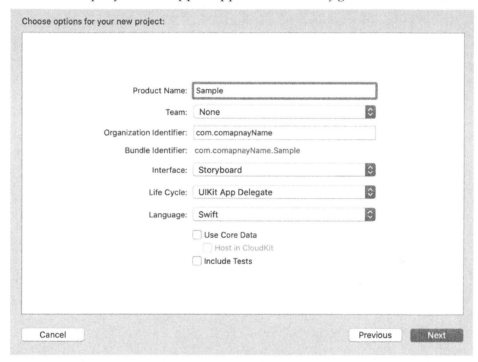

Figure 1.4: New iOS Project

- **Language**: This specifies the programming language to be used in app development. Select **Swift** from the drop box field.

- **User Interface**: For now, set this to Storyboard. We will discuss another type of user interface selection, SwiftUI.

- **Life Cycle**: When you create a new SwiftUI Application in an Xcode, you'd be given an option to choose between **SwiftUI App Lifecycle** and **UIKit App Delegate**. If the user interface is selected as Storyboard, it would be UIKit App Delegate by default.

- **Checkboxes**: These checkboxes are used to include the core data for the purpose of local database, unit test, and the UI unit test cases in the project. Keep them unchecked for now.

9. Choose the location where you want to save this project code in your Mac machine.

Xcode user interface

Before moving further towards app development, we first need to understand the navigation of Xcode, tools, and the options used during the development of the iOS applications. Let's discuss the different sections of Xcode Interface to understand clearly how we will use this IDE during app development, as follows:

- **ToolBar**: This toolbar on the top left side of Xcode is used to build, run the app, and view the execution progress of your app.

- **Windows pan bar**: This will help you configure the Xcode development environment.

   o **Object Library**: Addition or plus button will be used to add UI or object components to the project.

   o **Version Editor**: This will be used to check for differences of codes between two versions.

   o Open and close buttons for Navigator, Debug, and Editor Area in Complete windows pan.

- **Navigator area**: This provides quick access to all the parts of the project. The Navigation area is shown by default in the Xcode window.

- **Editor area**: The Editor area allows you to edit your code, user interface components, and resource files, if required in the project.

- **Inspector area**: This area will allow you to edit the information related to the items in the Navigator area and Editor area.

- **Debug area**: This area contains two portions – one for the view of variables and their values and another one for the console.

Here, we are trying to get familiar with the different parts of Xcode, so don't be overwhelmed by such information on the parts and their relation. We will study all these in detail and use each portion many times in the upcoming chapters.

Xcode search navigator

In the Project Navigator Area, when you click on the **Search** icon, it will open a search navigation bar form where you can search for any text and in the results.

Xcode Editor Navigation area will show all the results of that project containing the text which is searched in the Xcode search navigation bar.

To use it via a shortcut, you can use the command *cmd + shift + F*, which will open the search navigation bar. These command operations would be helpful when you need to search multiple times and be quick. Refer to *figure 1.5* as follows:

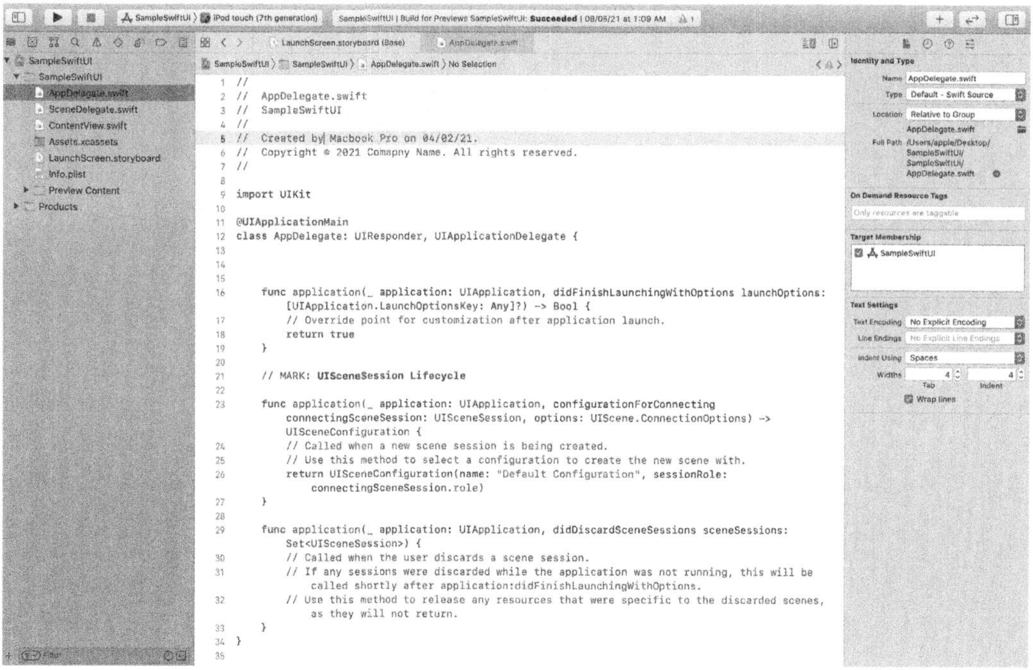

Figure 1.5: *Application Development window*

Xcode issue navigator

When there are some issues in the project while compiling and executing the app, the project navigation area shows warnings in the yellow symbolic icon and errors in red. A project can be built and run with warnings but not with errors. All errors need to be resolved to run a successful app.

Warnings could be potential issues in further development of the apps, so we should not ignore the warnings which are listed down in the issue navigation. Similarly, not only in coding but in the development of user interface, warnings and errors could occur in the same issue navigation.

Configuring Xcode project

The main or root node of the project navigator is the actual project configuration file, which is indicated by a blue icon. In this section, all the fields are already filled with optional content, and you can also edit those fields if required to change any such configurations of the project. Let's look at what we can change here, as follows:

- You can set or change the name of the project.

- Bundle Identifier related information can be edited.

- You can allow and disallow for multiple orientations of the screen for your app.

- Set the minimum required iOS version below which your app can't be installed.

- If required, add additional Apple libraries and frameworks.

- App icon and launch image linkage options can be edited.

Default project setup

When you create an Xcode project, it's created with some default components from which you can start the development of your app. We will discuss the default files and components created by Xcode automatically in the project, as follows:

- **AppDelegate**: **AppDelegate** requires very minimal or no change usually while development. This component initializes the app container and controls the lifecycle of the app which we will discuss and use in detail in the later chapters.

- **SceneDelegate**: **SceneDelegate** is responsible for what needs to be displayed on the app screen in terms of user interface and data. The app transfers some of the app handling responsibilities to the **SceneDelegate**. This will handle some of the app states which were handled in **AppDelegate** earlier to iOS 13, shown in *figure 1.6* as follows:

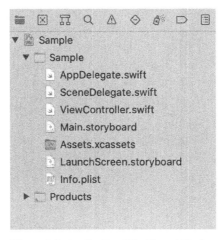

Figure 1.6: *Application File Menu Window*

- **ViewController**: This is a default view controller created by Xcode. We can create a new controller if required and can use the default one too. The **View Controller** class is mainly responsible for the lifecycle and functions of that view.

- **Main.storyboard**: The main storyboard is used for the development of the user interface of the app which we will discuss in detail in the User Interface section of this book.

- **Assets**: This component handles the images of different dimensions, such as 1x, 2x, and 3x. As we know, the same app will be run in different resolution Apple devices like iPhone 13 mini, iPhone 13, iPhone 13 Pro, etc.; therefore, we must give the respective resolution images in 2x and 3x forms, so that in any condition, the images and icons of the app do not get blurred.

  1x is the size (in terms of height and width) of the image component on the interface; so to get the 2x and 3x size information, we need to multiply it by 2 for 2x resolution and 3 for 3x resolution. Every item of a single image in the Assets component has three placeholders for the respective resolutions.

- **Info.plist**: A common property list which contains information about your project is **Info.plist**. Plist extension is used by Apple for file formats like XML type. We will discuss plist in *Chapter 8, File Handling in iOS*. Sometimes you need to add more information to this property list. For example, if your app wants to access a photo library, the app plist needs to contain a key which explains the reason for accessing the photo library.

Creating and adding new file

In the Project Navigator Area, when you right-click, a few options will be shown to you. To create the new code file in the project, you need to select the **Create New File** option, then a new option Pan will ask to choose the file type – as you know, we selected the Project language Swift, so you need to select Swift File type. Next, this will ask you to name the file and after naming it, this swift extension file will be added to your project.

If you want to add any existing file to your project, right-click on the project name and select the option of adding a **New File**. This will open a window for the selection of files from your Mac system. After the selection of a file, don't forget to select the copy option, because without the copy option, it will only create the reference of the file in your project, and when you change the location of the project in your Mac or any other Mac machines, that file will show as missing from the project as it never became a part of your project while adding.

Build Storyboard UI

After we created the new project, earlier in this chapter, and then selected the option of storyboard for the user interface, due to this, Xcode included the **main.storyboard** file. The main storyboard contains the UI screen for **ViewController** on which the user interface components such as labels, buttons, etc., will be placed to inspect or to change their properties as per requirements.

Assistant editor

To open Assistant editor, go to the **Editor** menu and choose **Assistant**. The Assistant editor view shows two pane views in the Xcode window in such a way that its storyboard screen and its relative view controller file can be seen together to edit or work on UI and its code efficiently. This editor will help connect the user interface elements from the storyboard view to the view controller code file, so that those elements can be manipulated via code at the time of execution as per the logic of code.

Utility area

- **File Inspector** is located in the first tab of the Utility area which shows the details about the current highlighted file in the project navigation area. This contains information such as type of file and the physical location of file on the Mac machine, so that you can locate the path of the file.

- **Quick Help Inspector** is located in the second tab of the Utility area, which shows you the documentation about the method, class, and the keyword that your typing cursor is currently on in the code file.

- **Attribute Inspector** and **Size Inspector** will only show as tabs in the Utility area when you select the user interface file's elements in the Storyboard. Using these two inspectors, you can change the properties and size of that selected element. We will further discuss these topics in detail in the *Chapter 5: TabBar, TableView and Collection View*.

Run and build Xcode iOS project

We already discussed some of the buttons in the beginning of this chapter. Now, we will see how these can be used to run and build your app or simulator. Before moving further, let's discuss simulators.

Simulator

In general, we can define a simulator as a machine designed to provide a realistic imitation of the controls and operations of complex systems. In our case, we are developing the apps which will run on iPhone, iPad, and the other Apple devices. It's good to have an Apple device to test, but it is not required to have these, instead the Xcode toolset provides Simulators of all the Apple devices with Xcode which we can choose while running your app, and test the app in almost a similar way as on the real device. Refer to *figure 1.7* as follows:

Figure 1.7: *iOS App in Simulator*

There is a limitation of the simulator, that it won't support the features which can be supported by the mobiles, such as network calling, network messages, Bluetooth communication, etc.

To run your app in the simulator, you need to complete the following steps:

1. Click on the **Scheme** menu in the upper toolbar of Xcode and you will see the list of simulators. Choose **iPhone 13** from the list of simulators.

2. Click on the **Run** button in the same toolbar to run your app in the currently selected simulator. You can also use the *command + R* shortcut on the keyboard for this same function.

3. In case your Developer Tool Access dialog box appears, then you need to enter the username and password of the Mac machine admin account.

4. The simulator application will launch in some time which will replicate the iPhone 13 and then your app will launch in that iPhone simulator.

5. To stop the running of the app again, switch back to Xcode and click on the Stop button in the toolbar to stop your currently running app.

Rather than just running a simple app, you can simulate some other action in the simulator to check the impact of these actions on the real devices. These actions are given as follows:

- **Device Rotation**: If you are developing your app for both the Portrait and the Landscape mode, then you need to check your app by switching to these two modes with the help of the device rotation feature on the simulator.

- **Simulating GPS**: From the menu in the **Debug** option, select **Location**; by choosing a custom location, you can set the latitude and the longitude of any location to test the GPS features with the Simulator.

- **Device Shake**: If you add an action which will happen only if the user of the app will shake the device, then you can test it by selecting the device shake option in the simulator and your code will trigger those actions which are attached to the shaking of the phone.

Run app on device

If you have an Apple device such as iPhone, iPad etc., you can run the developed app from Xcode directly. The step-by-step guide is given as follows:

1. First plug the Apple device into the Mac machine via USB.

2. When you try to run the app after selecting a device in the menu, it will give you an **Error: "Signing for <App Name> requires a development team"**.

3. A valid Apple digital certificate is required to run the app on the Apple devices. You can use either the Apple ID or the Apple developer account to add a team in the section **Signing and Certificates** which will generate the digital certificates.

4. Login with your Apple ID which you used for the Xcode download as well.

5. You will see a dialog box asking to trust this computer on the phone; to continue, click on **Yes**.

6. Xcode will ask you to confirm if you want to use this device for development purposes; to continue, click on **Yes**.

7. Now, you will be able to see your device in the list of devices, above the simulator list.

Almost all the instructions in this book won't require you to have an Apple device to learn and practice on the iOS 15 app development with Swift. Not setting up a device with Xcode will not affect your learning path. If you are not able to set up your device with Xcode (which could have many reasons, such as old device, not active Apple account etc., discussing all these cases here is out of the scope of this book), then please refer to the following Apple support link:

https://developer.apple.com/documentation/Xcode/running_your_app_in_the_simulator_or_on_a_device

Code with Xcode Playground

Playground in Xcode can be used to quickly write the Swift code and experiment on that code to see the results quickly without creating any new Xcode project. It's not a full-fledged project and is not intended for a complete app development; rather it is to practice or experience the Swift code on it. Playgrounds are a great learning, teaching, and practice tool for beginners. Refer to *figure 1.8* as follows:

Figure 1.8: *Choose Playground Template*

To create a new playground setup, go to the menu **File**, **New**, then select **Playground**. This will open the setup of a playground for Swift coding. If you just started the

Xcode, then on the Xcode welcome page, you will find the option to start **Get start with a Playground**. Let's do a quick tour of the Playground functions in Xcode, as follows:

- **Editor**: At the top left of the Playground window, you can write the Swift code in the editor. This is an area where you will do most of the work as coding for practice.

- **Console**: At the bottom left of the Playground window, you will see a console where you can see the output of your code. On the top of the console, there are two buttons from which you can close and open the console area.

- **Output**: When your code runs, you can see your intermediate results on the side output bar. These outputs are faster than the iOS project run results. You can also inspect the values of the variables in your code.

- **Status Bar**: On top of the Playground, you can see a status bar which shows that your code runs ok, or it might contain some errors.

Refer to *figure 1.9* as follows:

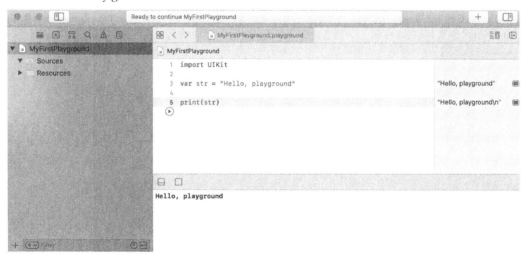

Figure 1.9: Playground Test

Now, run the Swift code in the editor. Click on the button **Run** at the bottom right of the playing area and wait for the execution to finish. Xcode will compile your code and show you the results. The default code doesn't return anything to Console, but you should be able to see the value of the variable on the sidebar to the right of Xcode.

Xcode Organizer

Xcode Organizer is a place which enables supportive components of the Apple software development. There are mainly four components in Xcode Organizer which are explained in detail as follows:

- **Archives**: The Archives section has the list of projects which you developed recently or in the past, and every project has Xcode build the archives with the file format as **xcarchives**. From this **xcarchives** file, you can create a **.ipa** file which is the final executable of the apps for the devices to run. (We will study about app distribution in detail in *Chapter 15: Publish Apps on the App Store.*)

- **Crashes**: Whenever there is any crash in your device for your app, you can just plug in your device via USB and see this section of crashes. This will give a file which includes the crash technical detail, which will help you resolve the crash.

- **Energy**: When your app consumes 80% CPU energy more than three minutes in the foreground mode of the app and one minute in the background mode of the app, then this section shows the energy logs.

- **Metrics**: When you release a build on the App Store, then you can see the app metrics in this section. You need to sign in with the same Apple ID from which you uploaded the app on the App Store.

Conclusion

In this chapter, you learned about downloading and installing the Apple Software development **Integrated Development Environment (IDE)** Xcode. Then, you got familiarized with the different parts of the Xcode user interface. Further, you created your first app iOS with Xcode and learned about it. Some of the key takeaways from this chapter are given as follows:

- While creating a new app, especially, when for the first time you are selecting the Single View app option, you can choose the other options such as master-detail or tab, but it is better to embed these controllers in a single view app.

- Initially, there will be a default file setup given by Apple on the new project creation. You can select the Swift file to code in the editor area, and the main storyboard file to design your app interface.

- We studied about Assistant editors, which can help you when you want to connect your code to the user interface components, so that at run time, you can control the interface actions via code.

- While developing the user interface components, we used the utility area for file inspection as well as for changing the properties and size of the UI elements.

- We studied simulators and their use while testing your developed app.

- We played with the Xcode Playground for development and experimentation of coding in Swift.

Whatever we used in this chapter is just limited to the introductory purposes and will be used again and again in the upcoming chapters in detail. For example, when we learn any new concept in Swift, we will experience our code on the Playground, rather than on the Xcode project, because initially it's not required. But when we come to the design section, we will start working on a full-fledged iOS project.

In the next chapter, we will start learning the Swift language, the core of all the new Apple Software development and experience it on Xcode Playgrounds.

Multiple choice questions

1. **Xcode Playground is used for _____.**

    a. Performance Analysis

    b. Swift Code Practice

    c. Command line tool

    d. App Building

2. **Which feature can we not test on a Simulator?**

    a. Device Shake

    b. Device Rotation

    c. Network Phone Calling

    d. GPS Simulation

3. **Assets Components used to have _____.**

    a. Font files

    b. Large video files

    c. Swift files

    d. 1x, 2x, and 3x Image files

4. **Attribute Inspector is used _____.**

    a.   To change the size of the UI element.

    b.   To change the properties of the UI element.

    c.   To inspect the file.

    d.   To run the simulator.

5. **Archives is part of which section of Xcode?**

    a.   Simulator

    b.   Xcode Organizer

    c.   Xcode Playground

    d.   Xcode Navigator

Answers

1.   b
2.   c
3.   d
4.   b
5.   b

CHAPTER 2
Swift Fundamentals

Introduction

Swift is a new Apple programming language, which is used in the development of the iOS, macOS, watchOS, and tvOS app. Apple released the Swift language and its supportive resources as an open-source project. With the open-source developments, the Swift language is improving every day.

Structure

In this chapter, we will cover the following topics:

- Swift features
- Types, constant, and variable
- Swift operators
- String and characters
- Collection types
- Control flow
- Conditional statements

- Control transfer statements
- Functions
- Closures

Objectives

In this chapter, you will learn how to use types, variables, and constants in Swift. You will also learn how to code in Swift with a conditional paradigm and how to code with strings and characters. You will then learn how to code with Collection types, Functions, and Closures.

Swift features

As most of the languages, Swift uses variables to store or save the values and refer to the values. Constant values can't be changed when ones are initialized. Swift also provides a mechanism to be *'Optional'* for the variables where it means that if a variable has a value, then it will return, or there isn't a value at all. Optional makes the variable safe to access which will never return you nil. Here, Apple solved the problem of Null Pointer Exception of language Objective C where your code got crashed when it tried to access a pointer with nil value.

Some of the features of the modern language Swift includes the following:

- **Clean syntax**: Syntax of Swift makes the code more readable and cleaner, which helps the developers to program efficiently.

- **Type safe**: Swift is a type-safe language which means the language itself is clear about the types of values. For example, if you require String type values, the language will stop you from passing an int value.

- **Type inference**: When you don't specify the type of a value, Swift uses the Type inference to enable the compiler to detect the type of the value by itself.

Types, constant, and variable

In Swift, we must declare the constant and variables before it gets used in your code structure. Apple provides two keywords, one for each constant and variable. You will use the **let** keyword for constant and **var** keyword for variable. Let's look at the following code:

```
let numberOfCounts = 10
var levelOfGame = 0
```

Let's understand that the code variable **numberOfCounts** has assigned value as **10** with the **let** keyword, which means, we want that value to be unchanged but **levelOfGame** has assigned value **0** with keyword **var**, which means that the value could be changed during further coding.

You can also declare comma separated variables or constants in a single line, as follows:

```
var a = 90, b = 20, c = 178
```

> If a stored value in your code won't change, always declare it as a constant with the let keyword. Use variables only for storing the values that need to be able to change.

You can declare the variables and constants with type annotations to give more clarity about the type of values, shown as follows:

```
var apple, orange, grapes: String
apple = "Apple"


var cube, cone, rhombus: Double
cube = 3.4
```

As we saw in the examples that we declared three variables with the type of String, you can save the string values to these variables. In the next code statements, the variables of type Double were declared where we assigned the double value 3.4 in one of the declared variables.

Swift 5.5 supports the following basic type annotations:

- **Int Or UInt**: This can be used in the form of **Int32** and **Int64**, more specifically for 32- and 64-bit signed Integers; for example, 67, -87.

- **Float**: This represents a 32-bit floating point number and holds only small decimal type values; for example, 9.3, 8.34.

- **Double**: Double is used to represent a 64-bit floating-point number and used when the floating-point values must be very large; for example, 78.908, 98.23445.

- **Bool**: Bool is a type of Boolean value which is either true or false.

- **String**: String is an ordered collection of characters, for example, "Hello World".

- **Character**: This is a single-character string literal, for example, "T".

- **Tuples**: Tuples is used to group multiple values in a single Compound Value.

Swift operators

Operators are special symbols from which you can check, change, and combine the values in Swift. There are mainly three types of Operators terminologies which are as follows:

- **Unary**: Operators operate on a single target, apply prefix just before their target, (**-c**) and postfix just after the target (**x-**).

- **Binary**: Operates on two targets and applied or infixed in between the target.

- **Tinary**: Operates on three targets. Swift only has a single ternary conditional operator, such as (**x ? y : z**).

Assignment operator

Assignment operators initialize and update the value of one from another. Let's understand from the following example (**x = y**), where (**=**) Equal to is the assignment operator:

```
let x = 90
var y = 20
y  = x
```

Arithmetic operator

Swift supports four types of arithmetic operators for the math number types, which are as follows:

- Addition (+)

- Subtraction (-)

- Multiplication (*)

- Division (/)

In Swift, the preceding operators perform their respective math in the programming language. Addition can be applied on the **String** type too as follows:

```
var classString = "My" + "Class" // will print as My Class
```

Compound assignment operator

The compound assignment operator combines the assignment (**=**) with another type of operation such as addition assignment operator (**+=**), as shown in the following example:

```
var x = 5
x  += 3
// Now x value will become 8
```

Comparison operator

Swift language supports the following type of comparison Operators:

- Equal to (**x == y**)
- Not equal to (**x != y**)
- Greater than (**x > y**)
- Less than (**x < y**)
- Greater than or equal to (**x >= y**)
- Less than or equal to (**x <= y**)

Let's look at the following example:

```
let x = "Class"
if x == "Class" {
print("My Class")
} else {
print("I'm sorry \(x), but I don't recognize you")
}
// Prints "My Class", because the name is indeed equal to "Class".
```

You can also compare two tuples if they have the same type. Tuples are formed in (**1, j**) manner where **i** and **j** are values which could have different types from each other. Let's look into this with a code example as follows:

```
(3, "Bird")  < (9, "Animal")
// return TRUE only first element of tuples matched with
// operator less than so Bird and Animal are not checked
(6, "Turtle") == (6, "Turtle")
// return TRUE for the first and second element too.
```

Ternary conditional operator

The ternary conditional operator has three parts as 1. query? 2. answer 1 3. answer 2. In this case, if the query returns true, then this conditional operator returns answer 1, otherwise it returns answer 2. This operator helps remove the small if - else structures, and in place of that, the following can be used:

```
heightCell1 = 50
heightOtherCell = 30
var height = cellIndix == 0 ? heightCell1 : heightOtherCell
```

In the preceding example, we want to set the height different for the cell index 0 and a different height for the others. If we try to write this code with **if:else**, then it will look like the following:

```
heightCell1 = 50
heightOtherCell = 30
var height = 0
If (cellIndix == 0)
{
  height = heightCell1
}
else
{
  height = heightOtherCell
}
```

We can see here that the ternary conditional operator shortens the whole code and makes it more readable and lucid. The overuse of the ternary operator in one combined sentence can make the code hard to read and understand.

Nil: Coalescing operator

To avoid crashes due to the nil values, Swift introduces the Nil:Coalescing operator (**x ?? y**) which can be used with optional values. Apple made this operator to shorten the following ternary operation:

```
x != nil ? x! : y
```

Check the value of **x** to see whether it is nil or not; if **x** has a value, then unwrap the optional **x** and return the **x** value, otherwise return the value of **y**. With the Nil:Coalescing operator, we can simply write the same operation in the following manner:

```
var safeValue = x ?? y
```

If the value of x is non-nil, the value of y is not evaluated. This is called a short-circuit evaluation.

Range operator

Swift uses several different types of range operators, which are shortcuts for expressing a range of values.

Closed range operator

The closed range operators (**x...y**) define a range that runs from **x** to **y**, including the values as well. In this case, the value of **x** must be greater than **y**. The closed range operator is helpful when you want to iterate a loop on all the values of the range given by the following operator:

```
for index in 1...3 {
    print("\(index) times 3 is \(index * 3)")
}
// 1 times 3 is 3
// 2 times 3 is 6
// 3 times 3 is 9
```

Half open range operator

The half-open range operator (**x..< y**) defines a range that runs from **x** to **y**. The reason why it's called half-open range is that here the range contains only the first value but not the last value. In case, the value of **a** is equal to **b**, the resulting range will be empty.

The half-open range operator is useful when you work with a zero-based list; in that case, the range starts from zero and is not required to include the last range point in the loop. Look at the following example:

```
let names = ["Ram", "Ajay", "Vijay", "Rubi"]
let countNumber = names.count
for i in 0..< countNumber {
    print("Person \(i + 1) is called \(names[i])")
}
// Person 1 is called Ram
// Person 2 is called Ajay
// Person 3 is called Vijay
// Person 4 is called Rubi
```

One sided range

The one-sided range operator has some form of the range that continues in one direction; for example, a range that includes all the elements of an array. In such cases, you can leave the value from the one side of the `range` operator. This kind of range is called a one-sided range because this operator has value only on one side. Look at the following example:

```
for name in names[2...] {
    print(name)
}
// Vijay
// Rubi

for name in names[...2] {
    print(name)
}
// Ram
// Ajay
// Vijay
```

The half-open range operator also has one-sided range because that's written only with the final value. Similarly, when you include a value on both sides, the final value is not part of the range.

Logical operator

The logical operator modifies or combines the Boolean logic value (true) and (false). The Swift language supports the following three logical operators:

- Logical NOT (`!x`)
- Logical AND (`x && y`)
- Logical OR (`x || y`)

Logical NOT operator

The logical **NOT** operator inverts the Boolean value. If the value is true after applying, this operator will become false and false will become true.

This **NOT** operator is a prefix operator and appears just before the value on which this is required to apply. It can be read as "**Not x**". Look at the following example:

```
let gateEntry = false
if !gateEntry {
    print("No Access")
}
// No Access
```

Logical AND operator

The logical **AND** operator (**x && y**) makes such expressions where both the values must be true for the whole expression to be true. If both the values are false, then the whole expression is false. More precisely, we can say that if the first value is false, there is no requirement to check for the second value. Look at the following example:

```
let enterCodeToUnlock = true
let fingerPrintToMatch = false
if enterCodeToUnlock && fingerPrintToMatch {
    print("Welcome To Office")
} else {
    print("NO ACCESS")
}
// Prints: NO ACCESS
```

Logical OR operator

The logical **OR** operator (**x || y**) is an infix operator. You can use it to create logical expressions in which only one of the two values has to be true. The logical **OR** operators use the short circuit evaluation for expressions. If the left side of a logical **OR** expression is true, the right side is not evaluated, because it can't change the outcome of the whole expression. Look at the following example:

```
let haveOfficeKey = false
let knowDigitalDoorPassword = true
if hasDoorKey || knowsOverridePassword {
    print("Welcome To Office")
} else {
    print("NO ACCESS")
}
// Output: Welcome To Office
```

Combining logical operators

You can combine multiple logical operators to form longer compound expressions. Look at the following example:

```
if enterCodeToUnlock && fingerPrintToMatch || haveOfficeKey ||
knowDigitalDoorPassword {
    print("Welcome To Office!")
} else {
    print("NO ACCESS")
}
// Output: Welcome To Office!
```

The preceding example uses multiple operators to form a longer compound expression. But as you can see, both the operators operate on only two values, so these are three smaller expressions formed together in a chain.

Suppose you entered the correct door code and passed the fingerprint match, or we have an office key or know the digital password, then you provide the office access, otherwise there is no access.

Swift logical AND && and OR || are left-associative, meaning that the compound expression with multiple logical operators evaluates the leftmost subexpression first.

Strings and characters

While formatting a user language or taking user inputs, you may require to use strings and perform the operations on it to enable the input changes which could reflect in a better way. Further character operations help make the strings even more advanced. We will discuss in detail how we can perform all these changes in the Swift language.

String literals

String literals are used to include a set of characters in the code; for this, you can pass this set in the form of the sentence, words, or just a list of some characters in double quotation marks ("). Let's see the following example:

```
let makeSenetence = "This is an example sentence."
```

Similarly, the multi-line string quotation can be used but that would have a little different syntax to use in Swift. The string begins on the first line after the opening quotation marks (""") and ends on the line before the closing quotation marks, as shown in the following example:

```
let makeSenetence = """This is an example sentence.
As well as multiline example for string lateral
"""
```

Special characters

String literals use the following list of special characters, as shown in *Table 1.1*:

\0	null character
\\	backslash
\t	horizontal tab
\n	line feed
\r	carriage return
\"	double quotation mark
\'	single quotation mark
\u{n}	Unicode char

Table 1.1: *Special Characters*

Empty strings

Empty strings can be initialized to use to assign blank. To do this, assign an empty string literal to a variable, or initialize a new **String** instance with the initializer syntax, as shown in the following example:

```
var empty = "" // Empty String
var initEmpty = String() // initialize String
```

String mutability

The approach of string mutability in Swift is different from Objective C. In objective C, **NSString** and **NSMutableString** are used for the mutable and non-mutable string types respectively. But the Swift string can be modified by assigning it to a variable when you want to modify, and keep it constant, when you don't want to modify. The string which is initialized with var is mutable string and can appended easily but string initialized with let is immutable and will give compile time error in case if you try to append new string in it. Look at the following example:

```
var mutableString = "This String is"
mutableString += "Mutable"
// mutableString Prints "This String is Mutable"
let immutableString = "This String is not"
```

```
immutableString += "Mutable"
// this reports a compile time error
```

Characters

You can get individual **Character** values for a **String** by iterating in the loop over the string with a **for-in** loop or while, as shown in the following example:

```
for character in "CHARACTER" {
    print(character)
}
// Will print every character of string "CHARACTER"
```

Similar to the **String** type, you can initialize a character by providing it to a **Character** type annotation, as shown in the following example:

```
let questionMark : Character = "?"
```

Concating Strings and Characters

The string type of values can be concating with the addition operators, as we studied in the arithmetic operator part that (**+**) addition can be applied to the string literals in a similar way that is used with string values. Look at the following example:

```
let string1 = "Hello"
let string2 = " World"
var firstLine = string1 + string2
// firstLine will print "Hello World"
```

You can append a character to the **string** variable as with the method **append()**, as shown in the following example:

```
var question = "What is the capital of India "
let questionMark : Character = "?"
question.append(questionMark)
// question print as "What is the capital of India ?"
```

String interpolation

The purpose of String interpolation is to construct a completely new **String** via concatenating or mixing variable, constant literals, and expression of string in a single literal. Every item that you insert into the string literal is wrapped with pairs of parentheses, prefixed by a backslash (****), as shown in the following example:

```
let addition = 3
```

```
let sentence = "\(addition) plus 10 is \(addition + 10)"
// sentence is "3 plus 10 is 13"
```

Collection types

Swift introduces some primary collection types which can hold collections of data, known as Array, Set, and Dictionary for storing the data values. Swift's array, Set, and dictionary types are implemented as generic collections. We will study about Generics in later chapters.

Mutability of Collections

In general, it is a good practice to create immutable collections always for the array, Set, and dictionaries. If you do, it will be easier for you to optimize the performance of your collections created by you.

Arrays

An array represents and stores the values of the same type in an ordered list where the same value can be in the list more than one time. In Swift, an array is written as **Array<Element>** where **Element** is the type of that array list. You can create an empty array list of a specific type with the array initializer, as shown in the following example:

```
var listOfString = [String]()
var listOfInt   = [Int]()
```

The method **count()** on the array variables gives you a count of items in the list, so you can check if there are any modifications and changes in the array, as shown in the following example:

```
let countList = "\(listOfString.count) string items"
// countList prints 0 items
```

When you use initialize array and are not sure of the type of array list, you can simply create it by using the blank list without the type information provided, as shown in the following example:

```
var array = []
```

The method of **append()** is used to add a data value to the array list as shown in the following example:

```
listOfInt.append(5)
listOfInt.append(9)
```

```
print("\(listOfString.count) string items") \\ ountList prints 2 items
print(listOfInt) \\ [5, 9]
```

The **remove(at:)** method is used to delete or remove using the index of a data value item from an array list. This operation on the arrays decreases the count and removes the items permanently, as shown in the following example:

```
listOfInt.remove(at: 1) // [5]
```

Deleting an element based on specific search or condition can be applied through closures with **removeAll { where:}**, as shown in the following example:

```
var numbers = [2, 3, 4, 8, 2, 7, 3, 2]
numbers.removeAll {$0 == 2} \\ [3, 4, 8, 7, 3]
```

Similarly, to remove all methods, the **filter()** method works; the difference is, it will return a modified array after the **filter** operation, as shown in the following example:

```
Numbers.filter { $0 != 3 } \\ [4, 8, 7]
```

Sets

A set stores distinct values which are of the same type of collection with no ordering. You can use **set** instead of **Array** if you want distinct values in the collection. The type of set values must be hashable in order to be stored in a set. All of Swift's basic types, such as **String**, **Int**, **Double** and **Bool**, are hashable by default. The syntax of set in Swift is written as **Set<Element>**, where **Element** is the type of elements that is allowed to be stored, as shown in the following example:

```
var characters = Set<Character>()
characters.insert("c")
characters.count()              // Prints: 1
characters = []
characters.count()              // Prints: 0
```

In the preceding example, we created a variable with a set of characters and inserted a new character in the set. A set type cannot be inferred from an array literal, so in such cases, the type **Set** must be explicitly declared. Although, because of Swift's type inference, you don't have to write the type of the set's elements if you are initializing it with an array literal.

You can access and modify a set through its methods and properties provided in Swift. To check whether the set is empty or not, **isEmpty** can be used to check. Similarly, **remove** can be used to remove the value in a set and **contains** can be used to check the existence of the value in a set, as shown in the following example:

```
characters.isEmpty  // returns true or false depending on the set
Elements.
characters.remove("c") // remove a element
characters.contains("c") // to check if set contains a value
```

Dictionaries

In Swift, a dictionary stores the associations between keys of the same type and values of the same type in a collection with no defined ordering. A dictionary key can be either int or string, but it should be unique within the dictionary.

The syntax of the Swift dictionary is written in full as **Dictionary<Key, Value>**, where **Key** is the type of value that is used as a dictionary key and **Value** is the type of value that is used to store the values in a dictionary. As with arrays, you can create an empty dictionary of a certain type by using the following syntax:

```
var friendsName = [Int: String]()
```

You can also initialize a dictionary with its literal, which has a similar syntax to the array literals. A key-value pair is a combination of a key and a value, the key and value in each value pair are separated by a colon. The key-value pairs are written as a list, separated by commas, surrounded by a pair of square brackets, as shown in the following example:

```
[<key 1>: <value 1>, <key 2>: <value 2>, <key 3>: <value 3>]
var roads: [String: String] = ["ABC": "Grand Trunk Road", "BCE":
"Delhi"]
```

This dictionary literal contains two **String:String** pairs. This key value type matches the type of the **roads** variable. You can also access and modify a dictionary via its methods and properties. Similar to array, you can find out the number of items in a **Dictionary** by checking its **count** property, as shown in the following example:

```
print(roads.count)  // prints: 2
```

You can also add a new key-value pair item to a dictionary with the subscript syntax. For this, you can use a new key of the correct type and assign a new value, as shown in the following example:

```
roads ["PVC"] = "MJ Road"
print(roads.count)  // Now prints: 3
```

You can also iterate over the key-value pairs in the dictionary with a **for-in** loop. Each item in the dictionary is returned as a (key, value) tuple, and you can decompose the tuple into constants and variables, as shown in the following example:

```
for (roadsCode, roadsName) in roads {
    print("\(roadsCode): \(roadsName))
}
// "ABC": "Grand Trunk Road"
// "BCE": "Delhi"
```

Control flow

The Swift language has multiple types of control flow statements, which can be used to either iterate or transfer the control of code. The **for-in** loop and **while** loop is used to perform an operation multiple times with the variation of data.

Other such statements like **if-guard**, **switch** execute different branches of code based on conditions, and **break**, **continue** is to transfer the flow execution to another point in code.

The for-in loops

You can use the **for-in** loop to iterate over a sequence, like the items of the array, some range of numbers or list of characters in string sentences. The following example code will iterate the list of the array:

```
let names = ["Ram", "Shaym", "Ajay", "Sunita"]
for name in names {
    print("Hey, \(name)!")
}
// Hello, Ram!
// Hello, Shaym!
// Hello, Ajay!
// Hello, Sunita!
```

You can use **for-in** with a numerical range. The following example will perform this iteration to explain further:

```
for index in 1...4 {
    print("\(index) times 4 is \(index * 4)")
}
// 1 times 4 is 4
// 2 times 4 is 8
// 3 times 5 is 12
// 4 times 5 is 16
```

The preceding sequence iterated over a range of numbers from **1...4**, with the use of a closed range operator (**...**). The value of the index sets the first number as (**1**) and then the statements in the loop start the execution. In this case, here we have only one statement inside the loop to be executed.

The while loops

The **while** loop performs a set of statements until a condition becomes false. These kinds of loops are best used when the number of iterations is not known before the first iteration begins. Swift provides the following two kinds of loops:

- **while** evaluating its condition at the start of each pass through the loop.
- **Repeat:while** evaluating its condition at the end of each pass through the loop.

While

The **while** loop starts by evaluating a single condition. If the condition is true, a set of statements under the loop will execute until the condition becomes false.

The following is the basic form of **while** loop:

```
while <condition> {
    <statements>
}
```

Repeat:while

The **repeat:while** is another variation of the **while** loop, which performs a single pass through the loop block first, before considering the loop conditions. Then, it continues the loop until the condition is false.

The following is the basic form of **repeat:while** loop:

```
repeat {
    <statements>
} while <condition>
```

The **repeat:while** loop in the Swift language is analogous to a **do-while** loop in other languages.

Conditional statements

Sometimes, you need to make parts in your codes which run conditionally. The Swift language provides two ways to add a conditional set of code branches – one is the if statements and other is the switch statements.

If there are more complex structures of code and multiple possible outcomes and a pattern matching that helps select which set of programs will execute, then the `switch` statements will be preferred.

if:else

The `if` statements have only a single `if` condition and it executes a single or multiple set of program statements only if that condition is true, as shown in the following example:

```
var bookprice = 400
if bookprice < 450 {
    print("I can buy this book.")
}
// prints: I can buy this book.
```

In the preceding example, we check if the price of the book is less than **450**, then we print off the statement about the buying decision. If the book price is greater than **450**, it will not print any message as per the given code block.

The `if` statements also provide an alternative way to set the execution of the program statements in case it's false, known as the **else** clause. These statements are indicated by the keyword **else**, as shown in the following example:

```
var bookprice = 500
if bookprice < 450 {
    print("I can buy this book.")
}
else {
    print("I cannot buy this book.")
}
// prints else clause: I cannot buy this book.
```

In such a case, one of the two branches of the code will execute for sure. You can chain multiple **if-else** clause statements to form more complex code execution decision branching, as shown in the following example:

```
var bookprice = 245
```

```
if bookprice > 450 {
    print("I can not buy this book.")
}
else if bookprice < 250 {
    print("It's too cheap, I can easily buy this book.")
}
else {
    print("It's in my budget, I can buy this book.")
}
// prints: It's too cheap, I can easily buy this book.
```

The final **else** in this example can be optional; if not needed, it will be excluded.

Switch

The **switch** statements consider a value to compare against many matching patterns. If it is matched, then it executes the appropriate block of code based on the matched expression. A **switch** statement provides an alternative to the **if:else** complex form of multiple potential states.

The simplest form of a **switch** structure compares a value against one or more values of the same type, as shown in the following example:

```
switch <some value to consider> {
case <value 1>:
    <respond to value 1>
case <value 2>,
     <value 3>:
    <respond to value 2 or 3>
default:
    <otherwise, do something else>
}
```

In this case, each **switch** statement consists of multiple possible cases, and each case starts with the **case** keyword.

Control transfer statements

The control transfer statements can change the order of the execution of your code, by transferring the control from one piece of code to another piece of code. The Swift language provides five control transfer statements, as follows:

- Continue
- Break
- Fallthrough
- Return
- Throw

We will learn, **continue**, **break**, and **fallthrough** in this section, the return statement in the following section of this chapter, and the throwing error handling part in the subsequent chapters.

Continue

The **continue** statement tells a loop that stops whatever is going on, starting again from the beginning of the next iteration through the loop. The following example will explain, if in case we want to skip printing some specific characters from the **English** statement, then **continue** can be used:

```
let inputStatement = "Welcome to this University !"
var outputStatement = ""
let characterRemove: [Character] = ["a", "e", "i", "o", "u", " "]
for character in inputStatement {
    if characterRemove.contains(character) {
        continue
    }
    outputStatement.append(character)
}
print(outputStatement)
// Prints "WlcmtthsUnvrsty!"
```

The given code in the example calls the **continue** keyword when it matches with a vowel or space, in such a way that the current iteration of the loop ends immediately and jumps to the start of the next iteration.

Break

The **break** statement ends the execution of an entire control flow statement. The **break** statements can be used inside the **switch** or loop when you want to terminate that execution. If you use it in any loop, the execution of the loop will completely stop, and the control of the program flow will come out from it.

Fallthrough

In Swift, the **switch** statements do not go to the bottom of each case, which means the entire switch case completes the execution when the first case is matching. Here you won't need to place a break, in the end, to end the execution of the case block. But in case you want to enable that the program flow doesn't stop and fall through in the next block of execution, then you can use the keyword **fallthrough**. The following example uses **fallthrough** to create a statement:

```
let integerToCheck = 5
var sentence = "The number \(integerToCheck) is"
switch integerToDescribe {
    case 2, 3, 5, 7:
        sentence += " a prime number, and also"
        fallthrough
    default:
        sentence += " an integer"
}
print(sentence)
// Prints: The number 5 is a prime number, and also an integer
```

Early exit

In Swift, the guard statement is the same as the **if** statement, executed based on the **bool** value of the expression. The **guard** statements always have an **else** clause, as shown in the following example:

```
var number =: 2
guard number >= 0 else {
    return nil
}
// code block will return nil
```

Functions

In Swift, functions are self-contained blocks of code that perform specific tasks under a specific function name. You can give a unique name to a function, and from that name, the function can be called to perform its task and may return some value in the execution of the program code.

Each function in Swift has a type, which consists of a function's parameter types and return type. You can pass type to functions as parameters to the other functions and return functions from the functions. Functions can be written within the other functions to encapsulate functionality within a nested function scope.

Defining and calling functions

Each function has a function name, which explains the task that the functions perform. You can call this function by its name and pass the input value (if required). These function input values are known as arguments which match the type of the function's parameters, as shown in the following example:

```
func meetToFriends(friendName: String) -> String {
    let meetMessage = "Hey, " + friendName + "!"
    return meetMessage
}
```

The preceding block of code is known as the definition of function, with the prefix of the keyword **func**. In this function block, we indicated the return value with keyword **return** and return type with arrow **-> <type>**. The function definition describes the tasks performed by the function, as shown in the following example:

```
print(meetToFriends(friendName:"Ashok"))
// Prints: Hey, Ashok!
print(meetToFriends(friendName:"Mohan"))
// Prints: Hey, Mohan!
```

Parameters and return values

Function parameters are very flexible in the Swift language. You can define simple string parameters to complex functions with expressive parameter names and different parameter options. There is a possibility of functions with no parameters as well as with multiple parameters. The following is an example of multiple parameters, written in single brackets, separated by commas:

```
func meetToFriends(friendName: String, isGreeted: Bool) -> String {
    if isGreeted {
        return meetAgain(friendName: person)
    } else {
        return meetToFriends(friendName: person)
    }
}
print(meetToFriends(friendName: "Ram", isGreeted: true))
// Prints: Hello again, Ram!
```

Nested functions

All the functions you have come across till now are examples of global functions. The global functions are defined at a global scope. In Swift, you can define functions in the function body – such functions are called nested functions.

By default, the nested functions are hidden in the outside world but can be used by their enclosing function. An enclosing function can also return one of its nested functions to be used in another scope of the program. The basic structure and syntax of the nested functions is given as follows:

```
func funcname() {
    //statements of outer function
    func anotherFuncname() {
        //statements of inner function
    }
}
```

Closures

Closures are self-contained blocks of code or programs which can be passed across and used in your code. Closures can maintain and capture references to any constants and variables from the context in which they are defined. Swift handles all the memory management of capturing the contexts.

Global and nested functions are special cases of closures. Closures usually take one of the following three forms:

- Global functions are closures that have a name but don't capture a value.

- Nested functions are closures that have a name and can capture values for their enclosing function.

- Closure expressions are unnamed closures written in a lightweight syntax that can capture values from their surrounding context.

Closure syntax expression optimizations include the following:

- Inferring parameter and return value types from context

- Implicit returns from single expression closures

- Shorthand arguments name

- Trailing closures syntax

Closure expression

Closure expressions are a way to write inline closures in a brief and focused syntax. Closure expressions provide many syntax optimizations for shorthand form without losing clarity.

The following example of a closure expression uses the **sorted(by:)** method to sort an array of **String** values in the reverse alpha order:

```
let friendsName = ["Suraj", "Vijay", "Pratibha", "Nirav", "Vishal"]
```

Here, one way to provide the sorting closure is to write a normal function of the correct type, and to pass it in as an argument to the **sorted(by:)** method, as shown in the following example:

```
func back(_ s1: String, _ s2: String) -> Bool {
    return s1 > s2
}
var reverseNames = friendsName.sorted(by: back)
// reverseNames: ["Vishal", "Vijay", "Suraj", "Pratibha", "Nirav"]
```
The closure expression syntax is given as follows:
```
{ (parameters) -> return type in
    statements
}
reverseNames = names.sorted(by: { (s1: String, s2: String) -> Bool in
return s1 > s2})
```

When the closure's body is started, it is introduced by the keyword **in**. This keyword explains that the definition of the closure's parameters and return type has finished, and the body of the closure is just about to begin.

Trailing closures

When you need to pass a closure expression to a function as the function's final argument and the expression is long, such that it can be useful to write, it as a trailing closure instead. A function call can include multiple trailing closures, but the first few examples use a single trailing closure, shown as follows:

```
func aFuntionThatTakesClosure(closure: () -> Void) {
    // function body goes here
}
// Here's how you call this function without using a trailing closure:
aFunctionThatTakesClosure(closure: {
```

```
    // closure's body goes here
})
// Here's how you call this function with a trailing closure instead:
aFunctionThatTakesClosure() {
    // trailing closure's body goes here
}
```

The string-sorting closure can be written outside of the **sorted(by:)** method's parentheses as a trailing closures, shown as follows:

```
reverseNames = friendsName.sorted() { $0 > $1 }
```

Autoclosures

In Swift, autoclosures is a closure that is automatically created to wrap an expression that's being passed as an argument to a function. It does not take any arguments, and when it's called, it returns the value of the expression that's wrapped inside of it. An autoclosure lets you delay the evaluation because the code inside isn't run until you call the closure. Delaying the evaluation is useful for the code that has side effects or is computationally expensive.

Conclusion

In this chapter, we started studying the Swift fundamentals while explaining the variable and constant behavior. We defined different operations of Strings and characters. Swift became stronger with the collection types provided by Apple. We learned that Array, Set, and dictionaries help you create better and viable collections of data to pass and use around the program code. We also learned that the control flow helps us make conditional and unconditional decision making while coding, further functions and nested functions make our code viable and readable such that every new task could have a separate function for better visibility. We then learned about Closures that usually capture and store references to any constants and variables from the context of code in which they are defined, and that Swift handles all the memory management of closures of capturing for your code.

In the next chapter, you will start learning the Swift topics, such as classes, structure, and enumerations.

Multiple choice questions

1. **Which of the following is the correct Data Type in Swift?**

   a. Double

   b. UInt

   c. Optional

   d. Char

2. **What are/is the control transfer statements used in Swift?**

   a. Continue

   b. Break

   c. Fallthrough

   d. All of the above

3. **What is the collection type in Swift?**

   a. Dictionary

   b. Optional

   c. Fallthrough

   d. Closure

4. **Swift is an _____ language, which means anyone can take the code, build it, and share it with a greater community?**

   a. Loose

   b. Open Source

   c. Optional

   d. Protected

5. **In Swift, what is similar to do-while?**

   a. while

   b. for-in

   c. repeat-while

   d. None of the above

6. **In Swift, which keyword is used for function?**

    a. function

    b. @function

    c. func

    d. @objc

7. **Which of the following correctly declares a mutable array?**

    a. let array = [Int]()

    b. var array = [Int]()

    c. let array = [Int]

    d. var array = [Int]

8. **What is the type of conditional statements?**

    a. Break

    b. Switch

    c. Optional

    d. Closures

Answers

1. d
2. d
3. a
4. b
5. c
6. c
7. b
8. b

CHAPTER 3
Classes, Struct, and Enumerations

Introduction

In the previous chapter, we discussed simple Swift syntax coding as well as the use of operators. In this chapter, we will discuss how we can use those Swift learning while implementing classes, structure, and enumerations (Enum). When we formulate the features or properties in one box, we use classes with encapsulation and inheritance, and for binding the data together, we can use structure as data models. Enum usually helps while giving you multiple options of the same type.

Structure

In this chapter, we will cover the following topics:

- Enumerations
- Structures and classes
- Properties
- Methods
- Inheritance
- Initialization
- Deinitialization

Objectives

After studying this chapter, you will be able to create classes, structure, and enumerations with their instances, property, and methods to perform the desired tasks and operations in Swift programming. You will also be able to perform advanced operations on classes, structure, and enumerations with the capabilities of inheritance, subclasses, and customized initializations.

Enumerations

Enumeration or enum is a symbolic name for a set of values of the same type. Enums are considered as data types that can be used as variables and properties. In Swift, enums are much more flexible compared to the other languages and are not required to provide the associated values for each case. If an original value is provided for every enumeration case, then the associated value can be a string, character, or a value of integer or floating-point type.

The Enums cases can specify the associated values of any type to be stored along with different values. Enumerations adopted many features which are supported by classes, such as computed properties to provide information about its current value. Enumerations can define the initializers to provide the initial case associated values and expand their functionalities beyond the original implementations that can conform to the protocols to provide the standard functionalities.

Swift enumerations use the **enum** keyword, as follows:

```
enum nameOfEnum {
    // Definition of Enumeration
}
```

The following is an example of storing points on the compass:

```
enum PointOfCompass {
    case north
    case south
    case east
    case west
}
```

Like any other data type in Swift, enumeration's name starts with a capital letter. Let's see how we can access the value of **enum** in a variable, as follows:

```
var mainDirection = PointOfCompass.south
```

Recursive enumeration

In Swift, when another instance of enumeration forms as an associated value for one or more enumeration cases, then these become recursive by writing the keywords indirectly before it. The following is the example of a recursive **enum**:

```
enum ArithmeticExp {
    case number(Int)
    indirect case addition(ArithmeticExp, ArithmeticExp)
    indirect case multiplication(ArithmeticExp, ArithmeticExp)
}
```

The given enumeration can save three kinds of arithmetic expressions – a number, addition of expressions, and multiplication of expressions. In this **enum**, the addition and multiplication cases have values that are also arithmetic expressions, and three associated values make it possible to nest expressions.

Structures and classes

Structure and classes are general purpose building blocks of your program code. You can define the properties and methods to add functionalities in structure and class. In Swift, there is no requirement to write a separate interface and implementation; you can define both in the same building block and file.

Comparison of classes and structure

Classes and structure, both have the following:

- Properties to store values

- Methods to provide functionalities

- Subscripts to provide access to values

- Initializers to set up their initial state values

- The availability for extension to expand functionality beyond a default implementation

- The confirmation to protocol which provides standard functionality

Classes have some extra features which the structure won't have, which are explained in *Table 3.1* as follows:

Feature	Class	Structure
Inheritance	Here one class inherits the features of another class.	Here one structure cannot inherit another structure.
Type Casting	Check and interpret the type of class instance at runtime.	Check and interpret the type of structure at compile time
Deinitialization	Free up resources from the instance of the class.	Deinitialization not allowed in structure due to non-reference type.
Reference	Reference counting allows more than one reference to a class instance.	Reference counting is not allowed.

Table 3.1: Classes vs. structure

Classes come with more complexities compared to structures. In general, most of the data types defined by you will be structure and enumerations.

Reference type classes

Reference types are not copied when they are assigned to a variable or passed to a function, but a copy to the same instance is used. The following is the example explanation of reference types:

```
let video = VideoPlayer()
video.resolution = hd
video.name = "10089"
video.frameRate = 25.0
```

Identity operator

Swift classes are reference types, so there is a possibility that the different multiple constants and variables refer to the same instance of a class. However, this case is not true for structure and enumerations due to the non-reference type instances, and they always perform copy whenever assigned to another variable or constant.

Swift provides the following two operators to identify or check if two constants or variables refer to the same instance of the class:

- Identical To (===)

- Not Identical To (**!==**)

We can use these operators to check whether two constants or variables refer to the same single instance, as follows:

```
if bigXObject === alsoBigXObject {
    print("bigXObject and alsoBigXObject referring to the same instance
of class")
}
// prints "bigXObject and alsoBigXObject referring to the same instance
of class"
```

Properties

Properties associate values with class, structure, and enum. These properties are constants and variables which can be used for calculation as part of instances. The computed values are also stored in type properties. Properties are associated with type itself which is known as type properties.

Property wrappers can be used to reuse the code in the getter and setter of multiple properties.

Stored properties

Stored property is a constant or variable that is stored as part of an instance of the class or structure. You can also provide a default value to the stored property or modify the value.

Computed properties

In computed property, classes, structure, and enumerations can define the properties in such a manner that it actually does not store the values, but instead they provide a getter and an optional setter to retrieve and set the properties and values indirectly.

Read-only computed property

A computed property with a getter but not a setter is known as a read-only computed property. Such type of read-only computed property always returns a value and can be accessed by dot syntax but can't be set to a value, as shown in the following example:

```
struct Cuboid {
    var width = 0.0, height = 0.0, depth = 0.0
    var volume: Double {
```

```
        return width * height * depth
    }
}
let fourByFiveByTwo = Cuboid(width: 4.0, height: 5.0, depth: 2.0)
print("the volume of fourByFiveByTwo is \(fourByFiveByTwo.volume)")
// Prints "the volume of fourByFiveByTwo is 40.0
```

Property observers

Property Observers observe the changes in the value for a property. Property observers are called every time when a change value is set to property which is being observed. You can add the property observers in the following mentioned cases:

- Stored properties defined by you

- Stored properties inherited by you

- Computed properties inherited by you

In case of inherited properties, you can add the property observers via overriding that property in a subclass. There are options to define either or both of these following observers on a property:

- **willSet** observer method is called just before the value is stored in case you want to perform any operation before a change of value on property.

- **didset** is called just after the new value is stored into the property which is observed.

Implementation of the **willSet** observer passed the new property value as a constant parameter. In case you do not write the parameter name and parentheses within your implementation, it will be made available as the parameter name **newValue**.

Similarly, in the case of implementation of the **didSet** observer, it will pass a constant parameter containing an old property value. You can name the parameter or use the default parameter name as **oldValue**. If you assign a value to a property within its own **didSet** observer, the new value of the property that you assign replaces the one that was just set. Look at the following example:

```
class TapCounter {
        var totalTaps: Int = 0 {
            willSet(newTotalTaps) {
                print("About to set totalTaps to \(newTotalTaps)")
            }
```

```
            didSet {
                if totalTaps > oldValue  {
                    print("Added \(totalTaps - oldValue) Taps")
                }
            }
        }
    }
    let tapCounter = TapCounter()
    tapCounter.totalTaps = 200
    // About to set totaltaps to 200
    // Added 200 taps
    tapCounter.totaltaps = 360
    // About to set totalSteps to 360
    // Added 160 taps
    tapCounter.totaltaps = 896
    // About to set totaltaps to 896
    // Added 536 taps
```

Property wrappers

Property wrappers add a layer of separation code and manage how the property is stored and defined. Let's suppose you are required to add the thread safety for every property in code, then there is no requirement to do it separately for each property and the property wrappers can do code management once you define the wrappers. That code can be reused for the other properties as property wrappers.

To make or define a property wrapper, you can use structure, enumeration, or class that defines the **wrapperValue** property, as follows:

```
@propertyWrapper
struct FifteenOrLess {
    private var number: Int
    init() { self.number = 0 }
    var wrappedValue: Int {
        get { return number }
        set { number = min(newValue, 15) }
    }
}
```

To apply the wrapper to a property, you can write the wrapper's name before the property as an attribute, as follows:

```
struct Rectangle {
    @FifteenOrLess var height: Int
    @FifteenOrLess var width: Int
}
var rectangle = Rectangle()
print(rectangle.height)
// Prints "0"
rectangle.height = 10
print(rectangle.height)
// Prints "10"
rectangle.height = 24
print(rectangle.height)
// Prints "15"
```

Global and local variables

Global variables are those variables which are defined outside of any function, closures, and method. Local variables are those variables which are defined within a function, method, and closures. Global and local variables, like stored properties, provide storage for the value of a certain type. You can define the computed variables and observers for the stored values, in either global or local variables.

Type properties

The Instance type properties are those properties which belong to instances of a particular type. Whenever you create a new instance type, it has its own set of values, different from any other instance. There will be only one copy of these properties, no matter how many instances are created by you; such type of properties is called type properties. Type properties are very useful for defining what are universal to all instances of a particular type, like constant properties which can be used by all other instances too. (This concept is similar to static variables in the C programming language.)

Stored type properties can be constant and variables, but computed type properties are always declared as variable properties.

The following example is for read-only computed type properties, but you can also define the read-write computed type properties with the same syntax as for computed instance properties:

```
struct SampleStructure {
    static var storedTypeProperty = "Sample value."
    static var computedTypeProperty: Int {
        return 1
    }
}
enum SampleEnumeration {
    static var storedTypeProperty = "Sample value."
    static var computedTypeProperty: Int {
        return 6
    }
}
class SampleClass {
    static var storedTypeProperty = "Sample value."
    static var computedTypeProperty: Int {
        return 27
    }
    class var overrideComputedTypeProperty: Int {
        return 107
    }
}
```

Querying and setting type property

Like instance properties, type properties are queried and set using dot syntax. Type properties, on the other hand, are requested and set on the type itself, not on an instance of that type. For example:

```
print(SampleStructure.storedTypeProperty)
// Prints "Sample value."
SampleStructure.storedTypeProperty = "Another value."
print(SampleStructure.storedTypeProperty)
```

```
// Prints "Another value."
print(SampleEnumeration.computedTypeProperty)
// Prints "6"
print(SampleClass.computedTypeProperty)
// Prints "27"
```

Methods

Methods are functions which are associated with a particular type. Classes, structure, and enumeration, all define the instance methods which can encapsulate some task and functionalities for the instances. Swift is very different from C and Objective C languages as structure and enumeration too have methods in Swift.

Instance methods

Instance methods are functions that belong to instances of classes, structure, or enumerations. You write an instance method within the opening and closing braces of the type it belongs to. The instance methods have implicit access to all other instance methods and properties of that type. An instance method can be called on a specific instance of the type it belongs to, and it cannot be called in isolation without an existing instance, as shown in the following example:

```
class IncreaseCounter {
    var count = 0
    func increment() {
        count += 1
    }
    func increment(by amount: Int) {
        count += amount
    }
    func reset() {
        count = 0
    }
}
```

Type methods

You can also define methods that are called on the type itself. These kinds of methods are called **type methods**. You can syntax it by writing the static keyword before the methods keyword **func**, although Classes can use the class keyword instead, to allow subclasses to override the superclass implementation of that method, as follows:

```
class AnyClass {
    class func anyTypeMethod() {
        // type method implementation
    }
}
AnyClass.anyTypeMethod()
```

Within the body of a type method, the implicit self-property refers to type itself. A type method can call another type method by the other method name without any prefix of its type name.

Inheritance

A Class can inherit properties, methods, and other features from another class. When one class inherits from another, the inheriting class is known as its superclass. Classes in Swift can call its methods and properties belonging to their superclass and can provide. In such cases, Swift ensures that your overrides are correct by checking it from the superclass method definitions.

Base class

Any class which does not inherit from another class is known as a base class. Swift classes do not inherit from the universal base class. Classes you define without the mention of superclass automatically become the base classes to build upon.

Subclassing

Subclassing is used to form a new class on an existing class as base. The subclass inherits all the features from the existing class, which can be redefined in the subclass. To form a subclass which has a super class, you need to write the subclass name before the superclass name, separated by a colon (:), as shown in the following example:

```
class SampleSubclass: SampleSuperclass {
    // subclass definition goes here
}
```

Other than a simple syntax given in the preceding example, we can understand it better by the following example:

```
class Vehicle {
    var currentSpeed = 0.0
    var description: String {
        return "traveling at \(currentSpeed) miles per hour"
    }
    func makeNoise() {
        // do nothing - an arbitrary vehicle doesn't necessarily make a
noise
    }
}
class Car: Vehicle {
    var hasBreak = true
}
```

The new **Car** class inherits all the features of the **Vehicle** class, such as its **currentSpeed**, description properties, and the **makenoise** method. From the instance of class **Car**, you can change the stored property values of the subclass as well as superclass, as follows:

```
let car = Car()
car.hasBreak = false
car.currentSpeed = 50.0
print("Car: \(car.description)")
// Car: traveling at 50.0 miles per hour
```

Overriding

A subclass can provide its own custom implementation of an instance method, type method, instance property, and type property which inherits from a superclass. This is known as **overriding**. The **override** keyword uses a Swift compiler to check that your overriding class's superclass has a declaration that matches with the one you provided.

You can use super prefix to access the property and methods of superclass from the instance of subclass. Let's see where it's appropriate to do so, as follows:

- An overridden method named **sampleMethod()** can call the superclass version of **sampleMethod()** by calling **super.sampleMethod()** within the overriding method implementation.

- An overridden property called **sampleProperty** can access the superclass version of **sampleProperty** as **super.sampleProperty** within the overriding getter or setter implementation.

- An overridden subscript for **someIndex** can access the superclass version of the same subscript as **super[someIndex]** from within the overriding subscript implementation.

Initialization

Initialization is the process of preparing an instance of a class, structure, or enumeration for use. This process includes the setting up of initial values of stored properties and performing any other setup or initialization which is required for that instance. You can set an initial value for a stored property either within an initializer or by assigning a default property value as part of the property definition.

Initializers

Initializers are called to create new instances of a particular type. An initializer is like a method without parameters, as shown in the following example:

```
init() {
    // perform some initialization process
}
```

The following example defines a new structure to store the temperature expressed in **Celsius** scale. The **Celsius** structure has one stored property of type **Double**, shown as follows:

```
struct Celsius {
    var temperature: Double
    init() {
        temperature = 35.0
    }
}
var c = Celsius()
print("The default temperature is \(c.temperature)° Celcius")
// Prints "The default temperature is 35.0° Celsius"
```

Customizing initialization

You can also customize the initialization via adding the input parameters that entail values of the stored property type. You can provide the initialization parameters as part of a definition of initializer, as follows:

```
struct Celsius {
    var temperatureInCelsius: Double
    init(fromFahrenheit fahrenheit: Double) {
        temperatureInCelsius = (fahrenheit - 32.0) / 1.8
    }
}
let boilingPointOfWater = Celsius(fromFahrenheit: 212.0)
// boilingPointOfWater.temperatureInCelsius is 100.0
```

In the preceding example, the initializer has a single initialization parameter with an argument label of **fromFahrenheit** and a parameter name of **fahrenheit**.

Deinitialization

The Deinitializers called before a class instance is deallocated. In Swift, the **deinit** keyword is used for deinitialization, similar to **init** used for initialization. This terminology is available only for class and not for structure and **enum**.

In Swift, every class definition can have at most one **deinit** per class. Deinitializers do not take any parameters and are written without parentheses, shown as follows:

```
deinit{
    // Here You can perform Deinit Operation
}
```

Deinitializers are automatically called before the instance deallocation takes place. You are not allowed to call a deinitializer yourself. Superclass deinitializers are inherited by their subclasses and are called automatically at the end of a subclass deinitializer implementation. It is not always required to use **deinit**, but if you want to do some cleanup before the deallocation of objects, you can do that. Let's understand this with an example – if your class manages a file or a different resource, you can close that handle in **deinit** to ensure that it doesn't live on after the object has been deallocated.

Conclusion

In this chapter, we learned how to clearly differentiate while choosing between classes and structure. It's definitely not always easy and possible to go with struct but that should always be default while programming with Swift. It is just recommended and will not harm any how if you use class instead of structure in any case. Once you start using struct more often, then you will get used to it. But when you require OOPs features while performing tasks and operations, then class is an obvious choice. In this chapter, we discussed the Inheritance with subclassing, and overriding method approach which make classes more capable than structures. Enumerations declared in class and structure and its value can be accessed by instances of the same class and structure.

In the next chapter, you will further learn about extensions, protocols, and error handling in Swift.

Multiple choice questions

1. **Which feature is part of Classes only?**

    a. Property

    b. Method

    c. Subscripts

    d. Inheritance

2. **The class which does not inherit from another class is called as _____.**

    a. Subclass

    b. Superclass

    c. Base class

    d. Main Class

3. **Which operator is used to check if two variables or constants refer to the same instance of class?**

    a. (==)

    b. (!==)

    c. (!=)

    d. (===)

4. **If you want to perform an action when a stored property value is changed, which feature will you use?**

   a.   Computed Property

   b.   Read-Write Property

   c.   Property Observer

   d.   Override

5. **A subclass provides the custom implementation of type method which inherits from superclass and is called _____.**

   a.   Property Observer

   b.   Initialization

   c.   Override

   d.   Inheritance

Answers

1.   d

2.   c

3.   d

4.   c

5.   c

CHAPTER 4

Protocols, Extensions, and Error Handling

Introduction

When you program complex solutions, you might make errors. Errors could be nightmares for new learners, but modern languages, such as Swift, come up with approaches to deal with it. So, whenever a program throws an error, we handle that with care. When you think of the word *'generic'* in terms or programming, you come across the idea of versatile and robust code which you can achieve with Generics in Swift. Similarly, Swift gives you the power to add more features to your class and structure with Extensions.

Structure

In this chapter, we will cover the following topics:

- Optional chaining
- Error handling
- Type casting
- Extension
- Protocols
- Generics

Objectives

After studying this chapter, you will be able to learn optional chaining and error handling while working on complex coding solutions of tasks. Also, you will learn the Swift language as a protocol-oriented language for the protocol-based communications between multiple code blocks and components with Extension and Generics for the flexibility, reusability, and extensibility.

Optional chaining

In Swift, optional chaining is a process with querying and calling properties, methods, and subscripts as optional to check what might be nil. The properties, methods, and subscripts called succeed if it has values, otherwise it returns nil. In optional chaining, multiple properties, methods, and subscripts query can be possible, and if in between, any value has nil, it will return nil.

Importance of optional chaining

In programming, forced unwrapping happens irrespective of its nil value. Forced unwrapping fails abruptly and can cause harm or crashes. When the optional is nil, optional chaining fails gracefully. The expected return value is the result of an optional chaining call of the same type but wrapped in an optional value. A property that normally returns an Int value will return an **Int** value with optional wrapping whenever accessed through optional chaining.

Optional chaining can be used by placing a question mark (**?**) after the optional value, on which, in programming, you wish to call property, methods, or subscripts. The following code snippets can give us a better understanding:

```
Class Letter {
    var address: Address?
}


Class Address {
    var houseNumber = 201,
}
```

Letter instances have a single Int property called **houseNumber**, with the default value of **201**.

Error handling

Error handling is the process of responding and handling your program from the error condition gracefully, such that the user flow continues and does not harm the system and the application in any manner. The Swift language provides firsthand support for throwing, catching, propagating, and manipulating the error at runtime.

Sometimes, some operations are not guaranteed to always complete the execution and produce meaningful results and fall under failed operations. In such cases, there is a requirement to understand or notify the user with reasons for the failure.

Throwing errors

In Swift, errors are represented by values of types that conform to the **Error** protocol (we will discuss protocol in detail, later in this chapter). Swift enumerations are well suited for modeling the error conditions with its associated values which communicate about the types of error, shown as follows:

```
enum CoffeeMachineError: Error {
    case invalidSelection
    case insufficientWater(waterNeedediInml: Int)
    case outOfStock
}
```

Throwing error from the program indicates that something unexpected happened and the normal flow of execution can't be continued in such a case. You can use the **throw** keyword statement to throw an error from the program code, shown as follows:

```
throw CoffeeMachineError.insufficientWater(waterNeedediInml: 5)
```

Handling errors

When the error is thrown by the program code, some piece of code would be responsible to handle the error gracefully to show and notify the user, the reason and type of the thrown error. There are mainly four ways to handle the errors in Swift, which are as follows:

- Errors using throwing function

- Handling error using do-catch

- Errors as optional values

- Disabling error propagation

Errors using throwing function

After the parameters of a function, method, or initializer, you write the **throws** keyword in the function's declaration to indicate that it can throw an error. A throwing function is a function that is marked with throws. You write the **throws** keyword before the return arrow (**->**) if the function specifies a return type, shown as follows:

```
func canThrowErrors() throws -> String
func cannotThrowErrors() -> String
```

Only the throwing functions can propagate the errors and any errors thrown inside a non-throwing function must be handled inside the function.

Handling error using do-catch

By running a block of code or a code clause, you can utilize a **do-catch** statement to handle the errors. If the code in the **do** clause throws an error, it is compared to the **catch** clauses to see which one can handle the condition.

The following is the general form of a **do-catch** statement:

```
do {
    try <expression>
    <statements>
} catch <pattern > {
    <statements>
} catch <pattern 2> where <condition> {
    <statements>
} catch <pattern 3>, <pattern 4> where <condition> {
    <statements>
} catch {
    <statements>
}
```

After you catch, you add a pattern to identify which mistakes that clause may handle. If a **catch** clause doesn't have a pattern, it matches any error and assigns it to a local variable named **error**.

Errors as optional values

You use **try?** to handle an error by converting it to an optional value. If an error is thrown while evaluating the **try?** expression, the value of the expression is **nil**. When you use **try?**, you write a concise error handling code when you want to handle all errors in the same way. For example, the following code uses several approaches to fetch the data, or returns **nil** if all the approaches fail:

```
func loadData() -> Data? {
    if let data = try? loadDataFromDisk() { return data }
    if let data = try? loadDataFromServer() { return data }
    return nil
}
```

Disabling error propagation

When you're confident that a throwing function or method won't actually throw an error at runtime, you can disable the error propagation by writing **try!** before the expression and wrapping the call in a runtime assertion that no error will be thrown. You'll get a runtime error if an error is truly thrown. The **loadImage(atPath:)** function in the following code example loads an image resource at a specified path or throws an exception if the picture cannot be loaded. Because no error will be thrown at runtime, as the picture is provided with the application, it is reasonable to disable the error propagation, as shown as follows:

```
let photo = try! loadImage(atPath: "./Resources/Mango.jpg")
```

Type casting

Type casting is a method of determining an instance's type. The **is** and **as** operators are used to implement type casting in Swift. These two operators make the checking of the type of a value or casting a value to a different type, simple and expressive. To check the type of a specific instance, you can use type casting with a hierarchy of classes and subclasses. Let's see the following example:

```
class Media {
    var name: String
    init(name: String) {
        self.name = name
    }
}
```

The preceding class **Media** provides the basic functionality of digital goods which declares a **name** property of the type string and an **init** name initializer. We can define two subclasses of **Media** superclass, first class is **Movie** which encapsulates the **movie name** and the **director** name information, and second class is **Song** which encapsulates the song name and artist information, as shown as follows:

```
class Movie: Media {
```

```
    var director: String
    init(name: String, director: String) {
        self.director = director
        super.init(name: name)
    }
}
class Song: Media {
    var artist: String
    init(name: String, artist: String) {
        self.artist = artist
        super.init(name: name)
    }
}
```

Checking Types

In type casting, we can use the type checker operator (**is**) to check whether an instance is of a subclass type. The type check operator returns true in case they are instances of that subclass type, and false in case they are not of that subclass type.

Downcasting

A constant or variable of a class type may actually refer to an instance of subclass behind the scenes; you can try downcasting it to the subclass type with a type cast operator (**as?** or **as!**). Because sometimes downcasting can fail, the type case operators come in the following two forms:

- The conditional form (**as?**) returns a value of the type you want to downcast to.

- The forced form (**as!**) attempts the downcast and force unwraps the results.

If you are not sure of the success of the downcast, then use the conditional form of a downcast operator; such form of the operator will always return an optional value and the value will be **nil** if the downcast is not possible. You can properly check for downcast using this method. Use the forced form of the type cast operator (**as!**) when you are confident that the downcast will always succeed. If you try to downcast to an improper class type with this type of operator, you will get a runtime error.

Casting for Any and AnyObject

Swift provides the following two special types for two non-specific types:

- Any, including the function types, can represent an instance of any type. Values of any type, including the optional types, are represented by the **Any** type. Swift warns you if you use an optional value in the place where a value of type **Any** is required. If you use an optional value as an **Any** value, you can use them as an operator to cast the optional to **Any**.

- Any object can be used to represent an instance member of any class type. When you specifically require the behavior and capabilities that **Any** and **AnyObject** give, you can utilize them. It is always preferable to be as clear as possible about the types you plan to work with in your code.

Nested Types

Swift allows you to create Nested Types, which allow you to nest the supporting enumerations, classes, and structures within the type of the nest declaration. Write a type's definition within the outer braces of the type it supports to nest it within another type. Types can be nested for as many levels as they are required to be.

Extensions

In Swift, Extensions add a new functionality to an existing class, structure, enumerations, or the protocol type. The extension includes the ability to extend the types on which you do not have access in the actual class or structure.

The extensions can be the following:

- Add the computed instance properties and computed type properties
- Define the instance method and type methods
- Provide a new initializer
- Define the subscripts
- Define and user a new nested type
- Make an existing type conform to a protocol

But there is one thing you need to understand, that extensions in Swift can add new functionalities to a type and they cannot override the existing functionalities. You can declare the Extension with the following **extension** keyword:

```
extension sampleExtension {
    // new functionalities can be added here
}
```

An extension can extend an existing type and adapt with one or more protocols as shown in the following code. To add the protocol for extending **Extension**, you write the protocol names as you write for the classes and structures, as follows:

```
extension sampleExtension: SampleProtocol, AnotherProtocol {
    // implementation of protocol requirements goes here
}
```

Computed properties

Extension can add the computed instances properties and computed type properties to the existing types. But we need to understand clearly that the extensions can add new computed property, but they cannot add the stored properties or add the property observers to the existing property types.

Initializers

Extensions can introduce new initializers to the existing types. In such a case, you can add new convenience initializers to a class, but the new designated initializers cannot be added by the extensions. You can call the default initializer and member-wise initializer for that value type if you apply an extension to add an initializer to it that offers the default values for all its stored attributes and doesn't define any custom initializers. Furthermore, if you use an extension to add an initializer to a structure declared in another module, the new initializer will not be able to access **self** until it calls an initializer from the defining module, as shown as follows:

```
struct Size {
    var width = 0.0, height = 0.0
}
struct Point {
    var x = 0.0, y = 0.0
}
struct Rect {
    var origin = Point()
    var size = Size()
}
```

Now, you can add the **Rect** structure to provide an additional initializer that takes specific points and size, as shown as follows:

```
extension Rect {
    init(center: Point, size: Size) {
```

```
            let originX = center.x - (size.width / 2)
            let originY = center.y - (size.height / 2)
            self.init(origin: Point(x: originX, y: originY), size: size)
    }
}
```

If you provide a new initializer with an expansion, you are still responsible for ensuring that each instance is fully initialized once the initializer completes.

Methods

Extensions can add new instance methods and type methods to the existing class or structure types, as follows:

```
extension Int {
    func repeat(task: () -> Void) {
        for _ in 0..<self {
            task()
        }
    }
}
```

After defining the extension, you can call the **repeat(task:)** method on any integer to perform a task, as shown as follows:

```
4.repeat {
    print("Hello World !")
}
// Hello World
// Hello World
// Hello World
// Hello World
```

Subscripts

Extensions can add new subscripts to an existing type. You can add an integer subscript or any other type which is taken to the Swift built-in type. This subscript returns the decimal digit n places in from the right of the number.

Protocols

In Swift, a protocol defines a blueprint of the methods, properties, and other requirements and functionality performed by the class or structure which will perform this protocol. Any type that satisfies the requirements of a protocol is said to confirm to that protocol. You can define the protocol simply, similar to class and structure, as shown as follows:

```
protocol SampleProtocol {
    // protocol definition
}
```

While implementing the protocols to the class and structure, multiple protocols can be listed, and are separated by commas, shown as follows:

```
struct SampleProtocol: FirstProtocol, AnotherProtocol {
    // structure definition
}
```

Property requirement

Swift protocols can require any confirming type to provide an instance with a particular name and type. Each property must be gettable or gettable and settable, according to the protocol. The property needs are always preceded with the **var** keyword and specified as the variable properties. After their type definition, the gettable and settable properties are expressed by writing **get set**, and the gettable properties are denoted by writing **{get}**, as shown as follows:

```
protocol SampleProtocol {
    var aSettable: Int { get set }
    var notNeedToBeSettable: Int { get }
}
```

You must always prefix the type property requirements with the **static** keyword when you define them in a protocol, shown as follows:

```
protocol LiveProtocol {
    static var liveTypeProperty: Int { get set }
}
```

Method requirement

Protocols which are implemented by confirming types require the instance methods and type methods. These methods are written in the definition of protocol similar to the normal instance and type methods. You are required to always prefix the type methods with the **static** keywords when they are defined in the protocol definition, shown as follows:

```
protocol SampleProtocol {
    static func sampleTypeMethod()
}
```

Sometimes, the methods need to modify (or mutate) the instance it belongs to. When you construct a protocol instance method requirement that is meant to mutate the instances of any type that uses the protocols, you must include the **mutating** keyword in the protocol specifications. You don't need to write a **mutating** keyword while implementing a **mutating** method type. The **mutating** keyword is only used by structures and enumerations, as shown as follows:

```
protocol ToggleProtocol {
    mutating func toggle()
}


enum OnOffSwitch: ToggleProtocol {
    case off, on
    mutating func toggle() {
        switch self {
        case .off:
            self = .on
        case .on:
            self = .off
        }
    }
}
var lightSwitch = OnOffSwitch.off
lightSwitch.toggle()
// lightSwitch is now equal to .on
```

Initializer requirements

You can write the initializers as part of the protocol's definition in exactly the same way as the normal initializers, but without the curly braces or an initializer body, as shown as follows:

```
protocol SampleProtocol {
```

```
    init(someParameter: Int)
}
```

Protocols as Types

Protocols do not implement any functionalities themselves and should be considered as types in your code. Using protocol as a type is called an existential type. You can use the protocol at many places, where the other prices are allowed, as follows:

- As a parameter type or return type in a function, method, or initializer
- As a type of a constant, variable, or property
- As a type of items in an array, dictionary, or other container

Delegations

Delegation is a design pattern in Swift that enables a class or structure to delegate (or hand off) some of its responsibilities to an instance of another type. The delegation design pattern implemented by defining a protocol that delegated the responsibilities is known as **delegate** and they are guaranteed to provide the functionality that has been delegated. Delegating objects keeps a reference to another object and, when required or at appropriate time, sends the message to it. Delegation then makes it possible for one object to alter the behavior of another object without the need to inherit from it, as shown as follows:

```
protocol ImageImporterDelegate: AnyObject {
    func imageImporter(_ importer: ImageImporter,
                       shouldImportImage image: Image) -> Bool

    func imageImporter(_ importer: ImageImporter,
                       didAbortWithError error: Error)

    func imageImporterDidFinish(_ importer: ImageImporter)
}


class ImageImporter {
    weak var delegate: ImageImporterDelegate?
    private func processFileIfNeeded(_ file: File) {
        guard let delegate = delegate else {
            return
        }
```

```
        let shouldImport = delegate.imageImporter(self,
shouldImportImage: file)
        guard shouldImport else {
            return
        }
        process(file)
    }
}
```

In the preceding code, **ImageImporterDelegate** is the protocol, and we declare this protocol type object named delegate in the class in which we want to implement this protocol.

Protocols inheritance

Similar to class and struct, a Protocol can also inherit from other protocols, and they can add to the criteria they inherit. Protocol inheritance uses the same syntax as class inheritance, with the addition of the ability to list several inherited protocols, separated by commas, as shown as follows:

```
protocol InheritingProtocol: SampleProtocol, AnotherProtocol {
    // protocol definition goes here
}
```

The following is an example of a protocol that inherits the **TextRepresentable** protocol:

```
protocol PrettyTextRepresentable: TextRepresentable {
    var prettyTextualDescription: String { get }
}
```

Class only Protocols

In case you want to specify a protocol specific to class and not to structure and enumerations, add the **Anyobject** protocol to its inheritance list. Use a class-only protocol when the behavior defined by those protocols' requirements assume or require that the type confirming has the reference semantics rather than the value semantics.

Generics

Generics enables you to write flexible and reusable code as functions which can work with any type. Swift Generics are the most powerful feature, such that many of the Swift Standard libraries build on Generics. Swift's Array and Swift's Dictionary types are generic collections. Generic functions can work with any type, shown as follows:

```
func swapTwoValues<T>(_ a: inout T, _ b: inout T) {
    let temporaryA = a
    a = b
    b = temporaryA
}
```

Instead of an actual type name, the generic version of the function utilizes a placeholder type name (named **T** in this example) (such as **Int**, **String**, or **Double**). The placeholder type name doesn't specify what **T** must be, but it does specify that both **a** and **b** must be of type **T**, whatever **T** stands for. Each time the **swapTwoValues(_:_:)** function is invoked, the actual type to use in place of **T** is determined.

The **swapTwoValues(_:_:)** function is based on the swap generic function, which is included in the Swift standard library and is immediately made accessible for use in your apps. If you need the behavior of the **swapTwoValues(_:_:)** function in your own code, instead of writing your own version, you can use Swift's **swap(_:_:)** function.

Type parameters

A type argument is represented by the placeholder type **T** in the given generics code. Type arguments are written directly after the function name, between a pair of matching angle brackets (such as **T>**) and they provide and name a placeholder type. You can also give several types of parameters by using commas to separate multiple type parameter names within the angle brackets.

Naming type parameters

The type parameters include descriptive names, such as "**Key**" and "**Value**" in **Dictionary Key**, **Value>** and **Element in Array Element>**, that inform the reader about the type parameter's relationship to the generic type or function it's used in. When there is no relevant relationship between them, it is customary to name them with single letters like **T**, **U**, and **V**.

Extending a generic type

When you extend a generic type, you don't provide a type parameter list as part of the extension's definition. Instead, the type parameter list from the original type definition is available within the body of the extension, and the original type parameter names are used to refer to the type parameters from the original definition.

The following example extends the generic **Stack** type to add a read-only computed property called **topItem**, which returns the top item on the stack without popping it from the stack:

```
extension Stack {
    var topItem: Element? {
        return items.isEmpty ? nil : items[items.count - 1]
    }
}
```

Conclusion

In this chapter, we learned how you can increase the efficiency of your code via Error handling which can make your code more proactive and protected against any unhandled cases. Further, we learned that the protocols as a communication key element in between classes and structure while doing complex tasks can make your code more robust and diligent. We also learned that the delegate pattern continues to be an important part of both the Apple's frameworks and our own codebases. We learned that Generics are important in terms of achieving reusability and flexibility while coding for Swift programs.

In the next chapter, we will learn in detail about the user interface building with different UI components and handling navigation flow with **UINavigationcontroller**.

Multiple choice questions

1. **Which of these keywords is not a part of exception handling?**

    a.   try

    b.   throw

    c.   thrown

    d.   catch

2. **If there is a direct communication between two objects, then which concepts we are talking about?**

    a.   Error handling

    b.   Generics

    c.   Delegate

    d.   Optional chaining

3. You can achieve reusability of code from _____.

    a. Protocols

    b. Error handling

    c. Generics

    d. Delegate

4. In case you want to add features to an existing class, you will use _____.

    a. Protocol

    b. Extension

    c. Generics

    d. Optional chaining

5. Which Swift concepts are used heavily in the Swift standard libraries?

    a. Protocol

    b. Extension

    c. Generics

    d. Optional chaining

Answers

1. c

2. c

3. c

4. b

5. c

CHAPTER 5

TabBar, TableView, and CollectionView

Introduction

An app that helps the users perform a serious task, can keep them focused by using robust and unobtrusive graphics, standard controls, and managed behaviors, and deliver captivating appearance with encouraging discovery. To maximize the overall impact and reach, the designs should follow clarity with depth, where the users feel like they are in control by keeping the interactive elements familiar and predictable, and making it easy to cancel the operations, even when they are already underway.

Structure

In this chapter, we will cover the following topics:

- Interface builder
- UI components
- UINavigationController

Objectives

After studying this chapter, you should be able to create your first UI page with Interface builder and Storyboard with different UI controls and Navigations, as well as create complex UI Components and Navigation flow of application with the List and grid style components.

Interface builder

Interface Builder (**IB**) is a Software development tool that is part of Xcode IDE. IB provides a collection of user interface objects for the app developers to use while designing the interface of applications. To make UI with the IB developer, simply drag the interface objects from the palette or collection onto a window or menu.

Storyboard

A Storyboard can represent the visual flow of single and multiple screen designs of an application, and it is composed of a sequence of scenes, each of which represents a view controller and its views; the scenes are connected by segue objects, which represent a transition between the two view controllers. On an iPhone, each scene corresponds to a full screen's worth of content; however, on an iPad, multiple scenes can appear on the screen at once, using the popover view controllers. Each scene has a dock, which displays the icons representing the top-level objects of the scene. The dock is used primarily to make the action and the outlet connections between the view controller and its views.

The reason why it's called a storyboard is that it actually tells the story of your app designs and flow in terms of segue and scenes which could have a little difference in the view as per the size of the screen in which you are viewing the app. Take a look at the following storyboard which shows the user flow of app as well as how each view is connected with other views in the app, as shown in *figure 5.1*:

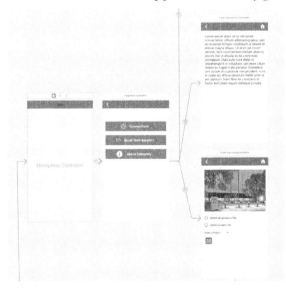

Figure 5.1: Storyboard

In the preceding figure, you can see a developed app with a storyboard that has more than 20 view controllers interconnected in a continuous flow, either navigated from the segue or with the program code.

View controller scene

To set up a project with a storyboard initially while creating your project, you need to select the **Interface** option as **Storyboard** and **Life Cycle** option as **UIKit App Delegate** with the language option Swift, as shown in *figure 5.2* as follows:

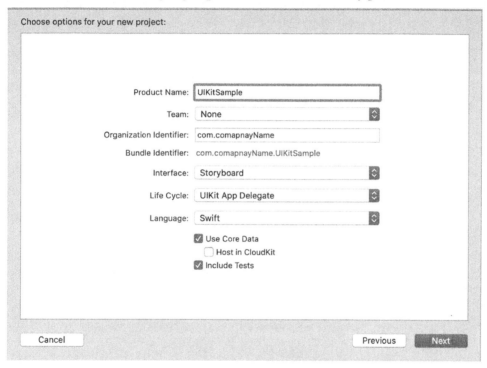

Figure 5.2: New Project

Moreover, when the Xcode window is opened for project, you will find the following files auto created by IDE:

- **AppDelegate.swift**
- **SceneDelegate.swift**
- **ViewController.swift**
- **Main.storyboard**
- **Assets.xcassets**
- **LaunchScreen.storyboard**

Here, the **Launchscreen** storyboard is used as a launch page screen which is not part of the actual app flow, and it will appear for as long as the app takes time to start the app to show its first screen. The **Main.storyboard** (by default) contains the start point of the app as well as the first screen of the app which is in general termed as the View Controller Scene. The Initial View Controller Scene represents and contains the view controller, first Responder, next moving flow (in the following case Exit), and the storyboard entry point. Every Storyboard contains a single-entry point. Whichever screen is pointed by the storyboard entry point will present first on the simulator of the iOS device, as shown in *figure 5.3* as follows:

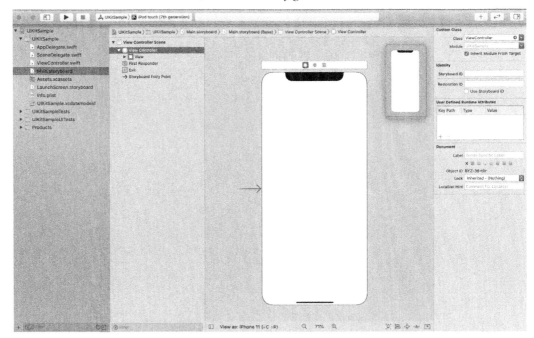

Figure 5.3: Interface Builder

Using Segue

From Segue, you can design and navigate the flow of the user interface. A segue defines a transition between the two view controllers in your app's storyboard file. When selecting the relationship type for your Segue, select an adaptive segue whenever possible. Adaptive segues adjust their behavior automatically based on the current environment. For example, the behavior of a Show segue changes based on the presenting view controller.

App Lifecycle

The App life cycle is responsible for responding to the system notifications when your app is in the foreground or background and handling other significant system-related events. When an iOS app launched main function of app is called which can initiate **UISceneDelegate** (in case you are using Scene based user interface flow) or **UIApplicationDelegate** (If you are using simple storyboard base flow). Let's take a look how they can be used to start app life cycle.

- **UISceneDelegate** is implemented from and after the iOS 13 supported apps to respond to the life-cycle events in a scene-based app.

- **UIApplicationDelegate** is implemented till and before the iOS 12 supported apps to respond to life-cycle events.

Responding to the launch of app: UIApplicationDelegate

Initialize your app's data structures, prepare your app to run, and respond to any launch-time requests from the system, as shown in *figure 5.4* as follows:

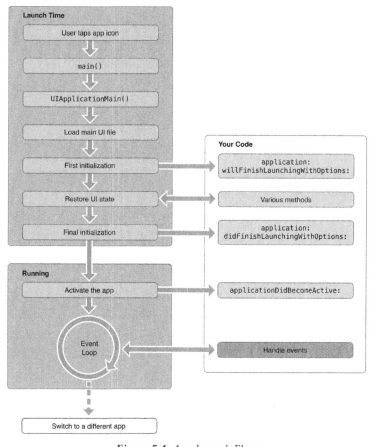

Figure 5.4: *App Launch Flow*

In Swift, **UIApplicationMain** class is represents the main function workflow, which required to be place before **AppDelegate** Class in such a way that main can transfer its control to application delegate implementations which initiates App life cycle.

```
@UIApplicationMain

class AppDelegate: UIResponder, UIApplicationDelegate {

var window: UIWindow?

func application(_ application: UIApplication,
didFinishLaunchingWithOptions launchOptions: [UIApplication.
LaunchOptionsKey: Any]?) -> Bool {

        return true

  }


    func applicationWillResignActive(_ application: UIApplication) {

            print("applicationWillResignActive")

    }

func applicationDidEnterBackground(_ application: UIApplication) {

            print("applicationDidEnterBackground")

    }

 func applicationWillEnterForeground(_ application: UIApplication) {

            print("applicationWillEnterForeground")

    }

func applicationDidBecomeActive(_ application: UIApplication) {

            print("applicationDidBecomeActive")

    }

func applicationWillTerminate(_ application: UIApplication) {

            print("applicationWillTerminate")

    }
```

Launch with UISceneDelegate

Moreover, if you are using the scene in your interface, it will add two **UISceneDelegate** methods, one for starting a new scene session and another one for discarding a scene session, as follows:

```
func application(_ application: UIApplication, configurationForConnecting
connectingSceneSession: UISceneSession, options: UIScene.
ConnectionOptions) -> UISceneConfiguration

{

    return UISceneConfiguration(name: "Default Configuration",
sessionRole: connectingSceneSession.role)

}
```

```
func application(_ application: UIApplication, didDiscardSceneSessions
sceneSessions: Set<UISceneSession>) {
        // Use this method to release any resources that were specific to
the discarded scenes, as they will not return.
}
```

Respond to the app-based life-cycle events

When the app launches, the system puts the app in the inactive or background state, depending on whether the UI is about to appear on the screen. When launching to the foreground, the system transitions the app to the active state automatically. After that, the state fluctuates between active and background until the app terminates. In app user may choose from Active state to Inactive and further either choose to keep it in background or may terminate the app which will lead to Not Running state. If the app is in background for long and operating system require more memory it may lead to Suspended state so that other app those are active can use run time memory. Refer to *figure 5.5* as follows:

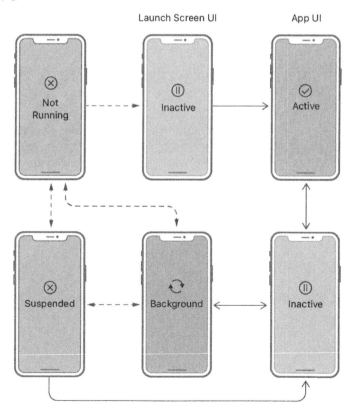

Figure 5.5: App States

When app go into active state it first starts the View Controller which should be shown initially as per storyboard app marking. When you run the app, it will show a splash screen which shows during the app start process and control flow further transferred to view controller. Let's take a look how view controller works as follows:

View Controller: View controller works as an intermediary between the views of the controller and the data which is going to appear on the view. Apple provides a class **UIViewController**, so whenever we make a new view controller scene, we must connect its view controller to a subclass of the **UIViewController**. This connection of the **UIViewcontroller** subclass and the view controller scene on the storyboard ensures that your code can now communicate with the UI elements present on the scenes. As you can see in *figure 5.3*, in place of the **Content** class, **ViewController** is present, which is a subclass of **UIViewController** auto created by Xcode IDE. Refer to the following code:

```
class ViewController: UIViewController {

    override func viewDidLoad() {
        super.viewDidLoad()
        // Do any additional setup after loading the view.
    }
}
```

View controller life cycle

The View controller life cycle talks about from what stages a view controller goes and what trigger is available for you to override while it gets initialized and becomes part of the application. Let's take a look on each view controller life cycle function which can be override while implementation of app controllers, as follows:

- **init**: View controllers are initiated by the storyboard usually, and internally calls **initwithCoder()** which you can override, if required.

- **loadView**: You override this method only in case you want to make your interface completely by the code instead of the storyboard or nib file. And don't use this method unless there is a valid reason to do so.

- **viewDidLoad**: When this method is called, it is ensured that the views of the view controller are created, and all the outlets of the view are in place. It is a good place to start the background activity and start the network calls when the view is loaded completely.

- **viewWillAppear**: You need to override this method when you want to repeat a task every time a view appears on the screen; a view controller loads one time when pushed to the navigation stack but can appear many times as per your app flow and navigation architecture. Good examples of this case would be network calls for refreshing the data of some animation which you want to show to a user every time the view appears on the screen.

- **viewWillLayoutSubviews**: This method is called every time the frame changes; for example, when the view rotates or is marked as needing layout.

- **viewDidLayoutSubviews**: You can make additional changes here in this method after the view layouts subviews.

- **viewDidAppear**: This method is called when the view controller completely appears on the screen.

- **viewWillDisappear**: Before transitioning to another screen and leaving the view of the current screen, this method is called.

- **viewDidDisappear**: When the current view controller is removed from the screen and another/next view controller loads on the screen, this method of the view controller of the previous VC (not which loads recently) is called.

- **deinit**: You can override this method to clean the resources that the view controller has allocated that are not freed by **Automatic retain Count** (**ARC**).

- **didReceiveMemoryWarning**: When the memory starts to fill up, the iOS does not automatically move the data from the memory to its limited hard disk space. It does, however, issue this warning, and as a developer, you are responsible for clearing the memory. Be aware that if the memory of your app goes over a certain threshold, iOS will shut down your app. And this will look similar to a crash to the end user.

- **viewWillTransition**: When the app interface orientation changes, the UIKit framework calls this method to the window's root controller which sends this message to all its child view controllers just before the size is going to make the changes.

Now, we will have a look how these life cycle function can be implemented in Swift language. Refer to the following code:

```
override func viewDidLoad() {
    super.viewDidLoad()
}
override func viewWillAppear(_ animated: Bool) {
    super.viewWillAppear(animated)
}
override func viewDidAppear(_ animated: Bool) {
    super.viewDidAppear(animated)
```

```
    }
    override func viewWillLayoutSubviews() {
        super.viewWillLayoutSubviews()
    }
    override func viewDidLayoutSubviews() {
        super.viewWillLayoutSubviews()
    }
    override func viewWillDisappear(_ animated: Bool) {
        super.viewWillDisappear(animated)
    }
    override func viewDidDisappear(_ animated: Bool) {
        super.viewDidDisappear(animated)
    }
    override func didReceiveMemoryWarning() {
        super.didReceiveMemoryWarning()
        // Dispose of any resources that can be recreated.
        print("Memory Warning %@", children)
    }
```

Self vs Super keyword

If a method is overridden, then self can be used to access the method in the subclass, otherwise for accessing the super class from a base class, the best practice is to use super.

Override keyword

When a subclass provides its custom implementation of an instance method, type method, instance property, type property, or subscript, that it would override otherwise it can inherit from a superclass. And while customizing the implementation of the instance method, the **override** keyword is used in front of those functions of super class.

UI components

An iOS app screens or pages under the navigation work similar to the **Stack** operations; the start point of this stack is the window object of the **UIWindow** class, which is a singleton in **AppDelegate.swift** (implements the **UIApplication** class delegate methods to achieve app initialization).

Exploring window

Window object in **AppDelegate.swift** consists of a root view controller which starts the app screen flow. The view controller's view will automatically be set as the contents of the window and presented to the user.

How to add the UI control on Storyboard View Controller?

In *figure 5.3*, on the right-side options on the upper menu, you will find a "**+**" action on Xcode. You can add the interface control objects from the window shown as in *figure 5.6*, which will appear after the plus action. Here, you can search and read about those controls to know better what they can achieve with their inclusion on the interface.

You can add these controls by dragging from this UI object pane to drop on the storyboard view controller. Refer to *figure 5.6* as follows:

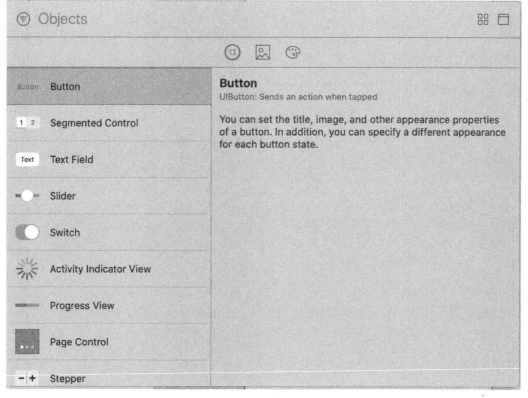

Figure 5.6: Add UI Control

Connect UI element to Swift code

When you add an UI element to View page that need to be connected to view controller class to implement the features that can be controlled by user interface actions as shown in following *figure 5.7*:

Figure 5.7: Connect UI Control

As shown in the preceding figure (*figure 5.7*), every UI element on the storyboard or view controller required a connection representation in code which is of type **@ IBOutlet** (Interface Builder Outlet). When you right select the UI element, there will be many options relevant to the user interface connection. In the *Reference Outlet* section, you need to attach a new reference outlet to the **IBOutlet** variable in code. After that, if you want to set the property or text for that element, you can set it from code and that will reflect when you execute the code.

UIControl

You never create any direct instance of **UIControl**. **UIControl** is used for the subclassing of the other controls, such that the common features and target actions of all the controls can be easily combined. The iOS system calls the action methods when the user interacts with the control in specific ways. The **UIControl.Events** enum has multiple events to send, such as **touchDown**, **touchUpInside**, etc. When a control-specific event occurs, the control calls any associated action methods immediately. The current **UIApplication** object dispatches the action methods and finds an appropriate object to handle the message, following the responder chain, if necessary.

First responder

In the UI designs components hierarchy, there is responder chain, which maintains the one-by-one chaining of the UI elements, such that when the user interacts with UI, the responder chain gets the response back from the related elements. So, the first responder is usually the first object in a responder chain which receives an event or action message.

UIButton

UIButton is the most used control in the iOS designs; after the iPhone 7+ changes, it looks simple like a text but a highly customizable component. Customizing the buttons allows you to style everything from the text style, drop shadow, choosing fonts, text weights, and color to an icon that is either prepended or centered if there is no text label, as well as fully customized backgrounds. Refer to *figure 5.8* as follows:

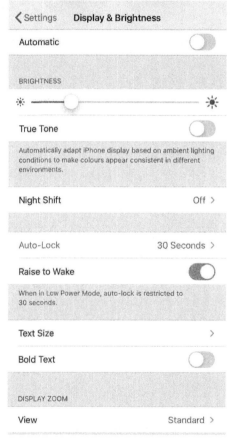

Figure 5.8: UI Controls

UILabel

A simple text could be as long<-->, which could have input as a string type in the text property. You can supply either a string or an attributed string that represents the content. In case you are using a non-attributed string, you can also configure the appearance of the label. Other than the text properties, you can set the font, font weight, color, text alignment, line break, number of lines, and many more such customizable properties which can enhance the overall appearance.

UITextField

UITextField is used for the display of an editable single line text area in your UI interface. In case, you would be required to take inputs or gather text-based information from the user, using an onscreen keyboard, you could use this control. The keyboard is configurable for many different types of input, such as plain text, emails, phone, numbers etc. The Text fields use the target-action mechanism and a delegate object to report the changes made during the editing.

UITextView

UITextView is used for the display of an editable multiline text area in the UI interface. This control has a scrollable area with text; so, if there is large content, then it would be visible correctly on a scrollable text field with one line. When the user taps in an editable text view, that text view becomes the first responder and automatically asks the system to display the associated keyboard. Because the appearance of the keyboard has the potential to obscure the portions of your user interface, it is up to you to make sure that does not happen by repositioning any views that might be obscured. Some system views, like the table views, help you by scrolling the first responder into the view automatically. If, however, the first responder is at the bottom of the scrolling region, you may still need to resize or reposition the scroll view itself to ensure that the first responder is visible.

The appearance of the keyboard itself can be customized using the properties provided by the **UITextInputTraits** protocol. The Text view objects implement this protocol and support the properties it defines. You can use these properties to specify the type of keyboard (ASCII, Numbers, URL, Email, and others) to display. You can also configure the basic text entry behavior of the keyboard, such as whether it supports the automatic capitalization and correction of the text. When the system shows or hides the keyboard, it posts several keyboard notifications. These notifications contain the information about the keyboard, including its size, which you can use for calculations that involve repositioning or resizing the views. Registering for these notifications is the only way to get some type of information about the keyboard. The system delivers the following notifications for the keyboard-related events:

- **keyboardWillShowNotification**
- **keyboardDidShowNotification**
- **keyboardWillHideNotification**
- **keyboardDidHideNotification**

UISlider

UISlider is used for selecting a single complete or in-fraction value from the minimum and maximum range of values. Refer to *figure 5.9* as follows:

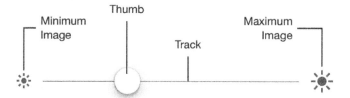

Figure 5.9: UISlider

When the thumb of the slider moves, it passes the action of **UIControl.Event valueChanged** to the targeted method. By default, the slider sends the value-changed events continuously as the user moves the slider's thumb control. Setting up the **isContinuous** property to false, causes the slider to send an event only when the user releases the slider's thumb control, setting the final value.

Use either a custom tint color or a custom image, but not both. When customizing the slider appearance with the images or tint, use one option or the other, but not both. Conflicting settings for the track and thumb appearance are resolved in favor of the most recently set value. The current value must be between the minimum and maximum values. If you try to programmatically set a slider's current value to be below the minimum or above the maximum, it is set to the minimum or maximum instead. However, if you set the value beyond the range of the minimum or maximum in the Interface Builder, the minimum or minimum values are updated instead. Set the custom images for all control states. If you use the custom track and thumb images for your slider, remember to set an image for every possible **UIControl. State**. Any control state that does not have a corresponding custom image assigned to it will display the standard image instead. If you set one custom image, be sure to set them all.

UISwitch

UISwitch controls the binary choice of option via On and Off. Similar to **UISlider**, when a user manipulates the switch control or just flips it on and off, the target method for the event action **valueChanged** triggers. You can also customize the appearance of the switch by changing the color used to tint the switch when it is on or off.

UIStepper

UIStepper is a user interaction control to increment and decrement by a single value. By default, pressing and holding a stepper's button increments or decrements the stepper's value repeatedly. The rate of change depends on how long the user continues pressing the control. To turn off this behavior, set the auto repeat property to false. The maximum value must be greater than or equal to the minimum value. If you set a maximum or minimum value that would break this invariant, both values are set to the new value.

UISegmentController

`UISegmentedControl` is a horizontal control that consists of multiple segments, such that each segment functions as a discrete button. You can customize the segment control with the button texts, background image, title, number of segments, as well as maintain the index at run time via code. When you add and remove the segments, you can request that the action be animated with the sliding and fading effects.

UIPageControl

`UIPageControl` displays a horizontal series of dots, each of which corresponds to a page in the app's document or other data-model entity. When a user taps a page control to move to the next or previous page, the control sends the `valueChanged` event for handling by the delegate. The delegate can then evaluate the `currentPage` property to determine the page to display. The page control advances only one page in either direction. The currently viewed page is indicated via a white dot. Depending on the device, a certain number of dots are displayed on the screen before they are clipped.

UIProgressView

A progress indicator view depicts the progress of a task over time. The `UIProgressView` class provides the properties for managing the style of the progress bar and for getting and setting the values that are pinned to the progress of a task.

UIPickerView

`UIPickerView` uses a spinning-wheel or a slot-machine metaphor to show one or more sets of values. It displays one or more wheels that the user manipulates to select the items. Each wheel has a series of indexed rows representing the selectable items. Each row displays a string or view, so that the user can identify the item on that row. The users select the items by rotating the wheels to the desired values, which align with a selection indicator.

UIDatePicker

`UIDatePicker` control is used for the inputting of date and time values. You can use a date picker to allow a user to enter either a point in time (calendar date, time value, or both) or a time interval (for example, for a timer). You use a date picker only for handling the selection of times and dates. If you want to handle the selection of arbitrary items from a list, use a **UIPickerView** object.

Date pickers use the *Target-Action* design pattern to notify your app when the user changes the selected date. To be notified when the date picker's value changes, register your action method with the **valueChanged** event. At runtime, the date picker calls your methods in response to the user selecting a date or time. You connect a date picker to your action method using the **addTarget(_:action:for:)** method or by creating a connection in the Interface Builder.

UIImageView

UIImageView is a UI container object that is used to display an image or to show a series of images in an animated manner. The image views let you efficiently draw any image that can be specified using a **UIImage** object. For example, you can use the **UIImageView** class to display the contents of many standard image files, such as JPEG and PNG files. You can configure the image views programmatically or in your storyboard file and change the images they display at runtime. The images are composited onto the image view's background and are then composited into the rest of the window. Any transparency in the image allows the image view's background to show through.

When scaling is required, the image view scales each image in the sequence separately. If the images are different sizes, scaling may not yield the results you want.

UITabBar

UItabBar displays one or more buttons in a tab bar for selecting between the different subtasks, views, or modes in your iOS app. You can use the tab bars in conjunction with a **UITabBarController** object, but you can also use them as standalone controls in your app. The tab bars always appear across the bottom edge of the screen and display the contents of one or more **UITabBarItem** objects. A tab bar's appearance can be customized with a background image or tint color to suit the needs of your interface. Tapping an item selects and highlights that item, and you use the selection of the item to enable the corresponding mode for your app. Here you can see a tab bar with three options to select with their icon and name. Refer to *figure 5.10* as follows:

Figure 5.10: *Tab Bar*

UITableView

UITableView displays multiple data in a single column of customizable rows which have vertically scrolling content, divided into rows and sections. Each row of a table displays a single piece of information related to your app. The sections let you group the related rows together. For example, the Contacts app uses a table to display the names of the user's contacts. The table view is not a complete element or control, and is built in collaboration with the different control objects, which are as follows:

- **Cell**: Each Item of **UITableView** consists of a single cell of class **UITableViewCell**. A cell provides the visual representation for your content. You can use the default cells provided by **UIKit** or define the custom cells to suit the needs of your app.

- **Data Source**: This data source object adopts the **UITableViewDataSource** protocol and provides the data for the table.

- **Delegate**: This delegate object adopts the **UITableViewDelegate** protocol and manages the user interactions with the table's contents.

Refer to *figure 5.11* as follows:

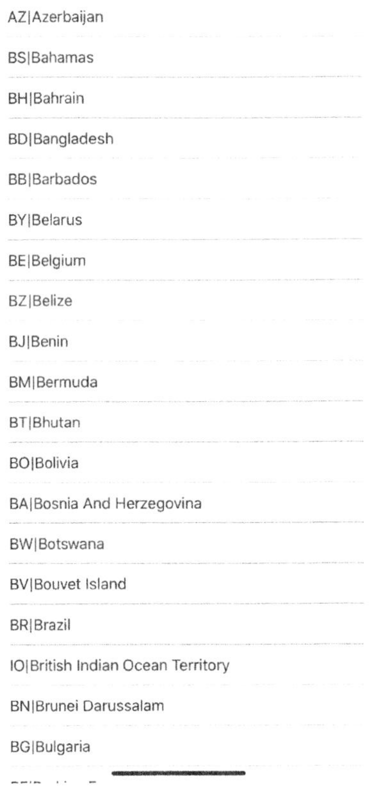

AZ|Azerbaijan

BS|Bahamas

BH|Bahrain

BD|Bangladesh

BB|Barbados

BY|Belarus

BE|Belgium

BZ|Belize

BJ|Benin

BM|Bermuda

BT|Bhutan

BO|Bolivia

BA|Bosnia And Herzegovina

BW|Botswana

BV|Bouvet Island

BR|Brazil

IO|British Indian Ocean Territory

BN|Brunei Darussalam

BG|Bulgaria

Figure 5.11: UITableView

View controller class implements the delegate and data source functions to use table view on user interface and show all relative data on it. The implementation code can be referred as follow:

```swift
import Foundation
import UIKit

class ViewController: UIViewController, UITableViewDelegate,
UITableViewDataSource
{
    var tableView: UITableView = UITableView()
    let country = ["AF|Afghanistan''","AL|Albania","DZ|Algeria",
"AS|American Samoa","AD|Andorra","AO|Angola","AI|Anguilla",
"AQ|Antarctica","AG|Antigua And
Barbuda","AR|Argentina","AM|Armenia","AW|Aruba","AU|Australia","AT|
Austria","AZ|Azerbaijan","BS|Bahamas","BH|Bahrain","BD|
Bangladesh","BB|Barbados","BY|Belarus","BE|Belgium","BZ|Belize","BJ|
Benin","BM|Bermuda","BT|Bhutan","BO|Bolivia","BA|Bosnia And
Herzegovina","BW|Botswana","BV|Bouvet Island","BR|Brazil","IO|British
Indian Ocean Territory","BN|Brunei Darussalam","BG|Bulgaria","BF|Burkina
Faso","BI|Burundi","KH|Cambodia","CM|Cameroon","CA|Canada","CV|Cape
Verde","KY|Cayman Islands","CF|Central African
Republic","TD|Chad","CL|Chile","CN|China","CX|Christmas
Island","CC|Cocos (keeling)
Islands","CO|Colombia","KM|Comoros","CG|Congo","CD|Congo,
The Democratic Republic Of The","CK|Cook Islands","CR|Costa
Rica","CI|Côte D'ivoire","HR|Croatia","CU|Cuba","CY|Cyprus","CZ|Czech
Republic","DK|Denmark","DJ|Djibouti","DM|Dominica","DO|Dominican
Republic","TP|East Timor","EC|Ecuador","EG|Egypt","SV|El
Salvador","GQ|Equatorial
Guinea","ER|Eritrea","EE|Estonia","ET|Ethiopia"]
    let cellReuseIdentifier = "cell"

    override func viewDidLoad()
    {
        super.viewDidLoad()
        self.view.backgroundColor = UIColor.white
        tableView.frame = CGRect(x: 0, y: 50, width: UIScreen.main.
bounds.size.width, height: UIScreen.main.bounds.size.height)
        tableView.delegate = self
        tableView.dataSource = self
        tableView.backgroundColor = UIColor.white
        tableView.register(UITableViewCell.self, forCellReuseIdentifier:
```

```
cellReuseIdentifier)

        self.view.addSubview(tableView)

    }

    func tableView(_ tableView: UITableView, numberOfRowsInSection
section: Int) -> Int
    {
        return country.count
    }

    internal func tableView(_ tableView: UITableView, cellForRowAt
indexPath: IndexPath) -> UITableViewCell
    {
        let cell:UITableViewCell = (tableView.
dequeueReusableCell(withIdentifier: cellReuseIdentifier) as
UITableViewCell?)!

        cell.textLabel?.text = country[indexPath.row]
        cell.textLabel?.textColor = UIColor.black
        cell.backgroundColor = UIColor.white
        return cell
    }

    private func tableView(tableView: UITableView,
didSelectRowAtIndexPath indexPath: IndexPath)
    {
        print("You tapped cell number \(indexPath.row).")
    }
}
```

UICollectionView

UICollectionView displays the nested views using a configurable and highly customizable layout. The collection view manages an ordered set of content in a grid fashion, such as the grid of photos in the Photos app and presents it visually. Similar to the Table view, the Collection View is not a complete element or control and is built in collaboration with the different control objects, which are as follows:

- **Cell**: Each Item of **UICollectionView** consists of a single cell of class **UICollectionViewCell**. A cell provides the visual representation for your content. You can use the default cells provided by **UIKit** or define the custom cells to suit the needs of your app.

- **Data Source**: This data source object adopts the **UICollectionView DataSource** protocol and provides the data for the table.

- **Delegate**: This delegate object adopts the **UIColelctionViewDelegate** protocol and manages the user interactions with the table's contents.

Refer to *figure 5.12* as follows:

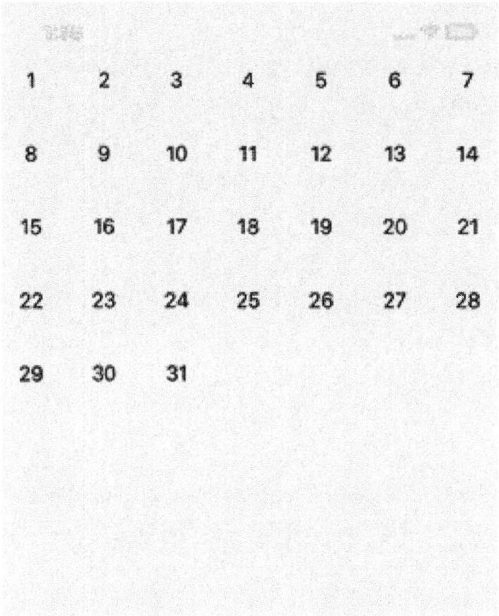

Figure 5.12: Collection View

Similar to table view, in this case view controller will implement the delegate and data source functions of collection view on user interface to show calendar data on it. The implementation code can be referred as follows:

```
import UIKit

class ViewController: UIViewController, UICollectionViewDataSource,
UICollectionViewDelegateFlowLayout, UICollectionViewDelegate {

    let leftAndRightPaddings: CGFloat = 80.0
    let numberOfItemsPerRow: CGFloat = 7.0
    let screenSize: CGRect = UIScreen.main.bounds
    private let cellReuseIdentifier = "collectionCell"
    var items = ["1", "2", "3", "4", "5", "6", "7", "8", "9", "10",
"11", "12", "13", "14", "15", "16", "17", "18", "19", "20", "21", "22",
"23", "24", "25", "26", "27", "28", "29", "30", "31"]

    override func viewDidLoad() {
```

```swift
        super.viewDidLoad()
        let flowLayout = UICollectionViewFlowLayout()
        let collectionView = UICollectionView(frame: self.view.bounds,
collectionViewLayout: flowLayout)
        collectionView.register(UICollectionViewCell.self,
forCellWithReuseIdentifier: "collectionCell")
        collectionView.delegate = self
        collectionView.dataSource = self
        collectionView.backgroundColor = UIColor.cyan

        self.view.addSubview(collectionView)
    }

    func numberOfSectionsInCollectionView(collectionView:
UICollectionView) -> Int {
        return 1
    }

    func collectionView(_ collectionView: UICollectionView,
numberOfItemsInSection section: Int) -> Int {
        return items.count
    }

    func collectionView(_ collectionView: UICollectionView,
cellForItemAt indexPath: IndexPath) -> UICollectionViewCell {
        let cell = collectionView.
dequeueReusableCell(withReuseIdentifier: "collectionCell", for: indexPath
as IndexPath)
        cell.backgroundColor = UIColor.clear
        let title = UILabel(frame: CGRect(x: 0, y: 0, width: cell.
bounds.size.width, height: 40))
        title.textColor = UIColor.black
        title.textAlignment = .center
        title.text = items[indexPath.row]
        cell.contentView.addSubview(title)
        return cell      //return your cell
    }

    //MARK: UICollectionViewDelegate
    func collectionView(_collectionView: UICollectionView,
```

```
didSelectItemAtIndexPath indexPath: NSIndexPath) {
        // When user selects the cell
    }

    func collectionView(_collectionView: UICollectionView,
didDeselectItemAtIndexPath indexPath: NSIndexPath) {
        // When user deselects the cell
    }
}
```

UINavigationController

UINavigationController is the container view controllers that define a stack-based scheme for navigating the hierarchical content which manages one or more child view controllers in a navigation interface. In such a case, only one child view controller is visible at a time, as shown in *figure 5.13* as follows:

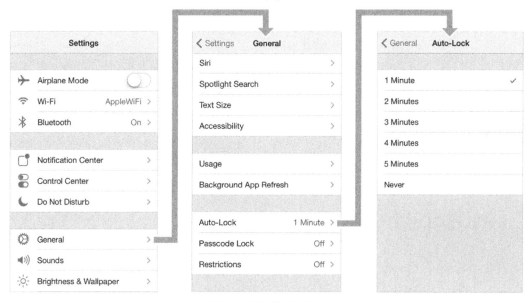

Figure 5.13: *Navigation*

Selecting an item in the view controller pushes a new view controller on the screen using an animation, thereby hiding the previous view controller. Tapping the back button in the navigation bar at the top of the interface removes the top view controller, thereby revealing the view controller underneath.

UINavigationBar

The navigational controls are displayed in a bar along the top of the screen, usually in conjunction with a navigation controller. It is most used within a navigation controller. The **UINavigationController** object creates, displays, and manages its associated navigation bar, and uses the attributes of the view controllers you add to control the content displayed in the navigation bar. If you use a navigation controller to manage the navigation between the different screens of content, the navigation controller creates a navigation bar automatically and pushes and pops the navigation items when appropriate.

Conclusion

Views and controls are the visual building blocks of your app's user interface. In this chapter, we discussed in detail about the storyboard and interface builder which is used for interface building of the Apple apps. Further, we studied the App launch life cycle and the view controller life cycle which are usually implemented in every subclass view Controller of the **UIViewController** class to understand the flow of the controller from the initialization to **deinit**. **UIControl** is the base class of every control and UI element, which is used for the designing of the app interface. We discussed all major elements, including **UItableView** and **UICollectionView** (both components used extensively for handling large sets of data on the Front-end UI). **UINavigationController** works as a container stack for the other view controllers.

In the next chapter, we will discuss SwiftUI, an option to build a UI from the interactive Swift coding without a storyboard or Interface builder. We will also discuss about the user interface designs with the UI coding techniques such as SwiftUI provided by Apple.

Multiple choice questions

1. The UI Control which used to select a single value from the range of values between the maximum and minimum values is _____.

    a. UIPicker

    b. UIStepper

    c. UISlider

    d. UISegmentControl

2. Which keyword is used for the UI variable that connects to a storyboard file?

    a. UIControl

    b. Interface Builder

    c.   IBOutlet

    d.   UIStepper

3. **Super Keyword used to access _____.**

    a.   The current class methods

    b.   The base class methods

    c.   The super class methods

    d.   None of the above

4. **The Delegate and Data Source is used for _____.**

    a.   UITableView

    b.   UIStepper

    c.   UISlider

    d.   UIProgressView

5. **The view which can have multiple rows and columns is _____.**

    a.   UICollectionView

    b.   UIStepper

    c.   UISlider

    d.   UIControl

6. **UINavigation Maintains the View as _____.**

    a.   Queue

    b.   Stack

    c.   Tree

    d.   Graph

Answers

  1. c

  2. c

  3. c

  4. a

  5. a

  6. b

CHAPTER 6

User Interface Design with SwiftUI

Introduction

In this chapter, you will be shown how the UI frameworks were shifted to SwiftUI for designing engaging application user interface designs across the Apple platforms. SwiftUI is a brand-new framework that is offered by Apple for the developers. It is a new way to create user interfaces. Basically, by using SwiftUI, you can build an application's user interface programmatically. SwiftUI is a new and exceptionally easy way of building the user interface designs across all Apple platforms. SwiftUI consists of a set of tools and APIs which are based on Swift. SwiftUI is not just a new framework, it fundamentally changes the way you think about how UI was designed and developed on iOS and other Apple platforms. Apple now encourages the functional programming style for creating the UI designs. It is now easier for you as a developer because you just need to focus on specifying what components are needed in designing the UI and what actions should they perform by programming in a declarative style.

Structure

In this chapter, we will cover the following topics:

- SwiftUI features
- SwiftUI elements

- SwiftUI drawings and animations

Objectives

After studying this chapter, you will be able to create your first UI page without Interface builder and with the SwiftUI interactive declarative coding style and learn how to design complex UI with the help of SwiftUI.

SwiftUI feature

SwiftUI is an incredible user interface designing framework with lots of features. It comes with views property, several controls, and design layouts which helps a developer in making amazing application UI designs.

Key features of SwiftUI

The following are some of the key features of SwiftUI:

- **Declarative syntax**: We declare the elements, and properties of the elements by stating them. You get your UI by declaratively stating it; you get what you type. SwiftUI is a powerful framework that simply organizes the code in an easy-to-read format.

- **Design tools**: SwiftUI provides amazing tools for designing in the native component's library, through which you can easily drag and drop the different controls directly in canvas. You can also replace or update them dynamically resulting in an automatic modification in the code editor according to the changes in canvas. From the preview, you can see what is going on with the project and how the changes are made.

- **Native**: This is an incredible feature where you can view the demo model/ prototype of your application on any platform of Apple with just a few lines of code. Isn't it amazing to design an application prototype for the Apple platform and at the same time view it on the iPad, Mac, and even the Apple Watch? Apple has paid close attention to bringing the controls and environment-specific experiences to SwiftUI. This feature has allowed us to make the application prototypes with all gesture and haptics-based interactions in the Apple platforms.

- **Dynamic type, localization, dark mode, and accessibility**: SwiftUI offers features like dark mode, localization, and accessibility tools including the voice-over, display customization captions and audio descriptions, and guided access. Incredibly anything you prototype with SwiftUI automatically supports these features as well.

This framework provides a friendly environment for the developer to build the UI designs with the help of the event handlers for handling different events, exceptions, and for delivering the taps, signs, and different types of input of application. It offers different tools to manage the data flow from the application's model to the views and controls that will be viewed and interacted with by the end-users. SwiftUI is the future of development as it provides one single platform to write and publish the UI code for all the Apple devices.

Let us learn a few basic concepts about SwiftUI. Knowing these concepts are equally important as writing a better code.

Declarative framework

What does declarative framework mean? We state SwiftUI elements for our design that we want, no matter how it gets and implements these elements. We declare the elements, and the properties of the elements. So, it is easier to design the user interfaces with the declarative Swift syntax. As compared to the previous UI frameworks like UIKit, you can build the same UI design with way less code. It means that the UI code is easier and more natural to write.

View protocol

A View is a simple protocol with a property *'body'* which is a mandatory property. Its type also implements the View protocol. It represents the parts of your app's user interface, and it provides the properties that you can use to organize the views. You can create your custom views by declaring the types that fit into the View protocol and combine them with the SwiftUI views for presenting different control values like texts, images, custom shapes using stacks, lists, and more. You must implement the 'body property' to provide the content for your custom view. To customize the rendering and interactivity of views, you can apply the powerful modifiers to the built-in views or your own.

Getting started with SwiftUI

Refer to *figure 6.1* that illustrates how to get started with SwiftUI, as follows:

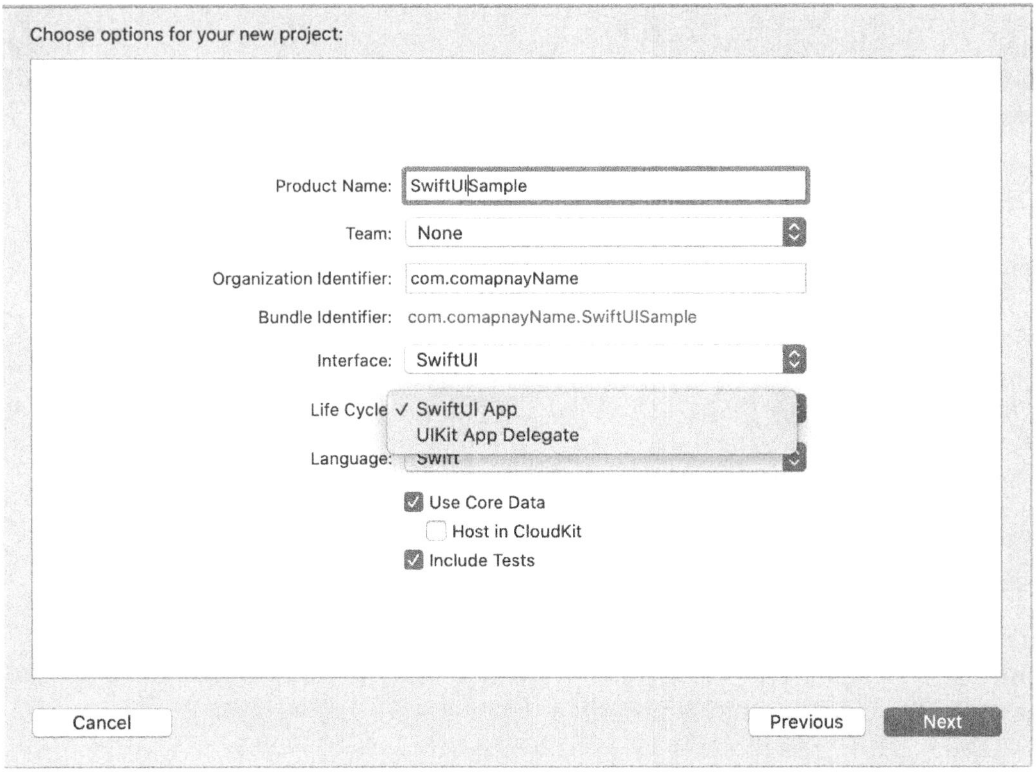

Figure 6.1: Create Project SwiftUI

While you create a new project, you need to first select SwiftUI in While interface and SwiftUI App in While lifecycle instead of While default selections, which will create a default set for you to start designing While UI components with SwiftUI. Refer to the following code:

```
var body: some View {
    return Text("Hello World")
}
```

The preceding code in Swift will create a view with While text **Hello World**, with a variable body which would be passed in While **ContentView.swift** struct. Let's further add more property to this simple text, as follows:

```
import SwiftUI

struct ContentView: View {
```

```
    var body: some View {
        Text("Hello, World!")
    }
}


struct ContentView_Previews: PreviewProvider {
    static var previews: some View {
        ContentView()
    }
}
```

SwiftUI elements

Let's compare UIView of UIKit vs View of SwiftUI, as follows:

- As we discussed earlier, View is a protocol rather than a class in SwiftUI.

- The view always returns a rendered view, and it may contain some other child view but must return a parent view.

Previews in Xcode

Preview Provider: To create a preview of the SwiftUI code, we need to confirm the protocol **PreviewProvider**. The Xcode preview system uses the same API to preview which is used by SwiftUI. Xcode statically discovers the types that conform to the **PreviewProvider** protocol in your app and generates the previews for each provider it discovers. This protocol does not run when the code is executed in the simulator.

Combining views using stacks

The next step in SwiftUI is to understand if there is no single element to return from the body and relatively multiple views and elements need to be shown. When creating a SwiftUI view, you describe its content, layout, and behavior in the view's body property; however, the body property only returns a single view. You can combine and embedded multiple views in stacks, which group the views together horizontally, vertically, or back-to-front. On the basis of combining views using stacks, there are mainly three types as follows:

- **VStacks**: VStacks represents the vertical alignment of the views in a stack manner. In the vertical stack of views, the three text views would be placed one above the other, shown as follows:

```
struct ContentView: View {
    var body: some View {
        VStack(alignment: .leading) {
            Text("Header")
                .font(.title)
            Text("First")
                .font(.subheadline)
            Text("Second")
                .font(.subheadline)
        }
    }
}
```

- **HStacks**: HStacks represents the horizontal alignment of views and other elements in a stack manner. In the horizontal stack of views, the three text views would be placed side by side to each other, shown as follows:

```
struct ContentView: View {
    var body: some View {
        HStack(alignment: .top) {
            Text("Title")
                .font(.title)
            Text("Content 1")
                .font(.subheadline)
            Text("Item 1")
                .font(.subheadline)
        }
    }
}
```

- **ZStacks**: The ZStack is in a category of its own because it groups the views together, seen back-to-front, along the z- or depth axis. The views will overlap in a ZStack, which means that it is great for creating the UI stacks that overlay the other views and assigns each successive child view a higher z-axis value than the one before it, meaning the later children appear on top of the earlier ones, shown as follows:

```
let colors: [Color] = [.orange , .red, .green,   .purple ,
.yellow, .blue]
struct ContentView: View {
```

```
var body: some View {
    ZStack {
        ForEach(0..<colors.count) {
            Rectangle()
                .fill(colors[$0])
                .frame(width: 100, height: 100)
                .offset(x: CGFloat($0) * 10.0,
                        y: CGFloat($0) * 10.0)
        }
    }
}
}
```

Refer to *figure 6.2* as follows:

Figure 6.2: ZStack Design View

Grids with ScrollView

In SwiftUI, two new view styles are lazy **VGrid** and lazy **HGrid** that SwiftUI provides us with to build a super custom grid-based interface. The axis of the layout is the only contrast between them. In the vertical direction, the lazy **VGrid** populates the space open. On the other side, in the horizontal direction, the lazy **HGrid** arranges its children. In these two views, the axis is the only distinction. It is similar to the **UICollectionView** of **UIKit**, shown as follows:

```
struct ContentView: View {
    private var columns: [GridItem] = [
        GridItem(.fixed(100), spacing: 16),
        GridItem(.fixed(100), spacing: 16),
        GridItem(.fixed(100), spacing: 16)
    ]
```

```
var body: some View {
    ScrollView {
        LazyVGrid(
            columns: columns,
            alignment: .center,
            spacing: 16,
            pinnedViews: [.sectionHeaders, .sectionFooters]
        ) {
            Section(header: Text("Section 1").font(.title)) {
                ForEach(0...10, id: \.self) { index in
                    Color.green
                }
            }

            Section(header: Text("Section 2").font(.title)) {
                ForEach(11...20, id: \.self) { index in
                    Color.orange
                }
            }
        }
    }
}
```

Refer to *figure 6.3* as follows:

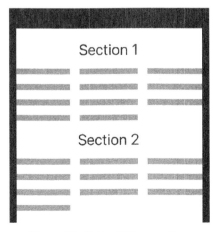

Figure 6.3: *Grid with two sections*

Grid Item: To customize the arrangement of objects in the lazy **HGrid** and lazy **VGrid** views, you can use the **GridItem** instances. Each grid object defines the layout properties, such as spacing and orientation, that all the objects in a given column or row will be sized and arranged by the grid view.

Container views

There are mainly the following four types of containers provided by Apple in the SwiftUI framework, although you can create your own custom containers if required or if the default containers won't work as expected:

- **List**: A grouping control container that is used for data entry, such as in settings or inspectors. In a way, suitable for the network, SwiftUI makes shapes. For starters, forms appear as grouped lists on iOS. A list in SwiftUI is similar to **UITableView** in **UIKit** Framework. Refer to the following code:

```
var body: some View {
        List {
            HStack {
                Text("1.").frame(width: 20.0, height: nil,
alignment: .leading)
                Text("Name: John Mathew \nAge: 32")
            }
            HStack {
                Text("2.").frame(width: 20.0, height: nil,
alignment: .leading)
                Text("Name: Marry Saldom \nAge: 24")
            }

        }
    }
```

Refer to *figure 6.4* illustrating the List View as follows:

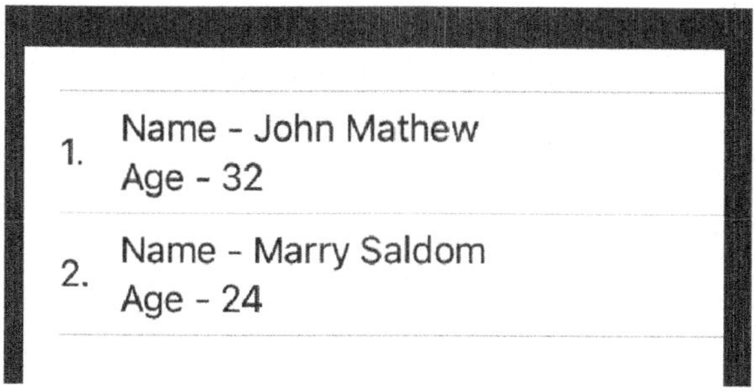

Figure 6.4: List View

- **Group**: When you want to list multiple views, you can use **VStack** but that has a limitation that the SwiftUI building system will let you design to add up to ten views in **VStack**; so, there you can use a group inside **VStack** to add more than ten elements to the designs.

- **GroupBox**: The GroupBox is a stylized view with an optional icon connected to a logical content classification. A plain card with the title and content is the default style on iOS. Let's have a look at that. SwiftUI provides us with the **GroupBoxStyle** protocol that enables us to fully alter the look and feel of every instance of **GroupBox**. For all the use-cases we require, we can build numerous types. A framework that conforms to the **GroupBoxStyle** protocol is created to create your own **GroupBox** style. The sole prerequisite is **GroupBoxStyle**. You must build a **makeBody** feature that accepts the **GroupBoxStyleConfiguration** type instance and returns a new view. **GroupBoxStyleConfiguration** provides us with the **GroupBox** mark as well as the material, within the **makeBody** feature as shown as follows:

```
struct HeartGroupBoxStyle: GroupBoxStyle {
func makeBody(configuration: Configuration) -> some View {
        VStack(alignment: .leading) {
            configuration.label
            configuration.content
        }
    }
}


struct ContentView: View {
    var body: some View {
        GroupBox(
            label: Label("Heart Rate: ", systemImage: "heart.
fill")
                .foregroundColor(.red)
        ) {
            Text("Your heart rate is 80 BPM.")
        }.groupBoxStyle(HeartGroupBoxStyle())
    }
}
```

Refer to *figure 6.5* illustrating the GroupBox, as follows:

Your hear rate is 80 BPM.

Figure 6.5: GroupBox

- **Section**: Much like **UITableView** in **UIKit**, SwiftUI's list view has built-in support for the sections and section headers. Start by placing a section around it and optionally adding a header and footer to add a section around those cells. Refer to the following code:

```
struct TaskRow: View {
var body: some View {
        Text("Task Link ")
    }
}


struct ContentView: View {
    var body: some View {
        List {
            Section(header: Text("Important Tasks")) {
                TaskRow()
                TaskRow()
            }
            Section(header: Text("Other Tasks")) {
                TaskRow()
                TaskRow()
            }
        }
    }
}
```

Refer to *figure 6.6* illustrating the Section in List, as follows:

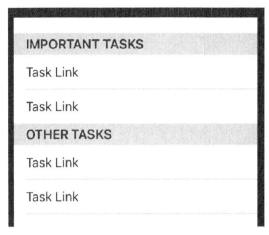

Figure 6.6: Section in List

Working with Form and Navigation in SwiftUI

The SwiftUI type is a container that allows you to group the controls for data entry, such as text fields, toggles, steppers, pickers, and others. In this tutorial, we will explore and apply each type of data entry control to a form. Now, we can learn how to build and use the forms in SwiftUI by constructing a basic UI type setup.

Wrap the content view in **NavigationView** to create a simple form with a text field, and then embed a form within it. By inserting a toggle with an option to keep our account private and making a section called **Profile** containing both the **TextField** and a Toggle, you can further change our form, shown as follows:

```
struct ContentView: View {
    @State var username: String = ""
    @State var isPrivate: Bool = true
    @State var notificationsEnabled: Bool = false
    @State private var previewIndex = 0
    var previewOptions = ["Always", "When Unlocked", "Never"]

    var body: some View {
        NavigationView {
            Form {
                Section(header: Text("PROFILE")) {
                    TextField("Username", text: $username)
                    Toggle(isOn: $isPrivate) {
```

```
                        Text("Private Account")
                    }
                }

                Section(header: Text("NOTIFICATIONS")) {
                    Toggle(isOn: $notificationsEnabled) {
                        Text("Enabled")
                    }
                    Picker(selection: $previewIndex, label: Text("Show
Previews")) {
                        ForEach(0 ..< previewOptions.count) {
                            Text(self.previewOptions[$0])
                        }
                    }
                }

                Section(header: Text("ABOUT")) {
                    HStack {
                        Text("Version")
                        Spacer()
                        Text("0.1.1")
                    }
                }

                Section {
                    Button(action: {
                        print("Perform an action here...")
                    }) {
                        Text("Reset All Settings")
                    }
                }
            }
            .navigationBarTitle("Settings")
        }
    }
}
```

Now, create a new segment called **Alerts Now**. This segment will include a toggle to turn the alerts on and off and a picker to select the options to preview the notifications. Create three new variables to keep track of the toggle range, the picker's chosen index, and a list of choices for the picker. Finally, at the very bottom of the form, let's add a button, allowing you to reset all the options to their default values, as shown in *figure 6.7* as follows:

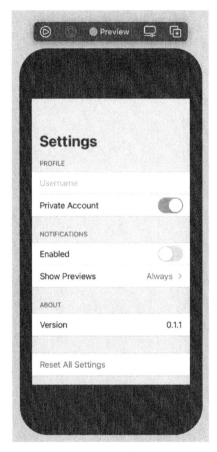

Figure 6.7: Form with Navigation

SwiftUI drawing and animations

In this section, we will discuss how we can draw different shapes with the help of the default available shapes as well as draw custom shapes with the path components. SwiftUI provides us with some of the following simple shapes that we can use in our app for drawing:

- Rectangle
- Rounded rectangle

- Ellipse
- Circle
- Capsule

The **Shape** doesn't know anything about its supposed size and position. Therefore, as long as we provide the shape with a frame, it tries to fill out the whole view. Here, we will understand how we can make use of the default shapes. Let's provide a **RoundedRectangle** with a certain width and height. We also define another fill color than the default black, and the following code will show a rounded rectangle with green color:

```
struct ContentView: View {
    var body: some View {
        RoundedRectangle(cornerRadius: 20)
            .frame(width: 250, height: 100)
            .foregroundColor(.green)
    }
}
```

If you want a shape not to be completely filled with color, but just to build some sort of boundary out of it, you can use a certain line width for your boundary by using the **.stroke** modifier (like the first one). Using another stroke form is also possible, such as using a dashed line as the boundary as shown as follows:

```
struct ContentView: View {
    var body: some View {
        RoundedRectangle(cornerRadius: 20)
        .stroke(style: StrokeStyle(lineWidth: 7, lineCap: .square, dash: [15], dashPhase: 2))
            .frame(width: 250, height: 100)
            .foregroundColor(.green)
    }
}
```

Refer to *figure 6.8* illustrating a shaded rectangle, as follows:

Figure 6.8: Shaded Rectangle

Drawing custom shapes with path

Reusability is the secret to recognizing the distinction between Path and Shape; paths are built to do one particular thing, while shapes have the freedom of drawing space and can also embrace the parameters to enable us to further modify them.

Take a quick look at what paths in SwiftUI are. You can imagine a path like a set of drawing instructions, including lines, curves, and other segments like arcs. Therefore, a shape is doing nothing different than using a specific path to define its appearance. Insert a Path instance followed by its corresponding closure. Inside the closure, we can actually define how our **path** should go. SwiftUI will fill out the resulting view with the black color. Now, draw our square by adding several lines to our **path**. We can do this by using absolute X- and Y-coordinates as shown as follows:

```swift
struct MySquare: Shape
{
    func path(in rect: CGRect) -> Path {
        var path = Path()

        path.move(to: CGPoint(x: 200, y: 0))
        path.addLine(to: CGPoint(x: 200, y: 200))
        path.addLine(to: CGPoint(x: 0, y: 200))
        path.addLine(to: CGPoint(x: 0, y: 0))
        path.closeSubpath()

        return path
    }
}


struct ContentView: View {
    var body: some View {
        MySquare()
        .frame(width: 250, height: 250)
    }
}
```

The given code will draw a simple black square which is by default completely filled, as illustrated in *figure 6.9* as follows:

Figure 6.9: *Square Rectangle*

Drawing curved shapes in SwiftUI

We will look at how curved shapes can be formed. We'll be able to create interesting shapes like a raindrop. A structure called **Raindrop** is proclaimed here and conforms to the **Shape** protocol. We initialize the **Raindrop** shape and add a stroke and frame to it within our SwiftUI window. We start pushing our **cursor** within our **Raindrop**'s route to the center of the upper edge of the **rect** as shown as follows:

```
struct Raindrop: Shape {


    func path(in rect: CGRect) -> Path {
        Path { path in
            path.move(to: CGPoint(x: rect.size.width/2, y: 0))
            path.addQuadCurve(to: CGPoint(x: rect.size.width/2, y: rect.
size.height), control: CGPoint(x: rect.size.width, y: rect.size.height))
        }
    }
}


struct ContentView: View {
    var body: some View {
        Raindrop()
            .stroke(lineWidth: 4)
            .frame(width: 200, height: 200)
    }
}
```

First, we want to draw the correct downward curve. To do that, we use the **addQuadCurve** approach. This function applies to the direction of a so-called Bézier curve. We first need to define an endpoint for the curve for such a Bézier curve; so, to really do the curve, we need to have a control point for the Bézier curve. Such a point of control is used to measure the curve's intensity and direction. For this, you don't need to know calculus. Only take a peek at the infographic shown in *figure 6.10* and get a feel for this, as follows:

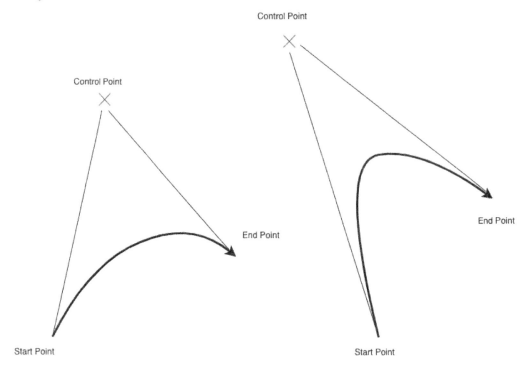

Figure 6.10: *Draw Curve*

To implement preceding scenario let's draw RainDrop Shape, adding the required moves and curves. Refer to the following code:

```
struct Raindrop: Shape {
    func path(in rect: CGRect) -> Path {
        Path { path in
            path.move(to: CGPoint(x: rect.size.width/2, y: 0))
            path.addQuadCurve(to: CGPoint(x: rect.size.width/2, y: rect.
size.height), control: CGPoint(x: rect.size.width, y: rect.size.height))
            path.addQuadCurve(to: CGPoint(x: rect.size.width/2, y: 0),
control: CGPoint(x: 0, y: rect.size.height))
        }
```

```
    }
}

struct ContentView: View {
    var body: some View {
        Raindrop()
        .fill(LinearGradient(gradient: Gradient(colors: [.white, .blue]),
startPoint: .topLeading, endPoint: .bottom))
        .frame(width: 200, height: 200)
    }
}
```

Let's complete our Raindrop form by drawing another curve that points to where we began our sketch. When we're done with our Raindrop form, by swapping the `.stroke` modifier, we can fill out this shape within our SwiftUI view. You may fill the form with a gradient, for example, as seen in the preceding code. And your Raindrop shape is expected to look like the image in *figure 6.11*, as follows:

Figure 6.11: *Draw Drop*

Animation views

You can animate updates to views, or to a view's condition, independently by using SwiftUI, no matter where the results are. The difficulty of these mixed, overlapping, and interruptible animations is managed by SwiftUI for you.

An interpolating spring animation that uses a damped spring model to create values within the range [0, 1] are then used to interpolate within the range of the animated property [from, to]. By incorporating the impacts of each animation, it maintains the speed through simultaneous animations. That image value can be toggled whenever a tap gesture is called. Let's take a working example with an image of a ball which will bounce on tap as shown as follows:

```
struct ContentView: View {
    @State private var bounceBall: Bool = false
```

```
var body: some View {
    VStack
    {
        Image("ball")
        .resizable()
        .frame(width: 150, height: 150)
        .foregroundColor(.black)
        .clipShape(Circle())
        .animation(Animation.interpolatingSpring(stiffness: 90,
damping: 1.5).repeatForever(autoreverses: false))
        .offset(y: bounceBall ? -200 : 200)
        .onTapGesture {
            self.bounceBall.toggle()
        }
    }
}
}
```

Architecture views

The Architecture views are used when we want the transitions of views with better management of the UI flow. In such a case, we can mainly use the following three architectural views other than the Navigation views:

- TabBar view

- Split view

TabBar view

A view that moves between the various views of children using elements of the immersive user interface is known as the **TabBar** view. Place the views in **TabView** to create a user interface with tabs and add the **tabItem(:)** modifier to the contents of each tab. A tab view with three tabs is generated as shown here:

```
struct ContentView: View {
    var body: some View {
        TabView {
            Text("The Home Tab")
                .tabItem {
```

```
                    Image(systemName: "heart.fill")
                    Text("Home")
                }
            Text("Featured Tab")
                .tabItem {
                    Image(systemName: "star.fill")
                    Text("Featured")
                }
            Text("The Profile Tab")
                .tabItem {
                    Image(systemName: "person.fill")
                    Text("Profile")
                }
        }
        .font(.headline)
    }
}
```

Refer to *figure 6.12* illustrating the TabBar view, as follows:

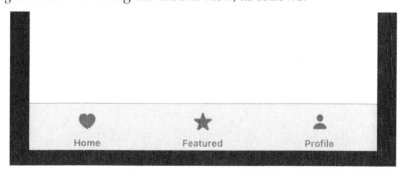

Figure 6.12: *TabBar View*

Split view

A layout container that arranges its children in a horizontal or vertical line and allows the user to resize them using the dividers placed between them, is known as the Split view, and is shown as follows:

```
struct ContentView: View {

 let requestUrls = ["https://Google.com", "https://bpbonline.com",
"https://twitter.com"]
```

```
    var body: some View {

        GeometryReader { geo in
            NavigationView {
                List(self.requestUrls, id: \.self) { url in
                    NavigationLink(destination: RequestDetailView(url:
url)) {
                        Text(url)
                    }
                }
                .navigationBarTitle("Links")

                Text("Nothing Selected.")
            }
            .padding(.leading, geo.size.height > geo.size.width ? 1 : 0)
        }

    }
}


// Detail view
struct RequestDetailView: View {
    let url: String
    var body: some View {

        Text("Detail view of request with url: \(url).")
    }
}
```

Refer to *figure 6.13* illustrating the Split View, as follows:

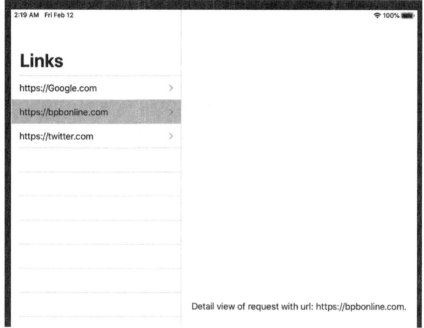

Figure 6.13: *Split View*

Presentation views

There are mainly two presentation views used to either inform the user or to give options to choose, which are as follows:

- Action view
- ActionSheet view

Action view

When you want the user to respond in response to the status of the app or the device, use a warning. Using the **alert(isPresented:content:)** view modifier, you can display an alert to generate an alert that occurs if the bound value **isPresented** is valid. A personalized instance of the **Alert** form is generated by the content closure you include for this modifier. In the following example, when tapped, the button shows a basic warning by updating the local **showAlert** property that links to the alert:

```
struct ContentView : View {
    @State private var showAlert = false
    var body: some View {
```

```
        Button("Tap to view alert") {
            self.showAlert = true
        }
        .alert(isPresented: $showAlert) {
            Alert(
                title: Text("Unable to Save Data"),
                message: Text("The connection to the server was lost."),
                primaryButton: .default(
                    Text("Try Again"),
                    action: saveData
                ),
                secondaryButton: .destructive(
                    Text("Delete"),
                    action: saveData
                )
            )
        }
    }


    func saveData() {
        // Save data code
    }
}
```

Refer to *figure 6.14* illustrating the Alert View, as follows:

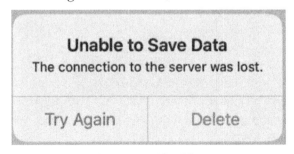

Figure 6.14: *Alert View*

ActionSheet view

When you want the user to decide between two or more choices, in reaction to their own action, use an action sheet. By using the **actionSheet(isPresented:content:)**

view modifier, you display an action sheet to construct an action sheet that occurs whenever the **isPresented** binding value is valid. A personalized instance of the **ActionSheet** form is generated by the content closure you include for this modifier. To include the alternatives, build an **ActionSheet.Button** instance to differentiate between the ordinary options, the destructive options, and the user's initial action cancellation, as shown as follows:

```swift
struct ContentView : View {
    @State private var showActionSheet = false
    var body: some View {
        Button("Tap to view action sheet") {
            self.showActionSheet = true
        }
        .actionSheet(isPresented: $showActionSheet) {
            ActionSheet(title: Text("Resume Workout Recording"),
                        message: Text("Choose a destination for workout
data"),
                        buttons: [
                            .cancel(),
                            .destructive(
                                Text("Overwrite Workout"),
                                action: overwrite
                            ),
                            .default(
                                Text("Append Workout"),
                                action: overwrite
                            )
                        ]
            )
        }
    }

    func overwrite() {
        // overwrite data code
    }
}
```

Refer to *figure 6.15* illustrating the Action Sheet, as follows:

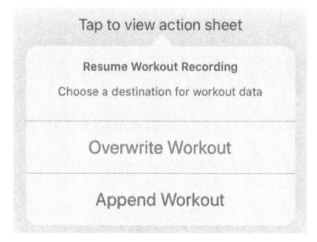

Figure 6.15: Action Sheet

Conclusion

It is surely an incredible improvement that Apple has made. It has simplified building a robust and flexible design system. Apple platforms are friendly, and its controls and platform-specific experiences are loved by everyone because of their presentation. SwiftUI is genuinely native, so your applications straightforwardly access the proven technologies of every platform with a limited amount of code and a collaborative design canvas. It is a powerful platform for the UI designers and developers who are compulsive about designing the user interfaces and about building real apps across all supported Apple platforms like (iOS, macOS, tvOS, iPad, and watchOS). While the code does not suit one-size-fits-all, the controls and methods involved can apply to all platforms. It provides an easy and friendly environment for the beginners as well, but it is also filled with tricks of designs and cool workflows for developing the best UIs and interactions.

In the next chapter, we will discuss the local data storage as a database with SQLite and Core Data.

Multiple choice questions

1. **What is View in SwiftUI?**

    a. Protocol

    b. Class

    c. struct

    d. UIKit component

2. **Why is the path used?**
    a. To add a Line
    b. To draw a curve
    c. As a default shape
    d. As a custom shape

3. **Alertview in SwiftUI is _____.**
    a. To show info to the user
    b. To show options to choose from
    c. To draw a curve
    d. A Shape

4. **What is the ActionSheet in SwiftUI used for?**
    a. A Shape
    b. To show options to choose from
    c. To show info to the user
    d. To draw a curve

5. **RoundRectangle in SwiftUI is a _____.**
    a. Custom shape
    b. Default shape
    c. Draw by curve
    d. Class

6. **Interpolating Spring is used in SwiftUI _____.**
    a. To show options to choose from
    b. As an Animation Component
    c. To draw a curve
    d. As a Custom Shape

Answers

1. a
2. a
3. a
4. b
5. b   6. b

CHAPTER 7

DataBase with SQLite and Core Data

Introduction

In the initial times of mobile development, when the network capabilities were not explored for the handheld devices, there were extensive requirements to save and persist data in the mobile memory. When simple operations, such as reading from the file in the directory and writing to a file in the directory were explored, those were good enough only for the small data sizes. But as the data started increasing gradually on the file, a few problems started in front of the developers, such as the searching results becoming slower and increasing the size of data files was another big issue for the handheld devices with limited memory allocations. There are distinct strategies to pick from for the iOS storage. However, the decision depends on when and how much knowledge you choose to hold. Most of the time, the implementation of the local storage in the iOS apps requires more than one process, as the device needs various persistence specifications. The most used approaches in iOS for the implementation of local storage are as follows:

- SQLite

- Property List

- Core Data

- UserDefaults

Structure

In this chapter, we will cover the following topics:

- UserDefaults
- SQLite
- CoreData

Objectives

After studying this chapter, you will be able to save the user inputs and experiences to persistent data and show them on UI after retrieval of the persistent data. You will be also able to save and retrieve the user credentials in the keychain to perform auto-login.

UserDefaults

UserDefaults provides access to the default user account, where you persistently store the key-value pairs during the launches of your app. A programmatic interface for communicating with the default framework is provided by the **UserDefaults** class. The default framework enables a programme to modify its actions to fit the needs of a user. You may allow the users to determine their desired measuring units or media playback speed, for example. The apps store these preferences in a user's default database by assigning the values to a series of parameters. The parameters are referred to as defaults because they are often used to decide the default state of an app at runtime or the default way it behaves. Refer to the following code:

```
let defaults = UserDefaults.standard
      defaults.set(30, forKey: "Age")
      defaults.set(true, forKey: "TouchID")
      defaults.set(CGFloat.pi, forKey: "PiValue")

      defaults.set("John Huge", forKey: "Name")
      defaults.set(Date(), forKey: "waitTill")
```

You can see in the preceding code that the **UserDefaults** class provides the convenience methods for accessing the common types such as floats, doubles, integers, Boolean values, and date.

It's still straightforward when it comes to reading back data, but it has a significant clause that if the configuration can't be found, **UserDefaults** will return a default value. You need to know what these default values are, so that you don't mistake them with the actual values that you set, which are as follows:

- **integer(forKey:)** returns an integer if the key exists, or 0 if not.

- **bool(forKey:)** returns a boolean if the key exists, or false if not.

- **float(forKey:)** returns a float if the key exists, or 0.0 if not.

- **double(forKey:)** returns a double if the key exists, or 0.0 if not.

- **object(forKey:)** returns **AnyObject?** so you need to conditionally typecast it to your data type.

UserDefaults singleton object can be accessed via standard function, and further values with respect to the unique keys, which are shown as follows:

```
let defaults = UserDefaults.standard
        let age = defaults.integer(forKey: "Age")
        let touchID = defaults.bool(forKey: "TouchID")
        let pi = defaults.double(forKey: "PiValue")
        print(age)
        print(touchID)
        print(pi)
```

Property list

Property list or plist is a simple form of XML data that can be kept in the key-value pair form of data with the file extension **.plist**. In *figure 7.1*, you can see how you can create a **plist** file in your project, shown as follows:

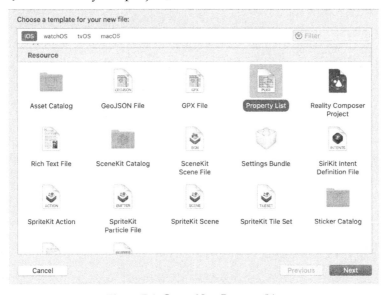

Figure 7.1: Create New Property List

The **plist** root item could have two types – Dictionary and Array. When you choose one type of root item, you could add more child items of types Dictionary, Array, Boolean, Data, Date, String, and Number. In XCode, you can see a structure of **plist** XML by right-clicking on a **plist** file and choosing **Open As | Source Code**. Let's see how a **plist** looks with data, as shown in *figure 7.2* as follows:

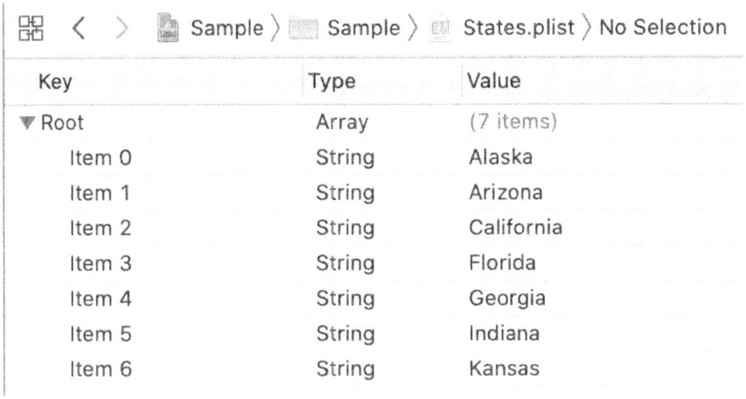
Sample 〉 Sample 〉 States.plist 〉 No Selection

Key	Type	Value
▼ Root	Array	(7 items)
Item 0	String	Alaska
Item 1	String	Arizona
Item 2	String	California
Item 3	String	Florida
Item 4	String	Georgia
Item 5	String	Indiana
Item 6	String	Kansas

Figure 7.2: *Property List*

Now, let's look at the source code, as follows:

```
<?xml version="1.0" encoding="UTF-8"?>
<!DOCTYPE plist PUBLIC "-//Apple//DTD PLIST 1.0//EN" "http://www.apple.
com/DTDs/PropertyList-1.0.dtd">
<plist version="1.0">
<array>
    <string>Alaska</string>
    <string>Arizona</string>
    <string>California</string>
    <string>Florida</string>
    <string>Georgia</string>
    <string>Indiana</string>
    <string>Kansas</string>
</array>
</plist>
```

Reading a plist with Swift

Property lists are great for your app to save quick, static key-value info. The following is how you can read the Swift plug-in:

```
func getPropertyList(withName name: String) -> [String]?
    {
        if  let path = Bundle.main.path(forResource: name, ofType:
"plist"),
            let xml = FileManager.default.contents(atPath: path)
        {
            return (try? PropertyListSerialization.propertyList(from:
xml, options: .mutableContainersAndLeaves, format: nil)) as? [String]
        }


        return nil
    }


if let states = getPropertyList(withName: "States") {
        print(states)
        }
// Output: ["Alaska", "Arizona", "California", "Florida", "Georgia",
"Indiana", "Kansas"]
```

Let's look into the code now, as follows:

- We are deserializing the XML data as a property list within the conditional clause. The property's list is returned as an array, but we will have to cast it to **[String]** because Any type is returned by **propertyList(from:options:format:)**.

- The feature returns zero when the conditional fails, or the typecasting fails, or when the **propertyList(from:options:format:)** call throws an error. If not, it returns an array of the form **[String]?** So, we use optional binding again to get the non-optional array states when we call **getPropertyList(withName:)**.

Writing data to plist

Adding data to plist and editing any data or key-value pair to plist is similar to writing to the file at a specific path location, which we will discuss in detail in the next chapter with File handling in iOS, and **NSFileManager**.

SQLite

SQLite is a library of applications that offers a framework for relational database management. In terms of configuration, database management, and the resources needed, the lite in SQLite means lightweight. SQLite is capable of building the databases in memory that are very easy to work with.

The following notable features are available for SQLite:

- Self-contained, serverless, zero-configuration, and transactional.

- SQLite is self-contained, ensuring that it requires a limited operating system or external library support.

- In any environment, this makes SQLite accessible, especially on embedded devices such as iPhones, Android phones, game consoles, mobile media players, etc.

- SQLite uses dynamic table forms. It means that in any column, regardless of the data type, you can store any value.

- SQLite facilitates a single database connection to concurrently view various database files. This brings several fun features, such as joining the tables in multiple databases or copying the data with a single command within the databases.

Working with SQLite in Swift

In this section, we will make a single class to manage all the SQLite files and CRUD operations. This class includes creating a database, creating tables, inserting in that table, reading from that table, and deleting from that table functions.

Refer to the following code:

```
import Foundation
import SQLite3


class DBManager
{

    let dbPath: String = "DB.sqlite"
    var db:OpaquePointer?

}
```

In the preceding code, we import the library SQLite3 to perform all the SQLite operations. The first variable **dbPath** has the name of the database file with its extension **.sqlite** and a variable of opaque pointer type will keep the reference of the database in the code at the time of execution.

Creating and connecting to database

We need to establish a database link before doing something. This feature is named **sqlite3 open()**, which opens or generates a new file for the database. It returns an **OpaquePointer**, which is a Swift sort for C pointers if it's efficient. You would have to grab the returned pointer when you call this function in order to communicate with the database. Many of the SQLite functions return the result code of **Int32**, which is normally a constant in the library of SQLite. SQLITE OK, for instance, represents the result code zero, shown as follows:

```swift
func openDatabase() -> OpaquePointer?
    {
        let fileURL = try! FileManager.default.url(for:
.documentDirectory, in: .userDomainMask, appropriateFor: nil, create:
false)
            .appendingPathComponent(dbPath)
        var db: OpaquePointer? = nil
        if sqlite3_open(fileURL.path, &db) != SQLITE_OK
        {
            print("error opening database")
            return nil
        }
        else
        {
            print("Successfully opened connection to database at \
(dbPath)")
            return db
        }
    }
```

Creating a table

You can create a table, now that you have a link to a database file. To store the data, you'll work with a very basic table. Here, the person table will have three columns, which are as follows:

- Id with int type and Primary Key

- Name of text type

- Age of int type.

Before preparing sqlite3 to create the table statement, we would need to frame the SQL query for creating the table with a given column; so, the query would be as follows:

```
CREATE TABLE IF NOT EXISTS person(Id INTEGER PRIMARY KEY, name TEXT,
age INTEGER)
```

Consider the following example:

```
func createTable()
{
        let createTableString = "CREATE TABLE IF NOT EXISTS person(Id
INTEGER PRIMARY KEY, name TEXT, age INTEGER);"
        var createTableStatement: OpaquePointer? = nil
        if sqlite3_prepare_v2(db, createTableString, -1,
&createTableStatement, nil) == SQLITE_OK
        {
            if sqlite3_step(createTableStatement) == SQLITE_DONE
            {
                print("person table created.")
            } else {
                print("person table could not be created.")
            }
        } else {
            print("CREATE TABLE statement could not be prepared.")
        }
        sqlite3_finalize(createTableStatement)
}
```

Let's understand the given code step-by-step for creating a table, as follows:

- First, take the defined constant table query and create a reference pointer in the next stage.

- **sqlite3_prepare_v2()** compiles the SQL statement into the byte code and returns a status code. To ensure the statement is correctly compiled, you match the returned status code. This mechanism moves to the next step.

Otherwise, you should print a message noting that the declaration was not compiled.

- The compiled statement is run by **sqlite3_step()**. You only move once in this situation since this argument has a single consequence.

- Finally, we call sqlite3 **finalize()** on your compiled statement to delete it and prevent the leakage of resources.

Before the implementation of create table, we are required to open the database with its name; this will ensure that a database SQLite file is created before any database operation. We can perform this as shown as follows:

```
class DBManager
{
    init()
    {
        db = openDatabase()
        createTable()
    }

    let dbPath: String = "DB.sqlite"
    var db:OpaquePointer?
```

>>>>

Inserting data

After the initial steps of opening the database and creating a table, we will insert some records into the person of **db.sqlite**, so that later, we can perform the retrieval operations and show that data. On the UI side, you will create a simple form with two or three input fields (you can choose **Id** to be autoincremented and maintain that as unique with the programming logic or you can take it as input too).

The syntax is as follows:

```
INSERT INTO person (Id, name, age) VALUES (?, ?, ?)
```

```
func insert(id:Int, name:String, age:Int)
    {
        let insertStatementString = "INSERT INTO person (Id, name, age)
VALUES (?, ?, ?);"
```

```
        var insertStatement: OpaquePointer? = nil
        if sqlite3_prepare_v2(db, insertStatementString, -1,
&insertStatement, nil) == SQLITE_OK {
            sqlite3_bind_int(insertStatement, 1, Int32(id))
            sqlite3_bind_text(insertStatement, 2, (name as NSString).
utf8String, -1, nil)
            sqlite3_bind_int(insertStatement, 3, Int32(age))

            if sqlite3_step(insertStatement) == SQLITE_DONE {
                print("Successfully inserted row.")
            } else {
                print("Could not insert row.")
            }
        } else {
            print("INSERT statement could not be prepared.")
        }
        sqlite3_finalize(insertStatement)
    }
```

Let's understand the given code step-by-step for inserting the records into the database, as follows:

- Initially, in the first step, you will compile the statement and verify that everything is working well.

- The name of the method, **sqlite3_bind_int()**, means that you bind an Int to the argument. The first function parameter is the argument to be added to, while the second is a non-zero-based index for the position of the **?** and the value itself is the third and final parameter. A status code is returned by this binding call; but for now, you presume it succeeds.

- To execute the sentence and check that it has been completed, use sqlite3 **step()**. While finalizing the assertion, if several connections were to be added, you would keep the argument and reuse it with different values.

Reading and retrieving data

There might be multiple records that we need to store into the objects of class **Person**. So, let's first create a new class with three variables, the same as columns, and default initialization for the table **person** in the database, as follows:

```
class Person
{
    var name: String = ""
    var age: Int = 0
    var id: Int = 0

    init(id:Int, name:String, age:Int)
    {
        self.id = id
        self.name = name
        self.age = age
    }


}
```

Now, we will read the records from **db.sqlite** which was stored by inserting the **Person** values via a calling function written for the insertion of records. The query statement for retrieving and reading the records from the database would be **SELECT * FROM person**. Here, * refers to all the records. You can use the other SQL query statements with conditions as well to practice this topic more precisely.

Refer to the following code:

```
func read() -> [Person] {
        let queryStatementString = "SELECT * FROM person;"
        var queryStatement: OpaquePointer? = nil
        var psns : [Person] = []
        if sqlite3_prepare_v2(db, queryStatementString, -1,
&queryStatement, nil) == SQLITE_OK {
            while sqlite3_step(queryStatement) == SQLITE_ROW {
                let id = sqlite3_column_int(queryStatement, 0)
                let name = String(describing: String(cString: sqlite3_
column_text(queryStatement, 1)))
                let year = sqlite3_column_int(queryStatement, 2)
                psns.append(Person(id: Int(id), name: name, age:
Int(year)))
                print("Query Result:")
                print("\(id) | \(name) | \(year)")
```

```
        }
    } else {
        print("SELECT statement could not be prepared")
    }
    sqlite3_finalize(queryStatement)
    return psns
}
```

Let's understand the given code step-by-step for retrieving the records, as follows:

- Prepare the statement with the given query string. Now, we will execute the statement. Here, we are checking the status of code **SQLITE_ROW**, which means that you retrieved a row record when you stepped through the result.

- Now, you're reading the values in the return lines. Provided what you know about the layout of the table and your question, you can access the column values of the row. The first column is an **Int**, so you use **sqlite3_column_int()** and pass a zero-based column index and a comment. The returned value is allocated to the locally scoped id constant.

Deleting data

While deleting a record, we will perform the delete SQL query statement, which will require a where condition to identify the identical records to delete, for which we will use **Id** (Id has the property of the primary key which is useful for selecting a unique person record from the person table).

The query syntax is as follows:

```
DELETE FROM person WHERE Id = ?
```

```
func deleteByID(id:Int)
{
    let deleteStatementStirng = "DELETE FROM person WHERE Id = ?;"
    var deleteStatement: OpaquePointer? = nil
    if sqlite3_prepare_v2(db, deleteStatementStirng, -1, &deleteStatement, nil) == SQLITE_OK {
        sqlite3_bind_int(deleteStatement, 1, Int32(id))
        if sqlite3_step(deleteStatement) == SQLITE_DONE {
            print("Successfully deleted row.")
        } else {
```

```
        print("Could not delete row.")
    }
} else {
    print("DELETE statement could not be prepared")
}
sqlite3_finalize(deleteStatement)
}
```

CoreData

We use CoreData to store the permanent data for offline use of your programme, to archive temporary data, and to add the undo capability on a single device to your app. You describe the types and relationships of your data using the CoreData's Data Model editor and create the respective class descriptions. To have the following functionality, CoreData will then handle the object instances at runtime. The developers are usually confused between CoreData and SQLite. You need to understand that the core data is not a database. CoreData is an object graph and persistence architecture supported by Apple. It makes it easier to serialise the data structured into XML, binary, or SQLite stored through the relational entity-attribute model.

Refer to *figure 7.3* that illustrates how to create a new iOS project with CoreData, as follows:

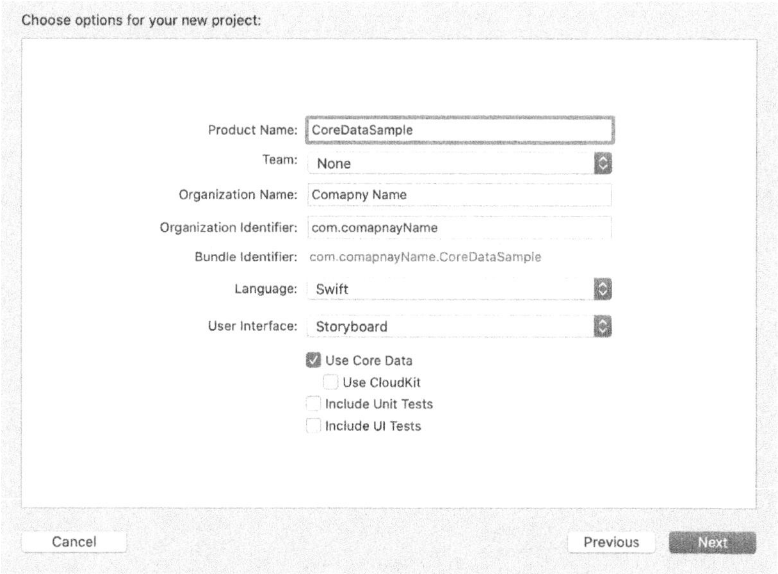

Figure 7.3: Create New iOS Project With CoreData

Difference between SQLite and CoreData

SQLite uses the basic SQL queries to perform the operations. To improve the performance of SQLite and local database management, Apple develops an **Object Relational Mapping (ORM)** framework named CoreData. Let's see in detail the difference between both the methodologies, as shown in *Table 7.1* as follows:

	SQLite	Core Data
1	These have data constrained features.	These do not have any data constrained features, if required implemented by business logic.
2	Stored on disk and directly operates on data.	Operates on in-memory data and regularly syncs to disk.
3	Drop table and edit table operation can be done without loading into memory.	In-memory data load is required before table drop and edit.
4	Slow as compared to CoreData.	Fast as compared to SQLite to perform all operations.

***Table 7.1:** SQLite vs CoreData*

CoreData create schema

When you want to use CoreData for saving your records and data, then you need to select the CoreData option while creating a new project from XCode, that will give you the default code setup in the **appdelegate.swift** file as well as the **<ProjectName>.xcdatamodel** file (a file view where you can create the database schema with properties). Let's first see the code of **appdelegate.swift** in terms of CoreData, and how that can help in creating and managing persistent storage for the app, as follows:

```
lazy var persistentContainer: NSPersistentContainer = {
        let container = NSPersistentContainer(name: "CoreDataSample")
        container.loadPersistentStores(completionHandler: {
(storeDescription, error) in
            if let error = error as NSError? {
                fatalError("Unresolved error \(error), \(error.
userInfo)")
            }
        })
        return container
    }()


    func saveContext () {
        let context = persistentContainer.viewContext
        if context.hasChanges {
            do {
                try context.save()
            } catch {
                let nserror = error as NSError
                fatalError("Unresolved error \(nserror), \(nserror.
userInfo)")
            }
        }
    }
```

Whenever **persistentContainer** is called to perform the CRUD operation on the database, it actually loads all the data into memory from the **sqlite** file managed internally and automatically by CoreData ORM. We should try not to access or interact with the **sqlite** databases directly; in fact, CoreData syncs regularly to storage, whenever we perform insert, update, and delete; also, the retrieval of data is fast due to the in-memory persistent storage.

Now, let's take a look at the `.xcdatamodel` file, and how you can play with that, as shown in *figure 7.4* as follows:

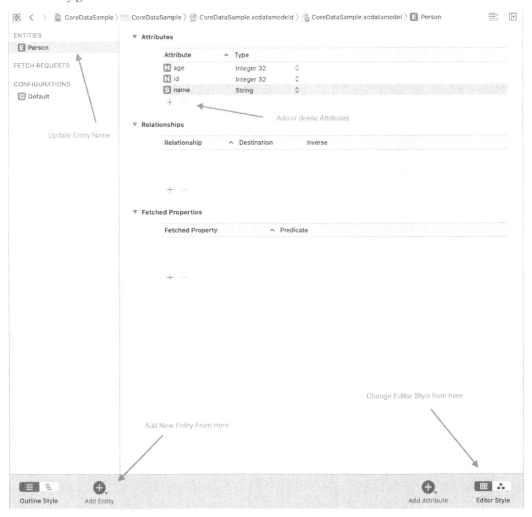

Figure 7.4: CoreData UI Schema

You can view the database model either in the form of entity attribute table style or in the pictorial form to clearly view the relationship between the entities if there is any. From the **Add Entity** action, you can add more tables (here we are talking in terms of SQLite, and in CoreData or ORM, it is not termed as a table but as one entity). In the attributes section, you can add the attributes with their types. Further, you need to add an **NSManagedObject** subclass with respect to the entity **Person**. However, that is not required to be added manually but could be done automatically, as shown in *figure 7.5* as follows:

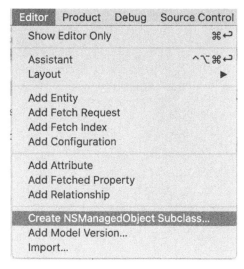

Figure 7.5: *Create NSManagedObject Subclasses*

When you select **Editor** | **Create NSManagedObject Subclass** from the menu, in the few following steps, the XCode system will create an extension subclass for **Person** entity (as per the case we took in the earlier part of this chapter). But remember one thing, in case you update the attributes of an entity, you need to create these extension subclasses again with similar steps. Refer to the following code:

```
import CoreData
extension Person {

    @nonobjc public class func fetchRequest() -> NSFetchRequest<Person>
{

        return NSFetchRequest<Person>(entityName: "Person")
    }

    @NSManaged public var id: Int32
    @NSManaged public var name: String?
    @NSManaged public var age: Int32

}
```

Inserting data

We need to create the records into the database similar to SQLite, but this time, with the help of CoreData ORM. From the **appdelegate** object, we will get the persistent storage context, which loads the entire data copy into memory and regularly gets synced to on desk memory. **NSEntityDescription** helps in code to get **Person** entity, so that we can perform inserting objects on this entity, which we did with a loop so that multiple records can be inserted, and then we saved that context so that the records are permanently stored into the database. Refer to the following code:

```
func insertData(){


        guard let appDelegate = UIApplication.shared.delegate as?
AppDelegate else { return }
        let managedContext = appDelegate.persistentContainer.viewContext
        let personEntity = NSEntityDescription.entity(forEntityName:
"Person", in: managedContext)!


        for i in 1...5 {


            let person = NSManagedObject(entity: personEntity,
insertInto: managedContext)
            person.setValue(i, forKeyPath: "id")
            person.setValue("Mike \(i)", forKey: "name")
            person.setValue(20 + i, forKey: "age")
        }
        do {
            try managedContext.save()


        } catch let error as NSError {
            print("Could not save. \(error), \(error.userInfo)")
        }
    }
```

Retrieving data

When we pass the entity name into **NSFetchRequest**, it prepares the fetch request to perform a retrieve operation. In case you want to apply some condition while fetching the records, you can apply with **NSPredicate**, which we will see while we perform the delete operation further. Now, you can fetch from the context with a **fetchrequest** statement that will give all the results and records of the **Person** entity. To check whether it's correct or not, you can check via printing the **name** attributes or any other attribute as well. Refer to the following code:

```
func retrieveData()
    {
            guard let appDelegate = UIApplication.shared.delegate as?
AppDelegate else { return }
            let managedContext = appDelegate.persistentContainer.
viewContext
            let fetchRequest =
NSFetchRequest<NSFetchRequestResult>(entityName: "Person")
            do {
                let result = try managedContext.fetch(fetchRequest)
                for data in result as! [NSManagedObject] {
                    print(data.value(forKey: "name") as! String)
                }

            } catch {

                print("Failed")
            }
    }
```

Deleting data

Similar to the other operations, initially, we will take persistent store context and prepare a fetch request with **NSFetchRequest**, adding a predicate condition to it that deletes the record whose name attribute is similar to the name given in the code. If there are non-zero fetch results, then we will delete the first record from the context, even if you want to delete all the records which you fetched from the fetch request; you can use a **for** or **while** loop to perform the delete operation on each result. Refer to the following code:

```
func deleteData()
    {
        guard let appDelegate = UIApplication.shared.delegate as?
AppDelegate else { return }
        let managedContext = appDelegate.persistentContainer.viewContext
        let fetchRequest =
NSFetchRequest<NSFetchRequestResult>(entityName: "Person")
        fetchRequest.predicate = NSPredicate(format: "name = %@", "Mike
3")
        do
```

```
        {
            let test = try managedContext.fetch(fetchRequest)
            let objectToDelete = test[0] as! NSManagedObject
            managedContext.delete(objectToDelete)
            do{
                try managedContext.save()
            }
            catch
            {
                print(error)
            }
        }
        catch
        {
            print(error)
        }
    }
```

Conclusion

In this chapter, initially, we started with how we can save the small key-value pairs in plist as well as in UserDefaults. Both the permanent storages have their own significance and usages. Further, we discussed in detail about the CRUD operations on the SQLite databases and the comparison of it with CoreData. From the outset, writing powerful CoreData code allows you to plan the app for the potential big datasets. Even if your app is running at the beginning, as your database and model expands, it will quickly slow down. You are now making the CoreData code more effective by using the background sense, smart fetch requests, and batch delete requests. There are also complicated things that we can do with improvements to CoreData monitoring, that is, adding predicates and dynamic database relationships. Things become more complicated as you use more CoreData.

In the next chapter, we will discuss in detail about the file handling operations such as creating, updating, deleting files, and managing efficiently in the iOS mobile apps.

Multiple choice questions

1. UserDefault key-value pair in real save in form of _____.
    a. JSON
    b. xml

    c.   plist

    d.   sqlite

2. **From the following, what is ORM used in?**

    a.   Plist

    b.   UserDefault

    c.   Core Data

    d.   SQLite

3. **Fetch request is used _____.**

    a.   To delete

    b.   To Update

    c.   To Retrieve

    d.   To Insert

4. **Xcdatamodel is used in _____.**

    a.   UserDefault

    b.   SQLite

    c.   Core Data

    d.   Plist

5. **Sqlite3_prepare_v2 is used _____.**

    a.   To prepare statement

    b.   To delete statement

    c.   To update Data

    d.   In Core data

Answers

1. b

2. c

3. c

4. c

5. a

CHAPTER 8

File Handling in iOS

Introduction

In iOS, Apple defines the rules and regulations with specific locations to save the files. For years, there was no managed access to the files, and it was only through the photo app for images, or via iCloud, which could be accessed from a desktop browser and from where you could download the image files on a desktop machine via photos. But that gives no information about how these files were managed in a folder or directory. From iOS 11, the file management via the iOS users changed altogether with the introduction of the Files app. In this chapter, we will discuss in detail how you can make the files and save them in the application's directory and expose those files to the other apps (such as File app by Apple or the other developers' file management app). As you know, every device has its limited local memory which can hold limited amounts of data in terms of the file size. Such a case explores the idea of further syncing those files to iCloud (an Apple service to save the data and files securely on an Apple server integrated with the user's Apple ID).

Structure

In this chapter, we will cover the following topics:

- File systems in iOS
- App file manager

Objectives

After studying this chapter, you will be able to save your app data and information to a file and place that file into the document directory in any file format. Further, you will be able to sync your app files to iCloud, so, in case a user changes their device, they will be able to get their files again with respect to the same app.

File systems in iOS

While you execute and run an iOS app in a device or a simulator, your app creates a Sandbox file system, as shown in *figure 8.1*. The iOS App Sandbox system mainly has the following three containers:

- App bundle container
- Data container
- iCloud container

Refer to *figure 8.1* as follows:

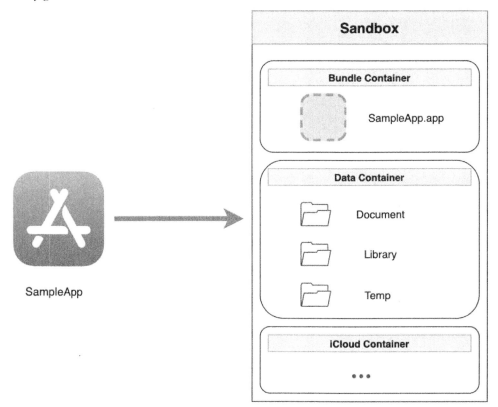

Figure 8.1: App File Architecture

App bundle container

This app bundle contains the application which is signed at the time of installation. A signed bundle cannot tamper, so it provides security from any time of manual or automated attacks. This directory has all the resources, such as image **assets**, **info.plist**, etc, of the iOS application. The contents of the bundle directory are not backed up by iTunes or iCloud. But in case of the In-App purchase, iTunes performs a sync to identify the old purchases for that app. We cannot write anything in the app bundle directory and can only access the files with the bundle path. Let's see how you can get the paths of the bundle and access the files of the bundle, as follows:

```
let bundlePath = Bundle.main.bundlePath
print(bundlePath)
let infoFilePath = Bundle.main.path(forResource: "Info", ofType: "plist")
print(infoFilePath)
```

Data container

The data containers have three directories into which the users can save the app data and files. This container contains the respective folders for the following directories:

- Document directory
- Library
- Temp

Document directory

In a document directory, either you can create the files at the top level, or you can create a subfolder or directory to store those files for better management and quick access. Apple reserves some subdirectory names for its own apps such as **Inbox**. So, you need to take care of the names while creating a subdirectory in the document directory. As a developer, you should save only those files here which you want the users to access.

Enable file sharing

When the file-sharing of an application is enabled, the directory is exposed, and all its files become visible in the Files applications and the user can put their files in the spotlight. All the content of the directory is persisted as well as included in the iCloud and iTunes backups. The storage settings UI under your app's **Document and Data** reported the disk space used in the directory. To enable File sharing for your app, you need to add **Application supports iTunes file sharing** or **UIFileSharingEnabled** with **YES** in the **info.plist** file, and to enable **Open in**

Place, add the **LSSupportsOpeningDocumentInPlace** or the **Support Opening Document in place** key with **YES** in **info.plist**, as shown in *figure 8.2* as follows:

Figure 8.2: *File Opening Permissions*

The same plist permissions can be given in the form of the source code in the.**plist** file as shown as follows:

```
<key>UIFileSharingEnabled</key>
<true/>
<key>LSSupportsOpeningDocumentsInPlace</key>
<true/>
```

Library – application support directory

You can save those files here which can be used by the app, but they will not be visible by the users like your database file. Either you can directly save the files on the top level, or a subdirectory can be used. All the contents of the directory are persisted as well as included in the iCloud and iTunes backups. The storage settings UI under your app's **Document and Data** reported the disk space used in the directory.

Library – cache

The files stored in the cache can be discarded by the OS system whenever the memory is low. This is a good place to save those files which can be re-downloaded whenever needed. The contents of this cache directory are not included into the backups. When the device is on low disk space, iOS starts clearing the cache. The file storage is not reported into the storage settings UI under your app's **Document and Data**.

Temp directory

This directory is used to store temporary files which are not needed for a longer time. Although the system removes such files periodically, it is good to have a habit to remove it by programming (later in this chapter, we will study those techniques).

iCloud container

The iCloud container or drive is the best place to put a document or file. Whenever the connection to the apple server is established, those files will be available on all the devices synced with the Apple account. When the network is inaccessible, the program reads and writes the data locally, and when the network is available, the data is immediately uploaded to the iCloud disk. Due to the likelihood of multiple machines accessing the files in the iCloud drive at the same time, file coordination is needed to prevent any conflicts.

App file manager

Now, we will start work on an App file manager which could be used across your multiple apps and would require very minimal or less changes while used in the other apps. This file manager will help you perform the directory, folder, subfolder, and files operations. There will be a singleton class (class which has only a single instance), **AppFileManager** which will implement the following three protocols, where every protocol has its own purpose:

- **AppFileStatusChecking** protocol

- **AppFileSystemMetaData** protocol

- **AppFileManipulation** protocol

AppFileStatusChecking protocol

In the **AppFileStatusChecking** protocol, we check the status of a file given to it as input. We can check for the write and read permission of the file as well as to know whether the file exists or not. We will write a protocol that will check the file status. The status could be writable, readable, exists, or not, as shown as follows:

```
protocol AppFileStatusChecking
{
    func isWritable(file at: URL) -> Bool


    func isReadable(file at: URL) -> Bool
```

```
    func exists(file at: URL) -> Bool
}
```

The status function gets the URL of the files that needs to be checked and returns the status in the Boolean values. Let's implement the **AppFileStatusChecking** Protocol, as follows:

```
extension AppFileStatusChecking
{
    func isWritable(file at: URL) -> Bool
    {
        if FileManager.default.isWritableFile(atPath: at.path)
        {
            print(at.path)
            return true
        }
        else
        {
            print(at.path)
            return false
        }
    }

    func isReadable(file at: URL) -> Bool
    {
        if FileManager.default.isReadableFile(atPath: at.path)
        {
            print(at.path)
            return true
        }
        else
        {
            print(at.path)
            return false
        }
    }

    func exists(file at: URL) -> Bool
```

```
    {
        if FileManager.default.fileExists(atPath: at.path)
        {
            return true
        }
        else
        {
            return false
        }
    }
}
```

Apple's Foundation framework contains the **FileManager** inbuilt class whose single instance can be accessed by **FileManager.default**, which can be used to access the functions to identify the status of the files.

AppFileSystemMetaData Protocol

The File meta info is not always required while you develop a general app, but it's good to have this feature. The **AppFileSystemMetaData** protocol will develop the following two main features:

List all the files from the directory

When you are required to get all the files at any path or directory, you can call the **contentOfDirectory** function on the file manager.

Get attributes of the file at a given path

When you are required to get the attributes of an item or a file, you can call the **attributesOfItem** function via giving the input of the file address, as follows:

```
protocol AppFileSystemMetaData
{
    func list(directory at: URL) -> Bool

    func attributes(ofFile atFullPath: URL) -> [FileAttributeKey : Any]
}

extension AppFileSystemMetaData
{
    func list(directory at: URL) -> Bool
    {
```

```
        let listing = try! FileManager.default.
contentsOfDirectory(atPath: at.path)

        if listing.count > 0
        {
            print("\n----------------------------")
            print("LISTING: \(at.path)")
            print("")
            for file in listing
            {
                print("File: \(file.debugDescription)")
            }
            print("")
            print("---------------------------\n")

            return true
        }
        else
        {
            return false
        }
    }


    func attributes(ofFile atFullPath: URL) -> [FileAttributeKey : Any]
    {
        return try! FileManager.default.attributesOfItem(atPath:
atFullPath.path)
    }
}
```

The list function of the protocol will get all the contents of the directory with the **contentsOfDirectory** function of **FileManger** and the attributes of the file with the **attributesOfItem** function.

The AppFileManipulation protocol

Before the manipulations of the files and folders, we need to have the paths of different directories. Let's get the path of all the directories, as follows:

```
enum AppDirectories : String
{
    case Documents = "Documents"
    case Inbox = "Inbox"
    case Library = "Library"
    case Temp = "tmp"
}


protocol AppDirectoryNames
{
    func documentsDirectoryURL() -> URL
    func inboxDirectoryURL() -> URL
    func libraryDirectoryURL() -> URL
    func tempDirectoryURL() -> URL
    func getURL(for directory: AppDirectories) -> URL
    func buildFullPath(forFileName name: String, inDirectory directory:
AppDirectories) -> URL
}
```

In the **AppDirectoryNames** protocol, we defined the functions to get the path of all the possible default directories as well as to get the path of a custom directory, as follows:

```
extension AppDirectoryNames
{
    func documentsDirectoryURL() -> URL
    {
        return FileManager.default.urls(for: .documentDirectory, in:
.userDomainMask).first!
    }


    func inboxDirectoryURL() -> URL
    {
        return FileManager.default.urls(for: .documentDirectory, in:
.userDomainMask)[0].appendingPathComponent(AppDirectories.Inbox.
rawValue)
    }
```

```
    func libraryDirectoryURL() -> URL
    {
        return FileManager.default.urls(for: FileManager.
SearchPathDirectory.libraryDirectory, in: .userDomainMask).first!
    }


    func tempDirectoryURL() -> URL
    {
        return FileManager.default.temporaryDirectory
    }


    func getURL(for directory: AppDirectories) -> URL
    {
        switch directory
        {
        case .Documents:
            return documentsDirectoryURL()
        case .Inbox:
            return inboxDirectoryURL()
        case .Library:
            return libraryDirectoryURL()
        case .Temp:
            return tempDirectoryURL()
        }
    }


    func buildFullPath(forFileName name: String, inDirectory directory:
AppDirectories) -> URL
    {
        return getURL(for: directory).appendingPathComponent(name)
    }
 }
```

Now, we will define the main protocol for the file and directory operations, such as write, read, rename, delete, move, copy, etc. **AppFileManipulations** will extend the **AppDirectoryNames** protocol as well, as follows:

```
protocol AppFileManipulation : AppDirectoryNames
{
    func writeFile(containing: String, to path: AppDirectories, withName
name: String) -> Bool

    func readFile(at path: AppDirectories, withName name: String) ->
String

    func deleteFile(at path: AppDirectories, withName name: String) ->
Bool


    func renameFile(at path: AppDirectories, with oldName: String, to
newName: String) -> Bool

    func moveFile(withName name: String, inDirectory: AppDirectories,
toDirectory directory: AppDirectories) -> Bool

    func copyFile(withName name: String, inDirectory: AppDirectories,
toDirectory directory: AppDirectories) -> Bool

    func changeFileExtension(withName name: String, inDirectory:
AppDirectories, toNewExtension newExtension: String) -> Bool
}
```

You would require a path of the directory and name of the file when you want to write, read, and delete the file. And when you want to either move the file or copy the file from one path/place to another path/place, that will take two directories as input in the functions.

Write file

While performing the write file operations, there are two options. One is to write the string data passed as input, which would then require you to convert that string into the UTF data and write a file. The second way is to directly pass the file data as input to write on the path as a file.

Copy file

Copy file requires a path of the file which needs to be copied and another or maybe the same path where the file needs to be copied. Copy file name logic could be implemented by you in the following code: number one (1) is added by default on every new copy of the file:

```
extension AppFileManipulation
{
    func writeFile(containing: String, to path: AppDirectories, withName
name: String) -> Bool
    {
        let filePath = getURL(for: path).path + "/" + name
        let rawData: Data? = containing.data(using: .utf8)
        return FileManager.default.createFile(atPath: filePath, contents:
rawData, attributes: nil)
    }


    func writeFile(containing: Data, to path: AppDirectories, withName
name: String) -> Bool
    {
        let filePath = getURL(for: path).path + "/" + name
        return FileManager.default.createFile(atPath: filePath, contents:
containing, attributes: nil)
    }


    func writeFileIn(folder: String, containing: Data, to path:
AppDirectories, withName name: String) -> Bool
    {
        let filePath = getURL(for: path).path + "/" + folder + "/" + name
        let fileManager = FileManager.default
        if let tDocumentDirectory = fileManager.urls(for:
.documentDirectory, in: .userDomainMask).first {
            let filePath =  tDocumentDirectory.appendingPathComponent("\
(folder)")
            if !fileManager.fileExists(atPath: filePath.path) {
                do {
                    try fileManager.createDirectory(atPath: filePath.path,
withIntermediateDirectories: true, attributes: nil)
                } catch {
                    NSLog("Couldn't create document directory")
                }
```

```
            }
            NSLog("Document directory is \(filePath)")
        }
        return FileManager.default.createFile(atPath: filePath, contents:
containing, attributes: nil)
    }


    func readFile(at path: AppDirectories, withName name: String) ->
String
    {
        let filePath = getURL(for: path).path + "/" + name
        let fileContents = FileManager.default.contents(atPath: filePath)
        let fileContentsAsString = String(bytes: fileContents!, encoding:
.utf8)
        print(fileContentsAsString!)
        return fileContentsAsString!
    }


    func deleteFile(at path: AppDirectories, withName name: String) -> Bool
    {
        let filePath = buildFullPath(forFileName: name, inDirectory: path)
        do
        {
            try FileManager.default.removeItem(at: filePath)
            return true
        }
        catch
        {
            print(error)
        }
        return false
    }


    func renameFile(at path: AppDirectories, with oldName: String, to
```

```
newName: String) -> Bool
    {
        let oldPath = getURL(for: path).appendingPathComponent(oldName)
        let newPath = getURL(for: path).appendingPathComponent(newName)
        do {
            try FileManager.default.moveItem(at: oldPath, to: newPath)
            return true
        } catch {
            return false
        }
    }


    func moveFile(withName name: String, inDirectory: AppDirectories,
toDirectory directory: AppDirectories) -> Bool
    {
        let originURL = buildFullPath(forFileName: name, inDirectory:
inDirectory)
        let destinationURL = buildFullPath(forFileName: name,
inDirectory: directory)
        try! FileManager.default.moveItem(at: originURL, to:
destinationURL)
        return true
    }


    func copyFile(withName name: String, inDirectory: AppDirectories,
toDirectory directory: AppDirectories) -> Bool
    {
        let originURL = buildFullPath(forFileName: name, inDirectory:
inDirectory)
        let destinationURL = buildFullPath(forFileName: name+"1",
inDirectory: directory)
        try! FileManager.default.copyItem(at: originURL, to:
destinationURL)
        return true
    }
```

```
    func changeFileExtension(withName name: String, inDirectory:
AppDirectories, toNewExtension newExtension: String) -> Bool

    {

        var newFileName = NSString(string:name)

        newFileName = newFileName.deletingPathExtension as NSString

        newFileName = (newFileName.appendingPathExtension(newExtension)
as NSString?)!

        let finalFileName:String =  String(newFileName)


        let originURL = buildFullPath(forFileName: name, inDirectory:
inDirectory)

        let destinationURL = buildFullPath(forFileName: finalFileName,
inDirectory: inDirectory)


        try! FileManager.default.moveItem(at: originURL, to:
destinationURL)


        return true

    }

}
```

Changing file extension

When you want to change an extension of a file with a file name and new extension, it would first be required to frame a new name with that new extension and rewrite that file with that new name, and later, the old extension file can be deleted.

Now, we need to implement our actual singleton class and use all these defined protocols in **AppFileManager**, as follows:

```
class AppFileManager: NSObject, AppFileStatusChecking,
AppFileManipulation, AppFileSystemMetaData

{

    static let sharedInstance: AppFileManager = {

        let instance = AppFileManager()

        return instance

    }()
```

```
override init() {
    super.init()
}
}
```

Class **AppFileManager** extends and uses all the protocols which we used earlier and initialized the singleton instance. Now you can make the functions as per your application requirements.

Save file

When you need to save an image file or PDF file, you would be required to pass the file data with a path. That path could be at the directory top-level or could be passed with the folder name to accommodate the file in the subdirectory. In the following code, if we are not required to save the file in the folder, we would send that as an empty string, so that we can take the decision to write the file directly on the path or with the folder path:

```
func savefile(folder: String, fileName: String, image: Data) -> Bool
    {
        if folder == ""
        {
            return writeFile(containing: image, to: .Documents,
withName: fileName)
        }

        return writeFileIn(folder: folder, containing: image, to:
.Documents, withName: fileName)
    }
```

Delete file

When you want to delete a file from any directory or path, you first need to check whether that file exists on that path or not, and if it exists on the path, then you can proceed with the delete file operations, as follows:

```
func fileExist(folder: String, file: String) -> Bool
    {
        return folder == "" ? exists(file: buildFullPath(forFileName:
file, inDirectory: .Documents)) : exists(file: buildFullPathWith(folder:
folder, forFileName: file, inDirectory: .Documents))
    }
```

```
func deleteFile(folder: String, fileName: String) -> Bool
    {
        let filePath = folder == "" ? buildFullPath(forFileName:
fileName, inDirectory: .Documents) : buildFullPathWith(folder: folder,
forFileName: fileName, inDirectory: .Documents)
        if fileExist(folder: folder, file: fileName)
        {
            do
            {
                try FileManager.default.removeItem(at: filePath)
                return true
            }
            catch
            {
                print(error)
            }
        }
        return false
    }
```

Get file list

In case you want to get all the files saved on the top level of the document directory, you would require to get the directory contents which will give you an array of files, and further, if you want, you can filter that directory content, so that more precise results would be there. Refer to the following code:

```
func getFileList() -> [String]
    {
        var documentsUrl =  FileManager.default.urls(for:
.documentDirectory, in: .userDomainMask).first!
        do {
            // Get the directory contents urls (including subfolders
urls)
            let directoryContents = try FileManager.default.
contentsOfDirectory(at: documentsUrl, includingPropertiesForKeys: nil,
options: [])
            print(directoryContents)
```

```
        // if you want to filter the directory contents you can do
like this:
        var pdfList = directoryContents.filter{ $0.pathExtension ==
"pdf"} as [URL]
        let txtList = directoryContents.filter{ $0.pathExtension ==
"txt"} as [URL]
        let csvList = directoryContents.filter{ $0.pathExtension ==
"csv"} as [URL]
        let gpxList = directoryContents.filter{ $0.pathExtension ==
"gpx"} as [URL]
        pdfList.append(contentsOf: txtList)
        pdfList.append(contentsOf: csvList)
        pdfList.append(contentsOf: gpxList)
        var fileList: [String] = []
        for item in pdfList {
            let str = item.absoluteString.components(separatedBy:
"/")
            fileList.append(str.last!)
        }
        print("PDF list:", fileList)
        return fileList

    } catch {
        print(error.localizedDescription)
    }
    return []
}
```

In the preceding programming example, four types of file extensions would be considered to be in the file list. If your app requires more such different extension files as well, you can use it in a similar way.

Using AppFileManager

You can use **AppFileManager** as the singleton classes are used. Let's see some of the example code, as follows:

```
if WSFileManager.sharedInstance.deleteFile(folder: folderName, fileName:
filename)
{
    print("File Deleted")
}
```

```
self.list = WSFileManager.sharedInstance.getFileList()
```

Conclusion

In this chapter, we discussed in detail about the Sandbox structure of an iOS app and how the folders and files could be kept in those default directories. We learned to read and write the files on the disk in the document directory folder or subfolder to manage it better. Accessing the data on the disk is one of the slowest operations that a machine can perform in contrast to the other operations. Reading the files from a disk-based hard drive can take anything from a few milliseconds to several minutes, depending on the size and number of files. Make sure that the code runs as well as possible under a range of workloads, from mild to moderate. We learned that using the Instruments app to capture any baseline measurements is a good practice, if the app slows down or becomes less sensitive while dealing with the files. The Instruments inform you how much time the app spends while dealing with the files and help you keep track of the different file-related events.

In the next chapter, you will study about the different types of app gestures with the custom gestures available for the iOS apps.

Multiple choice questions

1. `FileManager.default` is _____.
   a. Factory instance
   b. Singleton instance
   c. Protocol
   d. Extension

2. What does `appendingPathComponent` do?
   a. Add New Files
   b. Check if File Exists
   c. Add a new path or folder
   d. Make a file visible

3. **What does `contentsOfDirectory` return?**

    a. Size of the files

    b. Name of the files on the path

    c. Size of the directory

    d. Singleton Instance

4. **If you can download the content again and don't require to save that permanently, then you will save that file in the _____.**

    a. Document directory

    b. Temp directory

    c. Subdirectory of Document directory

    d. In-App Bundle

5. **If you want to delete a file, what would you check first before deleting it?**

    a. Whether Document Directory is empty or not

    b. Size of the file

    c. Whether the File exists at the given path or not

    d. Whether the Cache is empty or not

Answers

1. b

2. c

3. b

4. b

5. c

CHAPTER 9

App Gesture Recognizers in iOS

Introduction

When you create the iOS apps using the standard UIKit views and control, it handles the touch and multi-touch events. These touch events on the interface responses and act in return with multiple responders of the class **UIResponder** and Responder chain. In this chapter, we will further strengthen our knowledge in Gesture implementation and recognition, which is a core part of the iOS application development. We will briefly discuss the following two categories of Gestures in iOS:

- Standard gesture
- Custom gesture

There are in-build gestures by iOS SDK, such as taps, pinches, pans, and rotations which are used as user inputs in the apps to perform significant actions and are part of Standard Gestures. In case you want to use a gesture that is not supported on views, you can create a Custom gesture with the built-in **UIGestureRecognizer** classes.

Structure

In this chapter, we will cover the following topics:

- Standard gestures

- Implementing a custom gesture recognition
- 3D touch interactions

Objectives

After studying this chapter, you will be able to use some standard gestures such as taps, pinches, pans, rotations etc. You will also be able to implement the custom gestures that are not provided by Apple to implement in the iOS Apps.

Standard gestures

In general, the users are familiar with the standard gestures and usually don't like to learn the new styles of gestures that are used for the same purpose or actions. You have to avoid using the standard gestures for performing the non-standard actions. Redefining the definition of the traditional movements leads to uncertainty and ambiguity, unless the app is a game with active gameplay. Provide an easy, visible way to access or execute an operation wherever possible, even if it requires an extra tap or two. Many system apps have a navigation bar with a flat, tappable back to the previous screen button. The users can also return to the previous screen by swiping from the side of the screen. On the iPad, the users can return to the **Home** screen by pressing the Home button or pinching with four fingers. The following is the list of standard gestures which we will discuss in this chapter in detail:

- Tap Gesture Recognizer
- Pinch Gesture Recognizer
- Swipe Gesture Recognizer
- Pan Gesture Recognizer
- LongPress Gesture Recognizer
- Rotation Gesture Recognizer
- Hover Gesture Recognizer

Handling UIKit gesture

When we want to handle any touch from the user, we use gesture the recognizers to simplify the touch handling to create a consistent user experience. A touch by the user on the device screen recognizes via the gesture recognizers and that recognizer invokes the method on the view controller, as shown in *figure 9.1* as follows:

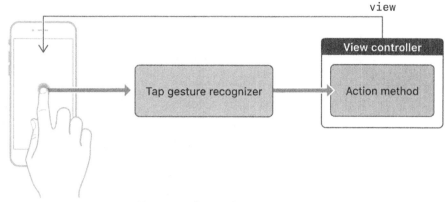

Figure 9.1: *Gesture Recognition Flow*

The best way to treat the tap or press cases with your views is to use the gesture recognizers. Any view will have one or more gesture recognizers attached to it. Gesture recognizers contain all of the logic necessary to process and interpret the incoming events for that view, as well as to align them to an established sequence. The gesture recognizer notifies its allocated target object, which may be a display controller, the view itself, or any other object in your app when a match is found.

There are two kinds of gesture recognizers – discrete and continuous. Once the gesture is understood, a discrete gesture recognizer calls the intervention procedure exactly once. A continuous gesture recognizer executes several calls to the action method after its initial recognition requirements are met, notifying you if the details in the gesture's event shift. Each of the basic **UIKit** gesture recognizers has an object in **IB** (**Interface Builder**). It also comes with a custom gesture recognizer object to represent your **UIGestureRecognizer** subclasses, as shown in *figure 9.2* as follows:

Figure 9.2: *Window to Add Gesture Objects*

If you want to add a gesture action recognizer, you can complete the following steps:

1. On Storyboard or Xib, drag one of the gestures onto the view.

2. Now, we will implement an action method which will be called when the gesture will be recognized from the user actions.

3. Then, we will connect your action method call to the gesture recognizer.

You can configure the action method programmatically using the **addTarget(_:action:)** method or create this connection in Interface Builder by right-clicking on the gesture recognizer and connecting its sent action selector to the object in your interface, as shown as follows:

```
@IBAction func gestureActionMethod(_ sender: UIGestureRecognizer)
    {
        // do your stuff here
    }
```

Tap Gesture Recognizer

This is a discrete gesture recognizer that interprets single or multiple taps. The tap motion senses one or two fingertips momentarily touching the screen. The fingers used in these movements do not wander far from their original contact points, and the number of times they must touch the screen can be personalized. You might set up the tap gesture recognizers to detect single, double, or triple taps. We first need to change the axis position values in the recognition view which will animate when we start the animation with the given duration in **UIViewPropertyAnimator**, as shown as follows:

```
@IBAction func tapHandle(_ gestureRecognizer : UITapGestureRecognizer )
{
    guard gestureRecognizer.view != nil else { return }

    if gestureRecognizer.state == .ended {
    let animator = UIViewPropertyAnimator(duration: 0.2, curve:
.easeInOut, animations: {
            gestureRecognizer.view!.center.x += 100
            gestureRecognizer.view!.center.y += 100
        })
        animator.startAnimation()
    }
}
```

Pinch Gesture Recognizer

This discrete gesture recognizer interprets the pinching gestures involving two touches. When pinching a view, the user must press two fingers on it. Zoom out is the traditional sense when the user moves the two fingers toward each other; zoom in is the conventional meaning when the user moves the two fingers away from each other. Pinching in and out are both continuous gestures. And the pinch gesture only ends when the user lifts their fingers from the view.

Changes in the space between the two fingers touching the screen are recorded by a pinch gesture recognizer. Since the pinch movements are constant, your action method will be named if the distance between the fingers varies. A scale factor is a measurement of the distance between the fingertips. The scale factor is 1.0 at the start of the gesture. The scale factor increases proportionally as the space between the two fingers grows. Similarly, as the space between the fingers reduces, the scale component decreases. The most frequent use of the pinch movements is to adjust the scale of the items or material on the screen. Map views, for example, use the pinch gestures to adjust the map's zoom level, as shown in *figure 9.3* as follows:

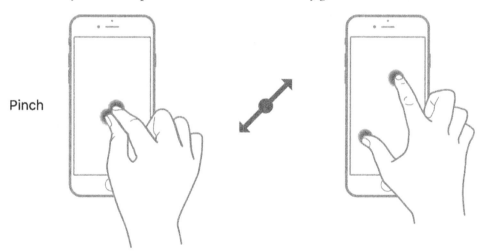

Figure 9.3: *Pinch Gesture*

When the handle pinch gets the gesture, first it will check for the state of the gesture. If the state is changed or has begun, we will transform the view of the gesture recognizer starting with the scale set to 1, as shown as follows:

```
@IBAction func handlePinch(_ gestureRecognizer :
UIPinchGestureRecognizer) {   guard gestureRecognizer.view != nil else {
return }

        if gestureRecognizer.state == .began || gestureRecognizer.state
== .changed {
```

```
        gestureRecognizer.view?.transform = (gestureRecognizer.view?.
transform.scaledBy(x: gestureRecognizer.scale, y: gestureRecognizer.
scale))!
        gestureRecognizer.scale = 1.0
    }
}
```

In case the code for the pinch gesture is not working correctly or it would not recognize the pinch gesture, check to see if the following conditions are true:

- At least two fingers of the user should be touched to perform this gesture.

- User interaction property of the view should be enabled to true.

- Scale factor should be applied correctly on the view.

Swipe Gesture Recognizer

This is a discrete gesture recognizer that interprets the swiping gestures in one or more directions. When the user pushes the specified number of touches in an allowable direction far enough to produce a swipe, **UISwipeGestureRecognizer** recognizes it as a swipe. The swipes may be made slowly or quickly. A slow swipe necessitates high directional precision over a short distance, while a quick swipe necessitates low directional precision over a long distance. The system only delivers the corresponding action message once per swipe since it is a separate gesture. We can also determine the location where a swipe begins. Refer to *figure 9.4* that illustrates the Swipe gesture, as follows:

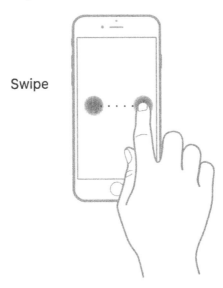

Swipe

Figure 9.4: Swipe Gesture

The motion of the user's finger over the screen, either horizontally or vertically, is tracked by a **UISwipeGestureRecognizer** object. Swipe requires the user's finger to move in a certain direction and not stray too far from the main path of travel. Since the swipe movements are distinct, your intervention method is only named after the gesture has been completed successfully. Therefore, the swipes are best used when you only think about the outcome of the gesture and not about monitoring the user's finger movement. You would use a method like this to perform a task when the gesture is recognized. Because the gesture is discrete, the gesture recognizer does not enter the beginning or changing states, as shown as follows:

```
@IBAction func handleSwipe(_ gestureRecognizer :
UISwipeGestureRecognizer) {
        if gestureRecognizer.state == .ended {
            // Perform action.
        }
    }
```

A Swipe Gesture will work properly and as per expectation when the following are true:

- The number of touches will be the same as specified for the property of **numberOfTouches**.

- Also, the direction of the swipe must be matched with the direction property.

Pan Gesture Recognizer

Panning the gestures are interpreted by a discrete gesture recognizer. Trace the motion of your fingertips through the screen and add it to your content. A pan gesture occurs at any time the user moves one or more fingers around the screen. A screen-edge pan gesture is a specialized pan gesture that originates from the edge of the screen. Use the **UIPanGestureRecognizer** class for the pan gestures and the **UIScreenEdgePanGestureRecognizer** class for the screen-edge pan gestures. For the tasks that enable you to watch the orientation of the user's fingers onscreen, use the pan gesture recognizers. Refer to *figure 9.5* that illustrates the Pan gesture, as follows:

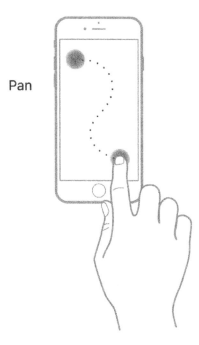

Pan

Figure 9.5: Pan gesture

A pan gesture recognizer may be used to move the objects around in the user interface or change their presence depending on the user's finger location. Since the pan movements are constant, the action method is named anytime the touch data changes, allowing you to refresh your content, as follows:

```swift
var initialCenter = CGPoint()  // The initial center point of the view.
 @IBAction func handlePan(_ gestureRecognizer : UIPanGestureRecognizer)
{
        guard gestureRecognizer.view != nil else {return}
        let piece = gestureRecognizer.view!

        let translation = gestureRecognizer.translation(in: piece.superview)
        if gestureRecognizer.state == .began {
            self.initialCenter = piece.center
        }
        if gestureRecognizer.state != .cancelled {
            let newCenter = CGPoint(x: initialCenter.x + translation.x, y:
initialCenter.y + translation.y)
```

```
        piece.center = newCenter
    }
    else {
        piece.center = initialCenter
    }
}
```

When panning a view, the user must touch one or more fingers on it. A constant panning gesture is used. It starts when the consumer moves the smallest number of fingers necessary to be recognized as a pan. When the user lifts a finger while pressing for the smallest number of digits, it adjusts. When the user lifts both of their fingers, it ends. To make the tracking easier, use the **translation(in:)** form of the pan gesture recognizer to determine how far the user's finger has moved from the initial contact spot. A pan gesture recognizer records the initial point of touch with the user's fingertips at the start of the gesture. (The gesture recognizer uses the middle point of the series of touches, if the gesture includes multiple fingers.) The **translation(in:)** process reports the distance from the original position each time the fingers pass.

Long Press Gesture Recognizer

Long-press gestures are interpreted by a discrete gesture recognizer. Detect the taps on the screen that last longer than a second and use them to reveal contextually meaningful information. Refer to *figure 9.6* that illustrates the Long-press gesture, as follows:

Long press
(>0.5 seconds)

Figure 9.6: Long Press Gesture

Before the operation is triggered, the user must press one or two fingers on a view and keep them there for a certain amount of time (more than 1 second). The user's fingertips can't go more than a certain distance when down, or the gesture fails. The long-press movements (also known as press-and-hold gestures) sense one or two fingertips (or a stylus) pressing the screen for a long time. You set the minimum time for the press to be recognized and the number of times the fingers would touch the frame. (The gesture recognizer is activated solely by the length of the touches, not by the intensity of which they are associated.) A long-press gesture may be used to perform an operation on the target being pressed. You could use it to display a context-sensitive menu too, as shown as follows:

```
@IBAction func showResetMenu(_ gestureRecognizer:
UILongPressGestureRecognizer) {
        if gestureRecognizer.state == .began {
            self.becomeFirstResponder()
            self.viewForReset = gestureRecognizer.view

            // Configure the menu item to display
            let menuItemTitle = NSLocalizedString("Reset", comment: "Reset
menu item title")
            let action = #selector(ViewController.resetPiece(controller:))
            let resetMenuItem = UIMenuItem(title: menuItemTitle, action:
action)

            // Configure the shared menu controller
            let menuController = UIMenuController.shared
            menuController.menuItems = [resetMenuItem]

            // Set the location of the menu in the view.
            let location = gestureRecognizer.location(in:
gestureRecognizer.view)
            let menuLocation = CGRect(x: location.x, y: location.y, width:
0, height: 0)
            menuController.setTargetRect(menuLocation, in:
gestureRecognizer.view!)

            // Show the menu.
            menuController.setMenuVisible(true, animated: true)
        }
    }
```

Rotation Gesture Recognizer

We can measure the relative movement of the two fingers on the screen and move the content on the view using the gesture. A rotating gesture happens as the first two fingers that contact the screen move around each other in a constant motion. To detect the rotation movements, use the **UIRotationGestureRecognizer** class, as shown in *figure 9.7*, as follows:

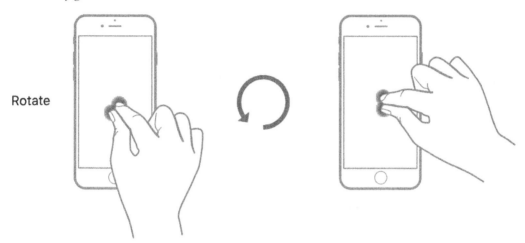

Figure 9.7: *Rotation Gesture*

In radians, the gesture recognizer registers the rotation values. If you envision a line between the user's fingertips, the line formed by the fingers in their original positions indicates the measurement's starting point, and thus represents a rotation angle of 0. At each new spot, a new line is formed between the fingers as the user's fingers move. The gesture recognizer determines the angle between the first and the subsequent lines and stores the effect in the rotation property, as shown as follows:

```
@IBAction func handleRotate(_ gestureRecognizer :
UIRotationGestureRecognizer)
{
        guard gestureRecognizer.view != nil else { return }


        if gestureRecognizer.state == .began || gestureRecognizer.state
== .changed {
            gestureRecognizer.view?.transform = gestureRecognizer.view!.
transform.rotated(by: gestureRecognizer.rotation)
            gestureRecognizer.rotation = 0
        }
}
```

Hover Gesture Recognizer

This is a discrete gesture recognizer that reads the pointer action around a screen. A user can pass the cursor over the user interface elements on the macOS computers. It's necessary to know when the pointer passes over an element without any other user interactions, such as pressing the mouse button, in some UI designs. As the pointer passes over a hyperlink, for example, the text can change colors or appear with an underline. A rollover effect is produced as a consequence of this. Add a hover motion recognizer to the app to have this feeling as the cursor passes over the view. Provide a target and action for the gesture recognizer to call as the cursor approaches, leaves, or moves around the display. When your app runs on iOS, **UIHoverGestureRecognizer** has no impact. A similar example is shown as follows:

```
class ViewController: UIViewController {
    @IBOutlet var button: UIButton!

    override func viewDidLoad() {
        super.viewDidLoad()

        let hover = UIHoverGestureRecognizer(target: self, action:
#selector(hovering(_:)))
        button.addGestureRecognizer(hover)
    }

    @objc
    func hovering(_ recognizer: UIHoverGestureRecognizer) {
        switch recognizer.state {
        case .began, .changed:
            button.titleLabel?.textColor = UIColor.red
        case .ended:
            button.titleLabel?.textColor = UIColor.link
        default:
            break
        }
    }
}
```

Implementing a custom gesture recognizer

You may identify the custom gesture recognizers if the built-in **UIKit** gesture recognizers don't have the action you want. To accommodate the touch sequences for touches, long press, pans, swipes, rotations, and pinches, **UIKit** describes highly configurable gesture recognizers. You may create a personalized gesture recognizer to accommodate the other touch sequences or movements involving the button presses. A gesture recognizer must be linked to a view in the responder chain in order to function. When a user taps on the screen, the touch event is passed down the stack of views, giving each view's gesture recognizers a chance to deal with the touch. The more requirements a gesture must meet in order to succeed, the more exact it will be. We anticipate the user to make the gesture with only one finger, making a downstroke from the left to the right, followed by a downstroke from the right to the left. So, initially you should try out with a simple conditioned custom gesture recognizer which we will build here in further steps.

Gesture recognizer state machine

Gesture recognizers are regulated by a state machine, which is used by **UIKit** to ensure that the events are handled correctly. Several critical activities are determined by the state machine, which are as follows:

- Whether a continuous gesture recognizer is allowed to enter the **UIGestureRecognizer.State.began** (begin) state.

- Whether a discrete gesture recognizer is allowed to enter the **UIGestureRecognizer.State.ended** (end) state.

- When the calls to attached action handlers occur.

You must update the state machine of a custom gesture recognizer at the right time while implementing it. In the discrete gesture recognizer, shift the state to **UIGestureRecognizer.State.ended** (end) when the incoming activities correctly fit the motion. Adjust the state to **UIGestureRecognizer.State.failed** (fail) as soon as you sense a failure when the circumstances do not follow your expected motion.

Handling cancellation

If the current event cycle is disrupted by a device event, such as an incoming phone call, the gesture is immediately cancelled. You may also programmatically cancel a gesture depending on the event details or circumstances in your app. The gesture recognizer is discouraged from executing the functions that the user did not expect. When you switch the gesture recognizer to the **UIGestureRecognizer**, it becomes a **UIGestureRecognizer**. **UIKit** calls the gesture recognizer's action methods one more time before resetting the **state.cancelled** (cancel) state.

Implementing a Discrete Gesture Recognizer

Discrete gesture recognizers have the advantage of being easier to execute because they require fewer state changes. One downside is that since the state transition happens later in the event series, recognition can easily be preempted by continuous gestures attached to the same view.

As shown in *figure 9.8*, a checkmark gesture is made by tracing one finger down and to the right, then up and to the right again. It makes sense to use a discrete gesture recognizer when the gesture takes a particular direction. Establish the criteria under which the identification can occur before applying your gesture recognizer code. The following are the criteria for matching a checkmark gesture:

- Only the first finger to touch the screen is tracked. All others are ignored.

- The touch always moves from left to right.

- The touch moves downward initially but then changes the direction and moves upward.

- The upward stroke ends higher on the screen than the initial touchpoint.

Refer to *figure 9.8* that illustrates the checkmark gesture, as follows:

Figure 9.8: Discrete Gesture

The checkmark gesture requires the gesture recognizer to know the gesture's starting point in order to equate it to the final point. It must also be able to tell whether the user's finger is going downward or upward, as shown as follows:

```
enum CheckmarkPhases {
    case notStarted
    case initialPoint
    case downStroke
    case upStroke
}
class CheckmarkRecognizer : UIGestureRecognizer {
    var strokePhase : CheckmarkPhases = .notStarted
    var initialTouchPoint : CGPoint = CGPoint.zero
    var trackedTouch : UITouch? = nil
```

Touch events

The **touchesBegan** method preserves the position of the touch in the initial touchpoint property since **UIKit** reuses the **UITouch** artefacts and thus overwrites their properties. All further touches applied to the sequence after the first are overlooked. If the original case involves two touches, the gesture automatically fails, as shown as follows:

```
override func touchesBegan(_ touches: Set<UITouch>, with event: UIEvent)
{
    super.touchesBegan(touches, with: event)
    if touches.count != 1 {
        self.state = .failed
    }

    if self.trackedTouch == nil {
        self.trackedTouch = touches.first
        self.strokePhase = .initialPoint
        self.initialTouchPoint = (self.trackedTouch?.location(in: self.
view))!
    } else {
        for touch in touches {
            if touch != self.trackedTouch {
                self.ignore(touch, for: event)
            }
```

```
        }
    }
}
```

When all the subsequent touches are missed, the touches moved verifies that the first touch is the right one. The touch's movement is then examined. This method sets the stroke phase property to down stroke while the original movement is down and to the right. The method switches the stroke step to **upStroke** as the motion changes direction and begins going upward. The method sets the gesture's state to fail if it deviates from this pattern in any way, as shown as follows:

```
override func touchesMoved(_ touches: Set<UITouch>, with event: UIEvent)
{
        super.touchesMoved(touches, with: event)
        let newTouch = touches.first
        guard newTouch == self.trackedTouch else {
            self.state = .failed
            return
        }
        let newPoint = (newTouch?.location(in: self.view))!
        let previousPoint = (newTouch?.previousLocation(in: self.view))!
        if self.strokePhase == .initialPoint {
            if newPoint.x >= initialTouchPoint.x && newPoint.y >=
initialTouchPoint.y {
                self.strokePhase = .downStroke
            } else {          self.state = .failed
            }
        } else if self.strokePhase == .downStroke {
            if newPoint.x >= previousPoint.x {
                if newPoint.y < previousPoint.y {
                    self.strokePhase = .upStroke
                }
            } else {
                self.state = .failed
            }
        } else if self.strokePhase == .upStroke {
                if newPoint.x < previousPoint.x || newPoint.y >
previousPoint.y {
                    self.state = .failed
```

```
            }
        }
    }
```

The touch ends decide if the gesture was going upward when it stopped and if the final point is higher than the initial point if the gesture had not yet collapsed. The procedure sets the state to accept if all the conditions are met; otherwise, the gesture fails, as shown as follows:

```
override func touchesEnded(_ touches: Set<UITouch>, with event: UIEvent)
{
        super.touchesEnded(touches, with: event)
        let newTouch = touches.first
        let newPoint = (newTouch?.location(in: self.view))!
        guard newTouch == self.trackedTouch else {
            self.state = .failed
            return
        }
        if self.state == .possible &&
                self.strokePhase == .upStroke &&
                newPoint.y < initialTouchPoint.y {
            self.state = .recognized
        } else {
            self.state = .failed
        }
    }


override func touchesCancelled(_ touches: Set<UITouch>, with event:
UIEvent) {
        super.touchesCancelled(touches, with: event)
        self.initialTouchPoint = CGPoint.zero
        self.strokePhase = .notStarted
        self.trackedTouch = nil
        self.state = .cancelled
    }

    override func reset() {
        super.reset()
```

```
        self.initialTouchPoint = CGPoint.zero
        self.strokePhase = .notStarted
        self.trackedTouch = nil
    }
```

Gesture interaction is one of the most intuitive user experiences on iOS, and the custom gesture recognizers provide an easy way for the apps to implement it.

3D touch interactions

In iOS 9, Apple has introduced a useful feature called Home-screen fast behavior. These fast steps on the iOS device's app icon assist the user in navigating to a certain part or screen of the app. Force Touch is a feature that is now available on the Mac and Apple iWatch. Since they made several improvements to differentiate the different layers of touches depending on how firmly you press, it was called 3D Touch in the case of iOS.

UIPreviewInteraction

UIPreviewInteraction is a class that registers a view to provide a custom user experience in response to the 3D Touch interactions. A 3D Touch interaction results in a preview interaction of two stages, the first of which is also known as a preview, and the second of which is known as a pledge. If the user adds more force with a touch, the interaction progresses through these stages. The association between the force of the user's touch and the phases of the preview interaction is shown in *figure 9.9*, as follows:

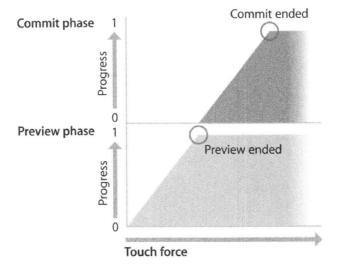

Figure 9.9: UIPreview Interaction

When using the view controller previewing, the preview process is represented by peek, and the commit phase is represented by pop. A preview interaction is in charge of controlling the 3D Touch interactions with a given view. It communicates the progress and state of the interaction to your code using a delegate object.

Conclusion

I hope this was sufficient to acquaint you with the use of gesture recognizers in the iOS applications. Gestures are an important feature of the iOS applications, and you should be able to use them now on your own. This chapter isn't intended to be comprehensive; rather, it serves as an introduction to the subject. There are a few other topics that this book does not cover. You may build your own gesture recognizers from scratch.

In the next chapter, we will discuss the use of GPS location in the mobile applications and show the pins of location on the maps with the help of the Core Location and MapKit frameworks.

Multiple choice questions

1. **Which type of gesture has a specific pattern of events?**
   a. Standard gesture
   b. Custom gesture
   c. Discrete gesture
   d. Continues gesture

2. **Which class represents the location, size, movement, and force of a touch?**
   a. UIPress
   b. UIEvent
   c. UITouch
   d. UIPressEvent

3. **Which of the following is an interface for responding to and handling the events?**
   a. UIEvent
   b. UITouch
   c. UIPressEvent
   d. UIResponder

4. **Which of the following is a discrete gesture recognizer that interprets the pointer movement over a view?**

   a.   Hover Gesture

   b.   Pan Gesture

   c.   Swipe Gesture

   d.   Tap Gesture

5. **Which of the following is a discrete gesture recognizer that interprets the rotation gestures involving two touches?**

   a.   Hover gesture

   b.   Rotation Gesture

   c.   Swipe Gesture

   d.   Pan Gesture

Answers

1. c

2. c

3. d

4. a

5. b

CHAPTER 10

Core Location with MapKit

Introduction

In today's time, with the advancements in technologies, the geo positional systems are an essential part of mobile hardware. And this GPS system can help write such apps, which show the users current location, positions on maps, distance between two or multi-geo positional points etc. The Apple embedded Core Location framework natively integrates with the GPS hardware of the iOS supported iPhones and iPads in such a manner that the developers can use this to build apps with features of the native maps and user's location. Core Location provides the services that determine a device's geographic location, altitude, and orientation, or its position relative to a nearby iBeacon device. The framework gathers the data using all the available components on the device, including the Wi-Fi, GPS, Bluetooth, magnetometer, barometer, and cellular hardware. Including location-based information in your app is an excellent way to keep your users connected to their surroundings. Location-based information should improve the overall user experience, whether you use it for practical purposes (such as navigation) or for entertainment.

Structure

In this chapter, we will cover the following topics:

- CLLocationManager

- AppLocation manager
- Show location on map

Objectives

After studying this chapter, you will be able to get significant positional location with less and high accuracy and perform the Map kit operations with the Core location points. You will also be able to perform the geo-position region monitoring.

CLLocationManager

The Core Location services are configured, started, and stopped using the instances of the **CLLocationManager** class. The following location-related tasks are supported by a location manager object:

- **Standard and significant location updates**: Track big or small changes in the user's current location with a configurable degree of precision.

- **Region monitoring**: When the user enters or leaves specific areas of interest, the location events are generated.

- **Beacon ranging**: Detect and locate the nearby beacons.

- **Compass headings**: Report heading changes from the onboard compass.

Add location permissions

Your app would require the location permission authorization from the user. There are mainly two types of location authorization that have different purpose and requirements for the app.

When in use

In this type of location authorization, your app will receive location events when the user is using the app, and if your app goes into the background, it will stop receiving the location updates and events. You can add in the **info.plist** of your app as **Privacy: Location When In Use Usage Description** property with a proper explanation of why your app required this permission. In the plist source code, you can add the following:

```
<key>NSLocationWhenInUseUsageDescription</key>
<string> To include location data with Project Report.</string>
```

Always use

In this type of location authorization, your app always receives the location events and updates even if the app is in the foreground or background. You can add in the **info.plist** of your app as **Privacy: Location Always Usage Description** property with a proper explanation of why your app required this permission. Alternatively, you can add the code with a change of reason as per your app in the **info.plist** source code as shown as follows:

```
<key>NSLocationAlwaysUsageDescription</key>

<string> To include location data with Project Report. </string>
```

App Location Manager

Now, we will start building a singleton class which will be single handedly responsible for managing the user location and start/stop tracking the user's live location.

Setup Location Manager

Location manager is required to set a delegate as a self-object which will be invoked when the app gets the user's real time location in the form of latitude and longitude. Refer to the following code:

```
var locationManager : CLLocationManager!
var kMinUpdateDistance = 5.0


 /*
     Setting up Location Manager Properties
     : type, filter, accuracy, enabled check
     */
    func setupLocationManager()
    {
        locationManager = CLLocationManager()
        locationManager.delegate = self

        locationManager.activityType = CLActivityType.
automotiveNavigation
        locationManager.distanceFilter = kMinUpdateDistance
        locationManager.desiredAccuracy =
kCLLocationAccuracyBestForNavigation
```

```
        locationManager.pausesLocationUpdatesAutomatically = false
        locationManager.allowsBackgroundLocationUpdates = false
    }
```

Activity type

The information in the activity type field is utilized by the location manager to decide when the location updates should be automatically halted. In circumstances where the user's position is unlikely to change, pausing the updates allows the system to conserve energy. The location navigation activity can be set to location manager as per your app's requirements of location, as follows:

- **Automotive Navigation**: It is used specifically during vehicular navigation to track the location changes to the automobile.

- **Fitness**: It is used to track the fitness activities such as walking, running, cycling, and so on.

- **Airborne**: The location manager is being used specifically during airborne activities.

- **Other Navigation**: It is used to track the movements for the other types of vehicular navigation that are not related to automobile.

Distance filter

Before an update event is created, a device must horizontally travel a minimum distance (measured in meters). This distance is measured relative to the previously delivered location.

Desired accuracy

Assign a value to this parameter that is appropriate for your use to decrease the impact of your app on the battery life. While the location service makes every effort to attain the desired precision, the applications must be prepared to work with less precise data. Changes to this property's value have no effect if your app isn't permitted to receive the precise location data; the accuracy is always **kCLLocationAccuracyReduced**. When you are making an app for navigation purposes, it is advisable to use **kCLLocationAccuracyBestForNavigation**.

Pause location updates

The location manager object's ability to halt the location updates is indicated by the bool value. Allowing the location manager to stop the updates on the target device helps extend the battery life while preserving the location data. This needs to be set to false, so that the location updates don't stop while the app is in use.

Allow background location

If an app wants to receive the location updates while it is suspended, it must include the **UIBackgroundModes** key (with the location value) in its **info.plist** file and set the value to true. The background updates need the availability of the **UIBackgroundModes** key with the location value; this property is used to programmatically activate and disable the background updates, as follows:

```
if CLLocationManager.locationServicesEnabled()
{
    requestLocationAuthorization()
}
```

Before requesting the user location permissions, we need to check for the location services, which must be enabled. In case the location services are not enabled for a device, we need to show an appropriate message in such a way that the user enables the location services on that device. If the location service enabled check returns true, then we will move forward for the user location permissions, as follows:

```
/*
    Check GPS Setting Status
    : Always, WhenIn Use, Not Determined etc


*/
    func requestLocationAuthorization()
    {
        let status = CLLocationManager.authorizationStatus()
        if status == CLAuthorizationStatus.notDetermined {
            locationManager.requestWhenInUseAuthorization()
        }
        else if status == CLAuthorizationStatus.authorizedWhenInUse
        {
            // perform any operation if required
        }
    }
```

In the preceding function, we check if the authorized location permission is already given as per requirements, and then we continue; otherwise, we need to request the location authorization. It could be of the following two types:

- **When in use:** This authorization is requested when your app requires the user location only when the app is in use and not in the background.

- **Always in use:** This type of authorization is given when your app has background modes permissions to be active in the background to get the location always.

Check location enabled

In some instances of the app features, the returning users might not have the location enabled, which we need before an important current location event. In such a case, you need a function that will tell you the current location status, and on the basis of that status, you can show the alerts to the user. Refer to the following code:

```
/*
	Check for location is enabled or not and return red/green image
*/
	func checklocationEnabled() -> UIImage
	{
	    if CLLocationManager.locationServicesEnabled()
	    {
	        switch CLLocationManager.authorizationStatus()
	        {
	        case .notDetermined, .restricted, .denied:
	            print("No access")
	            return UIImage(named: "RedGPS")!
	        case .authorizedAlways, .authorizedWhenInUse:
	            print("Access")
	            return UIImage(named: "GreenGPS")!
	        default:
	            print("Access")
	            return UIImage(named: "GreenGPS")!
	        }
	    } else {
	        print("Location services are not enabled")
	        return UIImage(named: "RedGPS")!
```

```
    }
  }
```

Although we already used all these statuses initially, the **checkLocationEnabled** function will give you the status of the device location enable conditions. Here, we are returning an image green as "*on location*" and red as "*off location*". You may use it as you want for your app development.

Start and stop location tracking

When you are tracking a user or an object with a location, ideally to save the battery, sometimes you need to stop or start the location tracking as per the feature implementation requirements. As we studied earlier, getting the user location depends on a significant location change or distance. Sometimes, we need to force an update such that we can get the current location of the device, as follows:

```
/*
    Trigger to start GPS Location Tracking
*/
func startTracking()
    {
        locationManager.startUpdatingLocation()

        updateTimer = Timer.scheduledTimer(timeInterval: 16.0, target:
self, selector: #selector(WSLocationManager.forceUpdateLocation),
userInfo: nil, repeats: true)
    }
```

The **locationManager** object can start the location tracking via **startUpdatingLocation** which will trigger the delegate methods with the updated locations which can be retrieved in the form of latitude and longitude points, as follows:

```
/*
    Trigger to stop GPS Location Tracking
 */

func stopTracking()
    {
        locationManager.stopUpdatingLocation()
        if (updateTimer != nil) {
            updateTimer!.invalidate()
```

```
        updateTimer = nil
    }
}
```

When the app features don't require location tracking, we can save the battery power by stopping the unnecessary location tracking. Location manager can stop tracking via **stopUpdatingLocation**. In the preceding case, a timer is used to force the location manager to get the current location which could help if the device movement is not significant, and we require regular location changes. Time calls **forceUpdateLocation** which simply requests for the location and notifies the app with the current location in the **delegate** method, shown as follows:

```
// Request Location Update

func forceUpdateLocation()

{

    locationManager.requestLocation()

}
```

Get current user location

When we need a location point of the current location, with the location object of **LocationManager**, we can get the latitude and longitude of the geo positional points to mark the destination of the user device, as follows:

```
/*

    Get current location latitude and longitude from Location Manager

*/

    func currentUserLocation() -> (Float, Float)?

    {

        var lat: Float

        var long: Float

        if let location = locationManager.location {

            lat = Float(location.coordinate.latitude)

            long = Float(location.coordinate.longitude)

            return (lat, long)

        }

        return nil

    }
```

Location Manager Delegates

After starting location tracking, the location manager sends the location updates as success or failure and will be listened to by the Location Manager delegate methods. We will add an extension to our singleton class with **CLLocationManagerDelegate**. Further, we will discuss in detail about these methods, as follows:

- **didchangeAuthorization**: This delegate method informs the delegates their authorization status when the app creates the location manager and when the authorization status changes.

- **didUpdateLocations**: The location data is stored in an array of **CLLocation** objects created by this delegate method. At least one item reflecting the current location is always present in this array. The array may contain extra entries if the updates were delayed or if numerous locations arrived before they could be provided.

- **didFailWithError**: When the location manager finds an error while attempting to retrieve the location or heading data, it calls this function. A **CLError** is reported if the location service is unable to get a location immediately.

With the proper implementation of preceding location delegate function, we can manage and update location as follows:

```
extension WSLocationManager: CLLocationManagerDelegate
{
    func locationManager(_ manager: CLLocationManager,
didChangeAuthorization status: CLAuthorizationStatus)
    {
        if status == CLAuthorizationStatus.authorizedWhenInUse
        {
            locationManager.startUpdatingLocation()
            locationManager.startMonitoringSignificantLocationChanges()
        }
    }

    func locationManager(_ manager: CLLocationManager,
didUpdateLocations locations: [CLLocation]) {
        userLocation = locationManager.location
        dLog("userLocation \(String(describing: userLocation))")
    }
```

```
    public func locationManager(_ manager: CLLocationManager,
didFailWithError error: Error)
    {
        dLog("LocationTracker: didFailWithError \(error)")
        if locationManager.location?.coordinate == nil
        {
            userLocation = CLLocation.init(latitude:
CLLocationDegrees(0.0), longitude: CLLocationDegrees(0.0))
        }
    }
}
```

Significant location change

When the location manager invokes a method for monitoring significant location updates, the location manager starts the generation of updates based on significant location changes. This method initiates the delivery of the location events asynchronously; the first event to be delivered is usually the most recently cached location event (if any) but may be a newer event in some circumstances.

When the smartphone goes 500 meters or more from its previous notification, the apps can anticipate a notice. It should not be expected to get alerts more than once every five minutes. The location manager is far more likely to provide the notifications in a timely way if the device can receive the data from the network.

Show current location on map

To show the user location on a map, you may opt for two ways -- one is with the Google maps and the other is with the Native Apple maps.

Location with Google maps

First, you need to install iOS SDK for the Google maps and Place API. Then, you need to get the API keys for further implementation. You can refer to the developer Google maps documentation.

In **AppDelegate.swift**, you need to add the following code:

```
import GooglePlaces
import GoogleMaps
```

Add the following to your **application(_:didFinishLaunchingWithOptions:)** method, replacing **YOUR_API_KEY** with your API key:

```
GMSPlacesClient.provideAPIKey("YOUR_API_KEY")
GMSServices.provideAPIKey("YOUR_API_KEY")
```

Add the following in the view controller where you want to implement the map view:

```
var mapView: GMSMapView!
var placesClient: GMSPlacesClient!
```

In the **didUpdateLocation** delegate method, we can set the camera position object to map view camera property in such a way that it contains the location coordinates with a zoom level of the map too. In the following code, the zoom level helps to point out that location on the map which we want to show accurately:

```
let location: CLLocation = locations.last!
print("Location: \(location)")


let zoomLevel = locationManager.accuracyAuthorization == .fullAccuracy ?
preciseLocationZoomLevel : approximateLocationZoomLevel
let camera = GMSCameraPosition.camera(withLatitude: location.coordinate.
latitude, longitude: location.coordinate.longitude, zoom: zoomLevel)
if mapView.isHidden {
   mapView.isHidden = false
   mapView.camera = camera
} else
{
   mapView.animate(to: camera)
}
```

Location with Apple Maps

The Apple iOS devices use the native **MapKit** framework to implement the map functions in the app. First, we must initialize a map view from **MapKit** which needs to be connected with **MapView** on the app, shown as follows:

```
@IBOutlet var mapView: MKMapView!

mapView.delegate = self
mapView.mapType = .standard
```

```
mapView.isZoomEnabled = true
mapView.isScrollEnabled = true
```

While setting the properties of the map, we can select the map type, zoom enabled, and scroll enabled for a smooth transition on the map. We can set a location if that is available in the location manager, shown as follows:

```
if let coor = mapView.userLocation.location?.coordinate {
    mapView.setCenter(coor, animated: true)
}


func locationManager(_ manager: CLLocationManager, didUpdateLocations
        locations: [CLLocation]) {
        let locValue:CLLocationCoordinate2D = manager.location!.coordinate

        mapView.mapType = MKMapType.standard

        let span = MKCoordinateSpan(latitudeDelta: 0.05, longitudeDelta:
0.05)
        let region = MKCoordinateRegion(center: locValue, span: span)
        mapView.setRegion(region, animated: true)

        let annotation = MKPointAnnotation()
        annotation.coordinate = locValue
        annotation.title = "You are Here"
        mapView.addAnnotation(annotation)
    }
```

To drop a location pin on the native map, we first need to set up a region on which the map needs to be focused. This map region takes the location as the center and spans the objects to show the location properly. Further, we can add a point annotation with the location coordinates and title to show the pin drop on the map view.

Convert location into place mark address

If you have a **CLLocation** object, use your geocoder object's **reverseGeocodeLocation(:completionHandler:)** function to get a **CLPlacemark** object for that place. When you wish to show the user information about a location, you usually transform the coordinates into placemarks, shown as follows:

```
func lookUpCurrentLocation(completionHandler: @escaping (CLPlacemark?)
                   -> Void ) {
     // Use the last reported location.
     if let lastLocation = self.locationManager.location {
         let geocoder = CLGeocoder()

         // Look up the location and pass it to the completion
handler
         geocoder.reverseGeocodeLocation(lastLocation,
                 completionHandler: { (placemarks, error) in
             if error == nil {
                 let firstLocation = placemarks?[0]
                 completionHandler(firstLocation)
             }
             else {
               // An error occurred during geocoding.
                 completionHandler(nil)
             }
         })
     }
     else {
         // No location was available.
         completionHandler(nil)
     }
}
```

Convert a place address to location coordinates

If you have a user-supplied address, use the **CLGeocoder** methods to get the associated location data. The **CLGeocoder** class allows you to transform either a user-typed string or a dictionary containing address-related information. This data is sent to the Apple servers, which evaluate it and deliver the findings, shown as follows:

```
func getCoordinate( addressString : String,
         completionHandler: @escaping(CLLocationCoordinate2D,
NSError?) -> Void ) {
```

```
        let geocoder = CLGeocoder()
        geocoder.geocodeAddressString(addressString) { (placemarks,
error) in

            if error == nil {
                if let placemark = placemarks?[0] {
                    let location = placemark.location!

                    completionHandler(location.coordinate, nil)
                    return
                }
            }


            completionHandler(kCLLocationCoordinate2DInvalid, error as
NSError?)
        }
    }
```

Types of Core Location Errors

CLError delivered the instances of **NSError** while there is an error specific to the location events. We will discuss some of them, as follows:

- **Location Unknown** indicates the location manager was unable to obtain a location value right now.

- **Denied** indicates the user denied access to the location service.

- **Prompt Declined** indicates the user didn't grant the requested temporary authorization.

- **Network** indicates the network was unavailable or a network error occurred.

- **Heading Failure** indicates the heading could not be determined.

- **Geocode Canceled** indicates the geocode request was cancelled.

- **Deferred Not Updating Location** indicates the location manager didn't enter the deferred mode because the location updates were already disabled or paused.

Monitoring the user's proximity to geographic regions

The Monitoring region service of Core location can be used for region monitoring to determine when the user enters or leaves a geographic region. When a user enters or departs a geographical region, region monitoring (also known as **geofencing**) allows your app to be notified. To execute the location-related tasks, you might employ region monitoring. The Reminders app, for example, utilizes them to send out the reminders when the user enters or exits a specific place.

When a user passes a set area border, the system monitors it and wakes up your app as needed. Region monitoring is only possible on macOS when the program is open (in the foreground or background), and the user's machine is awake, shown as follows:

```
func monitorRegionAtLocation(center: CLLocationCoordinate2D, identifier:
String ) {
        // Make sure the device supports region monitoring.
        if CLLocationManager.isMonitoringAvailable(for:
CLCircularRegion.self) {
            // Register the region.
            let maxDistance = locationManager.
maximumRegionMonitoringDistance
            let region = CLCircularRegion(center: center,
                radius: maxDistance, identifier: identifier)
            region.notifyOnEntry = true
            region.notifyOnExit = false


            locationManager.startMonitoring(for: region)


        }
    }
```

Handle region notifications

The delegate object of your location manager receives the boundary crossing notifications. The location manager specifically invokes its delegate's **locationManager(:didEnterRegion:)** or **locationManager(:didExitRegion:)** methods. If your app has already been launched, you must immediately create a **CLLocationManager** object and a delegate object in order to receive these alerts, as shown as follows:

```
func locationManager(_ manager: CLLocationManager, didEnterRegion
region: CLRegion) {
        if let region = region as? CLCircularRegion {
            let identifier = region.identifier
            triggerTaskAssociatedWithRegionIdentifier(regionID:
identifier)
        }
    }
}
```

The system waits until it is certain that a boundary crossing has occurred before delivering the notification. The user must cross the barrier a minimum distance and remain on the same side of the boundary for at least 20 seconds. These criteria assist to avoid the bogus calls to the methods of your delegate object.

Conclusion

Core Location and Map Kit frameworks help the developers to use GPS and the map base features and capabilities of the iOS devices. In this chapter, we discussed in detail about the use of location managers to track the location continuously, get the current user location, show the location coordinates on the map, etc. For showing the map features, you may opt for either google map capabilities or Apple map capabilities which are natively available with the MapKit framework. Both the maps have their own advantages and disadvantages, and you can make your decision of use as per the app requirements. Further, we discussed location region monitoring with a specific radius of range, and whenever a device entered that region, the app gets notified. The monitoring features are used mostly in locating the business and events as well as the service and product marketing apps to notify the users in real time, whenever they are around.

In the next chapter, we will discuss the use of core media such as camera and photo gallery images and video captures and their use in the mobile apps.

Multiple choice questions

1. **Which framework is used to get the locations in the iOS devices?**
   a. Beacon
   b. Map Kit
   c. Core Location
   d. UIKit

2. **Which delegate method gets an array of updated location coordinates?**

   a. changeAuthrizationStatus

   b. didUpdateLocation

   c. didfailwithError

   d. StartMonitoringRegion

3. **Reverse Geocoding is used for _____.**

   a. Getting updated location

   b. Location coordinates to Address

   c. Address to Location coordinates

   d. None of the above

4. **`startMonitoringSignificantLocationChanges` method is used for _____.**

   a. Starting location update

   b. Getting the location when there is a significant change in location

   c. Monitoring Region at location

   d. None of the above

5. **`CLCircularRegion` is used _____.**

   a. To start location update

   b. When there is a significant change in location

   c. Monitor the Region at location

   d. None of the above

6. **Which class of Core Location contains the location coordinates?**

   a. CLLocationCoordinate2D

   b. CLCircularRegion

   c. CLGeocoder

   d. MKCoordinateSpan

Answers

1.	c	2.	b
3.	b	4.	b
5.	b	6.	a

CHAPTER 11
Camera and Photo Library

Introduction

Nowadays, with the improvements in the mobile, the processing power and megapixels of the cameras are increasing regularly. The multimedia features in any app enhance the overall visibility while adding the capabilities to take pictures from the native camera and photo gallery as well as taking videos from the same into the app. In this chapter, you will learn in detail how you can use the native camera to take pictures inside any app and how you can use an image picker to get the pictures of the gallery into your app. Further, we will implement the customization features of the camera which can be used without a native app Camera.

Structure

In this chapter, we will cover the following topics:

- App media permissions.
- UIImagePickerController
- Working with movies and live photos
- Implement camera features

Objectives

After studying this chapter, you will be able to add an image from the mobile resources such as photo library and camera for the purpose of user image, image upload, album image etc., or any other such feature of your app, as well as be able to make use of the Image picker for loading the photo library and native camera app.

App media permissions

Before starting any coding for either loading the photo library and camera, you need to add the permissions to **info.plist** with a detailed specific reason explaining why and for which feature you want to access to the camera and photo library for your app. If there is no proper explanation, then there is a high chance that while going through the App Store Review at the Apple side, your app may get rejected. To add these permissions, first go to **info.plist** and add the rows, as shown in *figure 11.1* as follows:

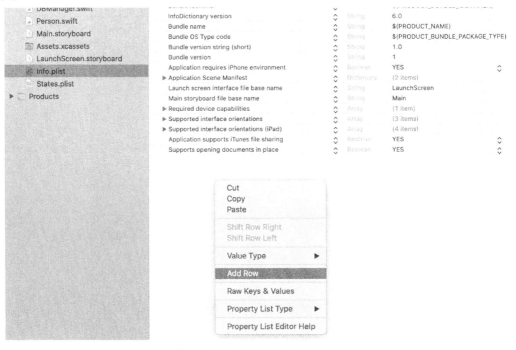

Figure 11.1: Add Media Permissions

Next, in that new row, you will start writing the word **Privacy**, select the option **Privacy - Camera Usage Description**. Further, this will give the option to write a string or statement where you need to explain the reason behind using this camera feature in your app (which you can see in *figure 11.2*). If you are writing the code for practice, you can write any sample string, as it will not affect your overall functionality, and is limited to the App store review cautions. Similarly, select the option for **Privacy - Photo Library Usage Description** for accessing the images from the photo library of the devices.

Other than directly adding into the **.plist**, you can add these via opening the **.plist** file as in the code and adding the following codes to it; this will work the same way as we added manual permissions:

```
<key>NSCameraUsageDescription</key>

<string>This app wants to take pictures.</string>

<key>NSPhotoLibraryUsageDescription</key>

<string>This app wants to use your photos.</string>
```

Refer to *figure 11.2* as follows:

Key	Type	Value
▼ Information Property List	Dictionary	(18 items)
Localization native development region	String	$(DEVELOPMENT_LANGUAGE)
Privacy - Camera Usage Description	String	To Upload User Image
Executable file	String	$(EXECUTABLE_NAME)
Bundle identifier	String	$(PRODUCT_BUNDLE_IDENTIFIER)
InfoDictionary version	String	6.0
Bundle name	String	$(PRODUCT_NAME)
Bundle OS Type code	String	$(PRODUCT_BUNDLE_PACKAGE_TYPE)
Bundle version string (short)	String	1.0
Bundle version	String	1
Application requires iPhone environment	Boolean	YES
▶ Application Scene Manifest	Dictionary	(2 items)
Launch screen interface file base name	String	LaunchScreen
Main storyboard file base name	String	Main
▶ Required device capabilities	Array	(1 item)
▶ Supported interface orientations	Array	(3 items)
▶ Supported interface orientations (iPad)	Array	(4 items)
Application supports iTunes file sharing	Boolean	YES
Supports opening documents in place	Boolean	YES

Figure 11.2: Add Reason to Take Permissions

Add option to choose camera and gallery

Now, we will give the options to choose one of the operations, either to take pictures from the camera or the image gallery, as shown as follows:

```
@IBAction func imagePickerAction(selectedButton: UIButton)
    {
```

```
        let alert = UIAlertController(title: "Choose Image",
message: nil, preferredStyle: .actionSheet)
        alert.addAction(UIAlertAction(title: "Camera", style:
.default, handler: { _ in
            self.openCamera()
        }))


        alert.addAction(UIAlertAction(title: "Gallery", style:
.default, handler: { _ in
            self.openGallery()
        }))


        alert.addAction(UIAlertAction.init(title: "Cancel", style:
.cancel, handler: nil))


        self.present(alert, animated: true, completion: nil)
    }
```

With the help of the action button operation, the users will be able to choose one of the choices out of the camera and the gallery. Now, we will perform the functions for open camera and open gallery code operation, using **UIImagePickerViewController**, as shown as follows:

```
func openCamera()
    {
        if UIImagePickerController.
isSourceTypeAvailable(UIImagePickerController.SourceType.camera) {
            let imagePicker = UIImagePickerController()
            imagePicker.delegate = self
            imagePicker.sourceType = UIImagePickerController.SourceType.
camera
            imagePicker.allowsEditing = false
            self.present(imagePicker, animated: true, completion: nil)
        }
        else
        {
            let alert  = UIAlertController(title: "Warning", message:
"You don't have camera", preferredStyle: .alert)
            alert.addAction(UIAlertAction(title: "OK", style: .default,
handler: nil))
```

```
        self.present(alert, animated: true, completion: nil)
    }
}
```

In the preceding code, we check if the source type as the camera is available; if it is not available, then the code will throw a message warning of not having a camera by this device. You will be able to test this code only on the devices that have a camera and not in a simulator. Now, refer to the following code:

```
func openGallery()
    {
        if UIImagePickerController.
isSourceTypeAvailable(UIImagePickerController.SourceType.photoLibrary){
            let imagePicker = UIImagePickerController()
            imagePicker.delegate = self
            imagePicker.allowsEditing = true
            imagePicker.sourceType = UIImagePickerController.SourceType.
photoLibrary
            self.present(imagePicker, animated: true, completion: nil)
        }
        else
        {
            let alert  = UIAlertController(title: "Warning", message:
"You don't have permission to access gallery.", preferredStyle: .alert)
            alert.addAction(UIAlertAction(title: "OK", style: .default,
handler: nil))
            self.present(alert, animated: true, completion: nil)
        }
    }
```

In the preceding code, we check if the source type as photo library is available; if it is not available, the code will throw a message warning of not having permission to access the photo library. You will be able to test this code on the devices as well as on the simulators.

Allow editing

Adding this property to the **UIImagePickerController** instance, if given as **TRUE**, allows the user to resize, zoom in, and zoom out the selected image before taking that into the app as the final selected image.

Source types

This chooses the type of picker interface that the controller will display. Set this value to the appropriate source type before executing the picker interface. If the source type you provide is not accessible, an exception is raised. If you modify this property while the picker is displayed, the picker interface will update to reflect the new value. There are mainly the following two source types:

- Camera

- Photo Library

UIIMagePickerController

When either a camera opens or a photo gallery after selecting and finalizing a picture, it returns that image in the picking media info delegate method. In the form of **InfoKey.OriginalImage** and in case the user does not select or capture any image, this will be returned in the **imagePickerControllerDidCancel** delegate method, as follows:

```
extension WSImageViewController: UINavigationControllerDelegate,
UIImagePickerControllerDelegate
{
    //Mark:- UIImagePicker delegate

    func imagePickerController(_ picker: UIImagePickerController,
didFinishPickingMediaWithInfo info: [UIImagePickerController.InfoKey :
Any])
    {
        imagePicker.dismiss(animated: true, completion: nil)

        projectImage.image =  info[UIImagePickerController.InfoKey.
originalImage] as? UIImage

        let imageName: String = WSCacheManager.sharedInstance.project.
value(forKey: "pName") as! String

        let fileName = String(format: "%@.png",imageName.
replacingOccurrences(of: " ", with: ""))

        let resizedImage = WSUtility.shared.
resize(info[UIImagePickerController.InfoKey.originalImage] as! UIImage)

    }


    func imagePickerControllerDidCancel(_ picker:
UIImagePickerController)
```

```
    {
        imagePicker.dismiss(animated: true, completion: nil)
    }
}
```

Dismiss the picture picker using your delegate object when the user presses a button to select a freshly taken or stored image or video or cancels the procedure. Your delegate can then store the newly captured media to the device's camera roll. Your delegate can then utilize the picture data according to the purpose of your program for the previously saved media. You may create your own picture picker controller to regulate the user interactions. To do so, create an overlay view with the controls you wish to show.

Working with movies and live photos

The default camera interface allows you to modify the videos that have already been saved. Trimming a movie starts or ends at the beginning or end, and then saves the reduced movie. The **videoMaximumDuration** parameter may be used to change the default duration limit of 10 minutes for the movie capture.

UIVideoEditorController

This is a view controller that manages the system interface for trimming the video frames and encoding a previously recorded movie. A video editor manages the user interactions and provides the filesystem path of the edited movie to your delegate object. The features of the **UIVideoEditorController** class are available only on the devices that support video recording. Use a video editor when your intent is to provide an interface for movie editing. Only the portrait mode is supported by the **UIVideoEditorController** class. This class is not meant to be subclassed and should be used as it is. Do not change the view hierarchy for this class because it is private. The usage of the overlay views to change the look of this class is not supported. Before initializing the edit controller, we will check whether the provided video can be edited by the edit view controller or not, then further, we will start allocating the video to the **videoPath** property and assign the delegate property, shown as follows:

```
if UIVideoEditorController.canEditVideo(atPath: video.path) {
        let editController = UIVideoEditorController()
        editController.videoPath = video.path
        editController.delegate = self
        present(editController, animated:true)
    }
```

Here, we will create an extension of the controller in which we executed the preceding code and implement the **UIVideoEditorControllerDelegate** methods. There are mainly the following three delegates:

- **didSaveEditedVideoToPath**: When the system has completed saving an edited video, this delegate method is called. The parameter **editedVideoPath** contains the path to the edited video file. **videoEditorControllerDidCancel**: When the user cancels a video editing process, this delegate method is invoked.

- **didFailWithError**: When the video editor is unable to load or save a movie, this delegate method is invoked. An incorrect filesystem path or an invalid media format might cause a movie to fail loading into the video editor. It's possible that saving will fail due to a lack of disk space or other factors. Refer to the following code:

WSViewController is extended by UIVideoEditorControllerDelegate such that this view controller can handle all video editing task, shown as follows:

```
extension WSViewController: UIVideoEditorControllerDelegate {
        func videoEditorController(_ editor: UIVideoEditorController,
            didSaveEditedVideoToPath editedVideoPath: String) {
            dismiss(animated:true)
        }


        func videoEditorControllerDidCancel(_ editor:
UIVideoEditorController) {
            dismiss(animated:true)
        }


        func videoEditorController(_ editor: UIVideoEditorController,
                didFailWithError error: Error) {
            print("an error occurred: \(error.localizedDescription)")
            dismiss(animated:true)
        }
    }
```

In every preceding case, we will dismiss the editor controller, so that we can get the control and handle the code appropriately with correct reasoning.

Live Photos

For Live Photos, the **PHLivePhoto** class functions in the same way as the **UIImage** or **NSImage** class does for the static pictures. A **UIImage** or **NSImage** object does not represent the data file from which an image is loaded, but rather a ready-to-use picture that can be presented in a view. Similarly, a **PHLivePhoto** object represents a Live Photo that is ready to display with motion and sound. This class may be used to import displayable Live Photo objects from the data obtained elsewhere (such as images posted through a social network) and to assign Live Photos to the **PHLivePhotoView** objects for display.

Implement camera features

You can use the iOS Camera app to take the photographs and videos with both the front and the back cameras. The Camera app also allows still capture of depth data, portrait effects matte, and Live Photos, depending on your device. We'll teach you how to include these capabilities into your own camera app. It takes advantage of the built-in front and back cameras on the iPhone and iPad, as follows:

```
private let session = AVCaptureSession()
```

Configure a capture session

The camera and microphone are examples of the capture devices that **AVCaptureSession** accepts the data from. Following the receipt of the data, **AVCaptureSession** marshals it to the relevant outputs for processing, finally producing a video file or a still picture. In **viewDidLoad**, our app creates a session and assigns it to the preview view, as shown as follows:

```
previewView.session = session
```

Setting up a capture session

At least one capture input and output are required for every capture session. Media sources, such as the cameras and microphone installed into an iOS device or a Mac, are used as capture inputs. The capture outputs create the media, such as picture and video files, using the data given by the capture inputs. Select an appropriate **AVCaptureDevice**, create a matching **AVCaptureDeviceInput**, and add it to the session to utilize a camera for the video input (to take images or movies), as shown as follows:

```
captureSession.beginConfiguration()
let videoDevice = AVCaptureDevice.default(.builtInWideAngleCamera,for:
.video, position: .unspecified)
```

```
guard let videoDeviceInput = try? AVCaptureDeviceInput(device:
videoDevice!),
            captureSession.canAddInput(videoDeviceInput)
            else { return }
captureSession.addInput(videoDeviceInput)
```

Display a camera preview

In the same way that a typical camera viewer allows the user to see the camera before snapping a photo or starting a video recording, the user wants to see the camera before snapping a photo or starting a video recording. Connecting an **AVCaptureVideoPreviewLayer** to your capture session, which shows a live video stream from the camera while the session is active, can offer such a preview, as follows:

```
class PreviewView: UIView {
    override class var layerClass: AnyClass {
        return AVCaptureVideoPreviewLayer.self
    }

    var videoPreviewLayer: AVCaptureVideoPreviewLayer {
        return layer as! AVCaptureVideoPreviewLayer
    }
}
```

Rear and front facing cameras switching

When a user touches a button in the UI, the change camera function handles the switching between the cameras. It employs a discovery session that lists the available device types in the order of preference and accepts the first device in the array. The **videoDeviceDiscoverySession** in the following code, for example, searches for the possible input devices on the device on which the program is running:

```
func changeCamera()
    {
        switch currentPosition {
        case .unspecified, .front:
            newVideoDevice = backVideoDeviceDiscoverySession.devices.first

        case .back:
```

```
        newVideoDevice = frontVideoDeviceDiscoverySession.devices.first


    @unknown default:
        print("Error capture position. Again to back, dual-camera.")
        newVideoDevice = AVCaptureDevice.default(.builtInDualCamera,
for: .video, position: .back)
        }
    }
```

Capture a photo

Taking a picture is done while waiting for a session. The method starts with matching the video orientation of the video preview layer to the **AVCapturePhotoOutput** connection. The following code allows the camera to record exactly what the user sees on the screen:

```
if let photoOutputConnection = self.photoOutput.connection(with: .video)
{
        photoOutputConnection.videoOrientation =
videoPreviewLayerOrientation!
    }
```

The picture captures the delegate here by using a distinct object, the **PhotoCaptureProcessor**. For Live Photos, when a single capture cycle may include the recording of many frames, this obvious separation of the capture cycles is required. This Project snaps a shot with the previously specified settings every time the user hits the center shutter button, shown as follows:

```
func photoCapture()
    {
        var photoSettings = AVCapturePhotoSettings()
        if  self.photoOutput.availablePhotoCodecTypes.contains(.hevc) {
            photoSettings = AVCapturePhotoSettings(format:
[AVVideoCodecKey: AVVideoCodecType.hevc])
        }
        if self.videoDeviceInput.device.isFlashAvailable {
            photoSettings.flashMode = .auto
        }
        photoSettings.isHighResolutionPhotoEnabled = true
        if let previewPhotoPixelFormatType = photoSettings.
availablePreviewPhotoPixelFormatTypes.first {
```

```
        photoSettings.previewPhotoFormat =
[kCVPixelBufferPixelFormatTypeKey as String:
previewPhotoPixelFormatType]
    }
    if self.livePhotoMode == .on && self.photoOutput.
isLivePhotoCaptureSupported {
        let livePhotoMovieFileName = NSUUID().uuidString
        let livePhotoMovieFilePath = (NSTemporaryDirectory() as
NSString).appendingPathComponent((livePhotoMovieFileName as NSString).
appendingPathExtension("mov")!)
        photoSettings.livePhotoMovieFileURL = URL(fileURLWithPath:
livePhotoMovieFilePath)
    }
    photoSettings.isDepthDataDeliveryEnabled = (self.
depthDataDeliveryMode == .on
        && self.photoOutput.isDepthDataDeliveryEnabled)

    photoSettings.isPortraitEffectsMatteDeliveryEnabled = (self.
portraitEffectsMatteDeliveryMode == .on
        && self.photoOutput.isPortraitEffectsMatteDeliveryEnabled)
    if photoSettings.isDepthDataDeliveryEnabled {
        if !self.photoOutput.
availableSemanticSegmentationMatteTypes.isEmpty {
            photoSettings.enabledSemanticSegmentationMatteTypes =
self.selectedSemanticSegmentationMatteTypes
        }
    }
    photoSettings.photoQualityPrioritization = self.
photoQualityPrioritizationMode
    self.photoOutput.capturePhoto(with: photoSettings, delegate:
photoCaptureProcessor)
  }
```

The following two arguments are accepted by the capture photo method:

- The settings your user configures through the app, such as exposure, flash, focus, and torch, are encapsulated in an **AVCapturePhotoSettings** object.

- A delegate that follows the **AVCapturePhotoCaptureDelegate** protocol and responds to the system's following callbacks during photo capture.

Further, the **AVCapturePhotoCaptureDelegate** methods handle all the listening of the events done with either the photo or the movie captures. The other visual effects, such as animating a preview thumbnail of the taken photo, can be applied in this delegate function. On a per-photo request basis, the camera adds depth and portrait effects matter as auxiliary information. The app displays an option to alter the settings for activating or removing the depth data, portrait effects matte, or Live Photos if the device supports them.

You may also require the authorization permissions for saving the files or taking pictures, which will work the same as explained in the initial part of this chapter. Also, you may consider uploading the media files directly to the cloud or different storage apps.

Conclusion

The Media enabled apps features can enhance the overall user experience and give better visual performances if handled with proper memory cache management and file management. In this chapter, we discussed in detail about the default camera app while taking photos or movie videos. We also learned about the implementation of the same features as in the custom camera app, so that you can embed the camera preview and its function as you want to show to your users and manage everything at your end.

In the next chapter, you will explore the domain of machine learning and get to know how Apple implemented the CoreML framework for the ease of the iOS app development.

Multiple choice questions

1. **UIVideoEditorController** is used for _____.

    a. Enabling Camera session

    b. Editing Videos

    c. Capturing photos

    d. None of the above

2. **Which class is the same for Live Photos as UIImage for static photos?**

    a. PHLivePhoto

    b. PHPhotoLive

    c. PLPhotoLive

    d. PHPhoto

3. **How do you get an Image from `UIImagePickerController`?**

   a. InfoKey.OriginalImage

   b. Key.OriginalImage

   c. Info.Key.OriginalImage

   d. OriginalImage

4. **Which class shows the camera preview?**

   a. PHLivePhoto

   b. AVcaptureDevice

   c. AVCaptureVideoPreviewLayer

   d. AVSession

Answers

1. b

2. a

3. a

4. c

CHAPTER 12
Machine Learning with Core ML

Introduction

In today's time, the AI and ML based applications gained popularity due to intelligent and fast decision making. The machine learning models have usually trained either on the server-side or on the high processing machines. But recent developments and research have come forward and made the mobile enabled training of the models that can use the mobile processing power and work efficiently. The Core ML framework is one of the efforts made by Apple for the iOS application developer community, so that the AI and ML base features can be embedded into the apps easily without much effort. In iOS with only a few lines of code, you can add the on-device machine learning functionality to your apps, such as object identification in photos and videos, language analysis, and sound categorization.

Structure

In this chapter, we will cover the following topics:

- Core ML
- Vision framework
- Natural language framework
- Speech framework
- Sound analysis

Objectives

After studying this chapter, you will be able to understand the basic concepts of the machine learning methodology which will help you enhance your knowledge to use vision, natural language, speech, and sound analysis in your iOS apps.

CoreML

The Apple technology with lowering memory footprint and battery consumption utilized efficiently for the on-device performance on a wide range of model types is widely known as Core machine learning framework. The Core machine learning models operate entirely on the user's device, eliminating the need for a network connection and making your app responsive while keeping your users' data safe. The Core ML converters can convert the models from the libraries like TensorFlow or PyTorch to Core ML. It works with the most up-to-date models, such as cutting-edge neural networks for understanding pictures, video, sound, and other forms of rich multimedia. The App-bundled models updated with the user data on-device, allows the models to remain relevant to the user behavior while maintaining privacy. You can also deploy the models to your app using CloudKit with the Core ML model deployment.

Core ML converters

The Core ML tools python package is the primary way to perform conversions from the third-party models (PyTorch, TensorFlow, etc.) to the CoreML models. Further, with this tool, we can read, write, and better optimize the CoreML models. You can then use Core ML to integrate the models into your app. The third-party tools may have their own type of trained model which can be converted to ML model packages, as shown in *figure 12.1* as follows:

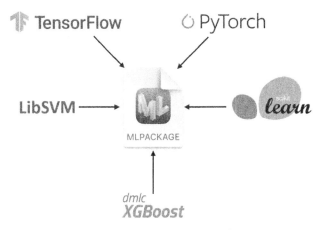

Figure 12.1: Core ML Conversion

Save a CoreML model package

The **mlmodel** (machine learning model) type binary file format, which encodes and stores the model's implementation details and complexity, has been used to represent the core ML models in the file system. A **mlmodel** file would be added to an Xcode project, and the code would be written to deal with it. The macOS package facility is used by the Core ML model package to store each of a model's components in its own file, isolating the model's information from its architecture and weights. You may update the model's metadata and input-output descriptions, as well as track the changes using source control, by saving it as a package. The ML package file contains the metadata in the form of JSON and other parameters in the form of binary, as shown in *figure 12.2*, as follows:

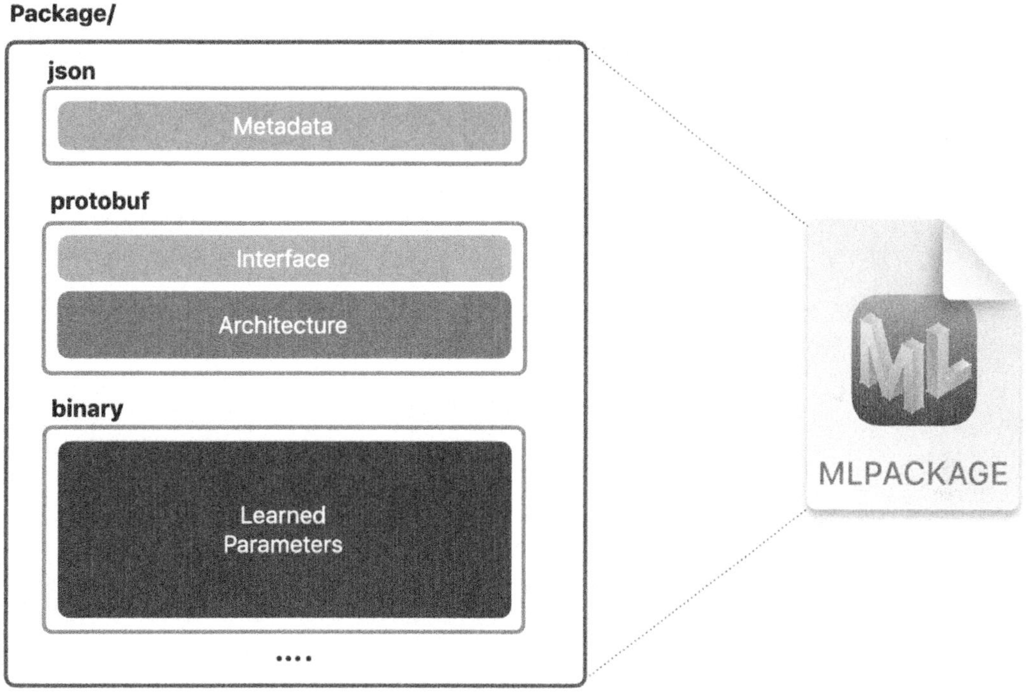

Figure 12.2: ML Package Format

The original **mlmodel** format is still supported by Core ML and Xcode, but you can save a model package for all the model types that the original **mlmodel** format supports.

Updating a model file to model package

A Core ML model package, like an app bundle, is a file-system structure that can hold a model in many files. Model packages, which include editable metadata and the separation of a model's architecture from its weights and biases, provide more flexibility and extensibility than the Core ML model files. By converting the model in Xcode, you may transform your model file to a model package. Before converting the model to the ML package format, Xcode displays a confirmation prompt. The original model file is automatically moved to the trash by Xcode. By deselecting the checkbox in the Xcode window, you can maintain your original model file. When you are ready to convert the model to a package, you can select update or edit, as shown in *figure 12.3*, as follows:

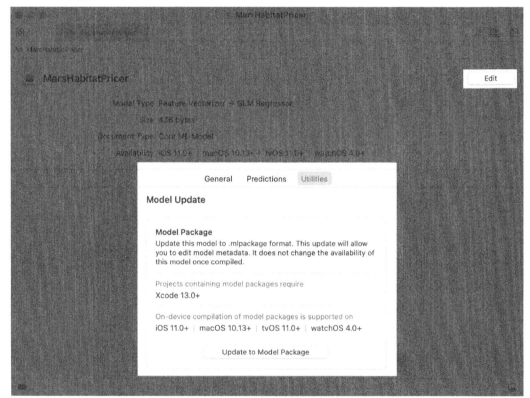

Figure 12.3: ML Package Update

Create ML

Create and train the new machine learning models on your Mac with the Create ML featuring familiar tools like Swift and macOS playgrounds. You could train the models to detect photos, extract meaning from text, and identify the relationships between quantities, among other things. By training a model to the representative samples, you may train it to spot patterns. For instance, you can train a model to detect the dogs by training it to a large number of images of various animals. After you've trained the model, you'll put that to test with the data it's not seen before and see how well it performs. When the model has proven to be robust, you could use Core ML to integrate it into your application. Create ML can take multiple types of inputs such as images and text to train the model with high accuracy which will generate the Core ML model output, as shown in *figure 12.4*, as follows:

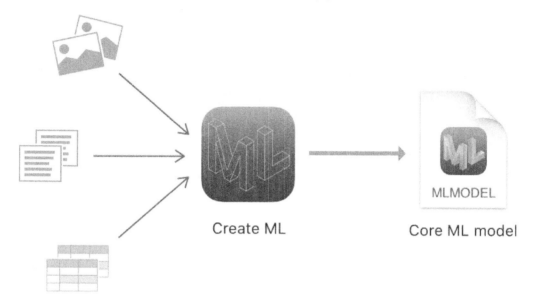

Figure 12.4: Create ML Process

Create ML makes use of the machine learning technology that is already present in the Apple products, such as Photos and Siri. As a result, your image classification and natural language models are smaller and train faster. Now, we will discuss how different types of classifiers can be used to create an ML model which can be used in your Core ML apps for the identification and detection of text, image, sound, action, etc.

MLImageClassifier

To classify the images, use an image classifier to train a machine learning model that you can incorporate in your app. You give the model a training dataset of labelled images as well as the parameters that control the training process when you create it. For example, you can train the model to detect the elephants and giraffes by placing the images of them in two folders labelled as 'Elephant' and 'Giraffe'.

MLTextClassifier

To identify the natural language text, use a text classifier to train a machine learning model that you can incorporate in your app. The model learns to link the labels with the aspects of the input text, which can range from phrases to paragraphs to complete documents. A text classifier is saved to a Core ML model file when it has been trained. The model file is then read into your app using an instance of the Natural Language framework's `NLModel` class.

MLActionClassifier

This is a model for classifying a person's body movements that you train with movies. A machine learning model that recognizes a person's body motions in a video is known as an action classifier. When given a video of a person performing jumping jacks, an action classifier that you train to recognize the exercise activities can predict the yoga forms and dance forms.

MLSoundClassifier

This is a machine learning model that can detect and identify sounds on a device after being trained with audio files. Create an audio dataset by recording or collecting the audio samples that best represent the sounds you want your app to recognize. Additionally, by collecting or recording the sample sounds, establish a negative class – a group of related noises that the sound classifier might perceive but aren't meaningful.

MLActivityClassifier

This is a model you train to classify the motion sensor data. A training dataset of a device's motion sensors, such as the accelerometer and gyroscope on an Apple Watch, is used to develop an activity classifier. You can, for example, gather the motion-sensor data from people who are waving, shaking hands, or throwing a ball to construct an activity classifier that detects those acts.

Improve model's accuracy

To improve the accuracy of your machine learning model, use metrics to fine-tune its performance. Looking at your model's performance across diverse data sets is the first step in evaluating and improving it. Each dataset's metrics reveal which adjustments have the greatest impact on your model's accuracy. If your model's training accuracy is low, it means that your current model setup can't handle the complexity of your data. Adjust the training parameters if necessary. In the `MLImageClassifierBuilder` playground UI, double the maximum number of iterations while dealing with the image data (the default value is 10).

You will require more data if your model's accuracy on the validation set is low or varies between low and high each time you train it. Data augmentation is a technique that allows you to produce extra input data from the examples you've already collected. In *figure 12.5*, we can see that by transforming one image into multiple examples, you can mix operations like cropping, rotation, blurring, and exposure modification for the elephant image data, as follows:

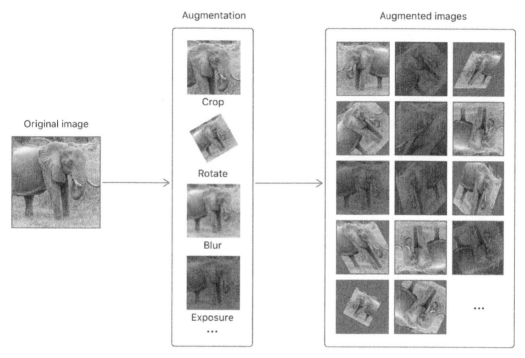

Figure 12.5: Improve Model Accuracy

Vision framework

When we need to apply the computer vision algorithms to input the photos and video to accomplish a number of tasks, Vision Framework could help out to achieve those tasks easily. Face and landmark detection, text detection, barcode recognition, picture registration, and general feature tracking are all performed by the Vision framework. Custom Core ML models can also be used for tasks like categorization and object detection using vision.

Object detection in still images

Rectangles, faces, text, and barcodes will all be detected by the Vision framework in any orientation. We will discuss in detail how to make requests to detect these items, as well as how to understand the results of those requests. We will use the Core Animation layers to draw the trails around the recognized features in the photos to help you visualize where an observation occurs and how it looks.

Create vision request

First, we will create a **VNImageRequestHandler** object with the input image to be processed, as follows:

```
let imageRequestHandler = VNImageRequestHandler(cgImage: image,
                                                orientation:
orientation,
                                                options: [:])
```

Create and bundle all the requests to pass into the image request handler if you're performing several queries from the same image (for example, recognizing facial characteristics as well as faces). On its own thread, Vision executes each request and its completion handler. After Vision completes all requests, you can pair each request with a completion handler to perform request-specific code. This code varies from request to request since the example draws the boxes differently depending on the kind of request. When initializing each request, specify your completion handler, as shown as follows:

```
        lazy var rectangleDetectionRequest: VNDetectRectanglesRequest =
{
        let rectDetectRequest =
VNDetectRectanglesRequest(completionHandler: self.
handleDetectedRectangles)
            rectDetectRequest.maximumObservations = 8
            rectDetectRequest.minimumConfidence = 0.6
            rectDetectRequest.minimumAspectRatio = 0.3
            return rectDetectRequest
        }()
```

When you have finished producing all of your requests, provide them as an array to the synchronous **perform(_:)** method in the request handler. Because vision computations might take a long time and demand a lot of resources, utilize a background queue to prevent blocking the main queue while it runs, as shown as follows:

```
DispatchQueue.global(qos: .userInitiated).async {
        do {
            try imageRequestHandler.perform(requests)
        } catch let error as NSError {
            print("Failed to perform image request: \(error)")
            self.presentAlert("Image Request Failed", error: error)
```

```
        return
    }
}
```

Detection results

When we get the results, the method **perform(_:)** returns a Boolean indicating whether the requests were successful or unsuccessful. If it was successful, the results property provides the observation or tracking data, such as the location and bounding box of a discovered object. The detector gives the **VNFaceObservation** findings with more detail, such as **VNFaceLandmarkRegion2D**, for the face landmark requests. The **characterBoxes** feature can be used to pinpoint specific characters in the text observations. Some supported symbol techniques have the payload information in the **payloadStringValue** attribute for the barcode observations, allowing you to parse the content of the detected barcodes. The Barcode detection, like a supermarket scanner, is designed to discover only one barcode per image. Before exiting the completion handler, it's up to the program to use or save the data from the observations. Rather than drawing pathways like the sample, create custom code to retrieve the information that your app needs from each observation.

Best way to use vision framework

Instead of creating numerous request handlers and submitting them multiple times on the same image, to save excessive computation, construct all of your requests before querying Vision, group them into a requests array, and submit the entire array in one call. Create a separate image handler for each image and issue queries to each handler on separate threads, so that they execute in parallel to perform detection across many, unrelated images. Each image request handler consumes additional processing time and memory, therefore avoid using the main thread for them. Send these handlers to separate background threads, only returning to the main thread for the UI modifications like displaying images or paths.

Natural language framework

The Natural Language framework offers a wide range of natural language processing (NLP) capabilities, as well as support for a wide range of languages and scripts. Use this framework to break down the natural language text into paragraphs, phrases, or words, and then tag the information about those segments, such as part of speech, lexical class, lemma, script, and language.

We can use this NL Framework to use the following:

- Language identification
- Tokenization

- Parts-of-speech tagging

- Named entity recognition

Identification of language in text

The task of automatically identifying the language and script of a piece of text is known as language identification. **NLLanguageRecognizer** does this task in Natural Language. You can get the most likely language for a piece of input text, or a list of possible language options with their associated probabilities, by using a language recognizer. You can additionally limit the identification procedure by providing a list of known probabilities for the languages or a list of languages against which the predictions must be made. **NLLanguage** lists the supported languages, but you can also create and use your own language tags. Further, we can create a language recognizer, as shown as follows:

```
let recognizer = NLLanguageRecognizer()
recognizer.processString("We are processing Language Recognizer")
```

Access the **dominantLanguage** property of the language recognizer to retrieve the most likely language for the specified input text. Because this is an optional setting, make sure to account for the possibility that the language recognizer will be unable to determine a dominant language, as shown as follows:

```
// Dominant language Identification.
    If let language = recognizer.dominantLanguage {
        print(language.rawValue)
    } else {
        print("Language not recognized")
    }
```

Use the **languageHypotheses(withMaximum:)** function to produce various possible language predictions. Set the maximum number of languages to be identified, as shown as follows:

```
// Two language hypothesis generation.
    let hypotheses = recognizer.languageHypotheses(withMaximum: 2)
    print(hypotheses)
```

Tokenizing text

When working with the natural language material, tokenizing the text into individual words can be quite useful. Using **NLTokenizer** to enumerate the words instead of just dividing the components by whitespace ensures consistent behavior across the scripts and languages. Chinese and Japanese, for example, do not utilize spaces to separate words. **NLTokenizer** can be used to count the number of words in a natural language document, as shown as follows:

```
let text = """
    Discrimination means being treated less favourably than others;
traditionally, for reasons related to factors that you could not change,
such as your colour, race, nationality, ethnicity or sex.
    """


    let tokenizer = NLTokenizer(unit: .word)
    tokenizer.string = text


    tokenizer.enumerateTokens(in: text.startIndex..<text.endIndex) {
tokenRange, _ in
        print(text[tokenRange])
        return true
    }
```

Let's take a detailed understanding of the code, as follows:

- Create a new instance of **NLTokenizer** with **NLTokenUnit.word** as the tokenization unit.

- Set the tokenizer's string property to the natural language text.

- By calling the method **enumerateTokens(in:using:)** function and specifying the complete range of the string to process, you can enumerate throughout the entire range of the string.

- To get each word, take a substring of the original text at **tokenRange** in the enumeration block.

- To get each word, take a substring of the original text at **tokenRange** in the enumeration block.

Parts of speech tagging

Identifying the parts of speech for the words in the natural language text can assist your apps in comprehending the sentence meaning. For example, if you have a transcription of a user request, you may establish a general-purpose program by looking simply at the nouns and verbs. **NLTagger** can be used to iterate over the natural language text and identify each word's part of speech, as follows:

```
let text = "This is a sample text to test NSTagger"

    let tagger = NLTagger(tagSchemes: [.lexicalClass])

    tagger.string = text

    let options: NLTagger.Options = [.omitPunctuation, .omitWhitespace]

    tagger.enumerateTags(in: text.startIndex..<text.endIndex, unit:
.word, scheme: .lexicalClass, options: options) { tag, tokenRange in

        if let tag = tag {

            print("\(text[tokenRange]): \(tag.rawValue)")

        }

        return true

    }
```

Named entity recognition

Identifying the identified things in natural language text can aid in the intelligent development of your software. A messaging app, for example, may search for names of the people and locations in the text to display relevant information such as contact information or directions. **NLTagger** enumerates over the string which contains the names of places, person, and organizations with options to remove white spaces and punctuations for better results, as follows:

```
let text = "The American Red Cross was established in Washington, D.C.,
by Clara Barton."


    let tagger = NLTagger(tagSchemes: [.nameType])

    tagger.string = text


    let options: NLTagger.Options = [.omitPunctuation, .omitWhitespace,
.joinNames]

    let tags: [NLTag] = [.personalName, .placeName, .organizationName]


    tagger.enumerateTags(in: text.startIndex..<text.endIndex, unit:
.word, scheme: .nameType, options: options) { tag, tokenRange in

        if let tag = tag, tags.contains(tag) {

            print("\(text[tokenRange]): \(tag.rawValue)")

        }

        let (hypotheses, _) = tagger.tagHypotheses(at: tokenRange.
lowerBound, unit: .word, scheme: .nameType, maximumCount: 1)
```

```
    print(hypotheses)


    return true
}
```

Speech framework

Receive transcriptions, alternate interpretations, and confidence levels of the results after performing speech recognition on live or prerecorded audio. To recognize the spoken words in a recorded or live audio, use the Speech framework. Speech recognition is used by the keyboard's dictation feature to convert the audio material into text. This framework has similar functionality; however, it may be used without the usage of a keyboard. For example, in other portions of your program, you might use speech recognition to recognize the spoken commands or manage text dictation.

Permissions to use speech recognition

The speech recognition process begins with the user's voice being recorded and sent to the Apple's servers for processing. You must make every effort to protect the audio you record because it contains sensitive user data. Before transferring the data across the network to the Apple's servers, you must additionally get the user's consent. The Speech framework's APIs are used to obtain authorization. Add the **Privacy - Speech Recognition Usage Description** key to the **Info.plist** file of your app in Xcode. **NSSpeechRecognitionUsageDescription** is the key's full name. Set this key's value to a string describing how you intend to use any recognized speech. The value of this key is displayed to the user as part of the system prompt when your app requests the authorization later.

When your app requests the permission to utilize voice recognition for the first time, the system prompts the user to agree or deny the request. The system keeps track of the user's choices, so that subsequent requests don't have to prompt them again. Subsequent inquiries, on the other hand, respond almost instantly with the already recorded findings. Further, we can check and control the UI on the basis of authorization access, as shown as follows:

```
override public func viewDidAppear(_ animated: Bool) {
        speechRecognizer.delegate = self


        SFSpeechRecognizer.requestAuthorization { authStatus in


        OperationQueue.main.addOperation {
            switch authStatus {
```

```
            case .authorized:
                self.recordAction.isEnabled = true

            case .denied:
                self.recordAction.isEnabled = false
                self.recordAction.setTitle("User Access Denied
                          to speech recognition", for: .disabled)

            case .restricted:
                self.recordAction.isEnabled = false
                self.recordAction.setTitle("Speech Recognition
restricted on this device", for: .disabled)

            case .notDetermined:
                self.recordAction.isEnabled = false
                self.recordAction.setTitle("Speech recognition not yet
                                    authorized", for: .disabled)
            }
          }
        }
    }
```

Live audio speech recognition

In this section, we will look at how to perform speech recognition on audio from an iOS device's microphone. **SpokenWord** communicates with the device's microphone using the AV Foundation. The app configures an **AVAudioEngine** object to retrieve the microphone input and a shared **AVAudioSession** object to manage the app's audio interactions with the rest of the system.

The program fetches the shared **AVAudioSession** object, configures it for recording, and makes it the active session when you start recording audio. The system is notified that the app requires the microphone resource by activating the session. The **setActive(:options:)** method throws an exception if that resource is unavailable, as shown as follows:

```
private let audioEngine = AVAudioEngine()


    let audioSession = AVAudioSession.sharedInstance()
    try audioSession.setCategory(.record, mode: .measurement, options:
```

```
.duckOthers)
    try audioSession.setActive(true, options:
.notifyOthersOnDeactivation)
    let inputNode = audioEngine.inputNode
```

The app obtains the **AVAudioInputNode** object from its audio engine and stores it in the local **inputNode** variable once the session is active. The current audio input path, which can be the device's built-in microphone, or a microphone attached to a set of headphones, is represented by the input node. To start recording, the app places a tap on the input node, which activates the audio engine and begins collecting the samples into an internal buffer. The audio engine calls the specified block when a buffer is full. The app's implementation of that block sends the audio samples directly to the request object's **append(_:)** method, which collects them and sends them to the speech recognition system.

Sound analysis

Create an **SNClassifySoundRequest** to analyze an audio file or stream and identify the distinct noises in your app, such as laughter or applause. Over 300 sounds can be identified using the sound requests. Alternatively, you can identify a specific group of sounds by attaching a custom Core ML model to the sound request. Create an **MLSoundClassifier** with the audio data to train a custom sound classification model in Create ML.

Audio file sound classification

Process the audio files with a **SNAudioFileAnalyzer** to recognize the sounds like laughter and applause when they occur in a recording. An audio file analyzer, for example, can be used by a sound recording software to assign searchable metadata tags to each sound file in its library. The analyzer might also be used by the same program to add the timestamps to each recording, allowing the user to skip to a certain sound.

Now, we will create a sound request that uses a custom Core ML model, as shown as follows:

```
let defaultConfig = MLModelConfiguration()
let soundClassifier = try SoundClassifier(configuration: defaultConfig)
let request = try SNClassifySoundRequest(mlModel: soundClassifier.model)
```

Implement the **SNResultsObserving** protocol to create a type that accepts the results from an audio analyzer. When an analyzer generates the results or errors, or when it completes a task, the protocol describes the methods it calls, as shown as follows:

```
let resultsObserver = ResultsObserver()
    class ResultsObserver: NSObject, SNResultsObserving {

        func request(_ request: SNRequest, didProduce result: SNResult)
{

            guard let result = result as? SNClassificationResult else {
return }
            guard let classification = result.classifications.first else {
return}
            let timeInSeconds = result.timeRange.start.seconds
            let formattedTime = String(format: "%.2f", timeInSeconds)
            print("Result Analysis  for audio at time: \
(formattedTime)")
            let percent = classification.confidence * 100.0
            let percentString = String(format: "%.2f%%", percent)
            print("\(classification.identifier): \(percentString)
confidence.\n")
        }

        func request(_ request: SNRequest, didFailWithError error:
Error) {
            print("The the analysis failed: \(error.
localizedDescription)")
        }

        func requestDidComplete(_ request: SNRequest) {
            print("The request completed successfully!")
        }
    }
```

In this case, the observer outputs the prediction result to the console, which includes a timestamp, a classification name, and the classifier's confidence. Implement your observer to take the proper action for your app based on the outcome.

Conclusion

In the pre context of mobile, the devices can use camera photos, audio, and video movies in the form of user inputs, the application horizon getting wider day-by-day with the advancements of machine learning and artificial intelligence focus. In this chapter, we discussed details about the Core ML framework which can help build real time ML applications on the pre-trained models which can be trained from the Create ML tools and techniques. Apple introduced Vision and NL and Speech frameworks to achieve computer vision and NLP algorithms and techniques, so that there is no need of diving deep into technology while implementing those into the mobile iOS apps.

In the next chapter, you will study about networking and communication to the backend server, so that your apps could easily integrate with the cloud databases and show dynamic data on user requests.

Multiple choice questions

1. **Speech Framework is used for _____.**
    a. Recognition of Text
    b. Recognition of Sound
    c. Analysis of Sound
    d. None of the above

2. **Sound Classifier is used for _____.**
    a. Recognition of Text
    b. Recognition of Sound
    c. Analysis of Sound
    d. None of the above

3. **Language Identification is part of _____.**
    a. Vision Framework
    b. Natural Language Framework
    c. Speech Framework
    d. Sound Framework

4. **Create ML is used for _____.**
    a. Training models
    b. Creating Vision task
    c. Creating NL Task
    d. None of the above

5. `MLImageClassifierBuilder` **is used for** _____.

    a.   Training models

    b.   Model Accuracy

    c.   Creating NL Task

    d.   None of the above

Answers

   1. b

   2. c

   3. b

   4. a

   5. b

CHAPTER 13

Networking in iOS Apps

Introduction

When you want to support dynamic content and sync the data from one device and also access it from anywhere on the Internet via the website or other cloud accounts, then the developers need to build the systems that integrate with the server-side implementations. In this chapter, we will discuss the basics of client-server networking architecture, by accessing REST APIs with Postman or Advance rest-client tools. We will see how an iOS app can request the data from the cloud and send and update the data to the cloud with the help of the Alamofire library as well as with the Apple Networking Frameworks.

Structure

In this chapter, we will cover the following topics:

- REST architecture
- Connection reachability
- Alamofire
- URLSession

Objective

After studying this chapter, you will be able to understand the communication and data transfer between the client-side app and server that will help you to identify the user accounts across multiple clients with credentials that can share the data to the server and vice versa as well.

REST architecture

The acronym for **REST** is **REpresentational State Transfer** which is an architecture for the distributed hypermedia systems used for portability of the user interface data across multiple platforms. **Application Programming Interface (API)** is a set of protocols and definitions used for the purpose of service request contract between the information provider and the information consumer, and work as a middleman for the web server content and content consumer client.

A mobile iOS app can implement the client request for RESTful APIs which will enable the app to handshake successfully with the server securely and further sync the data and get the content for the end user consumption.

Information content type

When we require to use RESTful APIs, the communication content needs to be defined such that the client and the server can parse and understand the data easily. The Content Types of APIs are as follows:

- **JSON**: JSON is the most popular content type in client requests due to its lightweight structure, and it is easily readable by both the humans as well as the machine algorithms.

- **XML/XSLT**: XML stands for eXtensible Markup Language. It was created as a language with the basic formal syntax, making it straightforward for both the programs and the people to produce and manipulate the documents, with a focus on the Internet use.

- **Binary File**: The Binary file is used when there is a need to send a file attachment with the text information in an API request.

- **Plain Text**: Plain text can be sent when there is no need for structured data and is used very rarely in the context of the best API communication.

HTTP structure

Data is transferred between a server and a client via the HTTP messages. There are different kinds of messages – requests, which are delivered by the client to cause the server to perform an action, and responses, which are the server's responses. The HTTP messages are made up of textual data encoded in ASCII that spans many lines. The HTTP Structure consists of mainly two components – one is **Request** and the other is **Response**. The HTTP requests are messages sent by the client to initiate an action on the server. The request target, usually a URL, or the absolute path of the protocol, port, and domain are usually characterized by the request context.

Request methods

HTTP specifies a variety of request methods for expressing the desired action for a given resource. These request methods are frequently referred to as HTTP verbs, despite the fact that they can also be nouns. Each of them implements a different semantic, although a number of them have certain similar properties. The list of HTTP methods are as follows:

- **GET**: The **GET** method is used to get a representation of a resource. Requests made using the **GET** method should only return the data.

- **HEAD**: The **HEAD** method requests a response that is equivalent to a **GET** request, but without the body.

- **POST**: The **POST** method is being used to submit an entity to the given resource, which frequently causes the server's state to change or have side effects.

- **PUT**: All existing representations of the target resource are replaced with the request payload when using the **PUT** method.

- **DELETE**: The **DELETE** method removes the provided resource from the system.

- **CONNECT**: The **CONNECT** method creates a tunnel between the client and the server specified by the destination resource.

- **OPTIONS**: The **OPTIONS** method is used to describe the communication options for the target resource.

- **TRACE:** A message loop-back test is performed via the **TRACE** technique along the way to the target resource.

Client in the form of either desktop or mobile makes the API requests with one of the request methods explained earlier to the Application server which validates the request and saves to the storage as well as sends back the data to the client, as shown in *figure 13.1*, as follows:

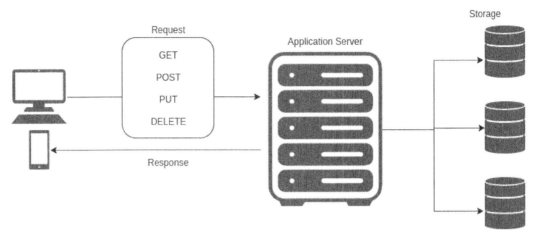

Figure 13.1: API Request Architecture

HTTP headers

The HTTP headers allow the client and server to send extra data with an HTTP request or response. The name of an HTTP header is case-insensitive, followed by a colon (:), and then the value. The headers can be grouped mainly into the following four types:

- Request
- Response
- Representation
- Payload

More information about the resource to be obtained, or about the client seeking the resource, can be found in the request headers. Additional information about the response, such as its location or the server that sent it, is stored in the response headers. The representation headers provide information about the resource's body, such as the MIME type or the encoding/compression used. The Payload headers provide the representation-agnostic information on the payload data, such as the content length and transport encoding.

The credentials providing the user agent's authentication information for the realm of the resource being requested make up the Authorization field value. The Accept-Encoding request-header element is identical to Accept, except it limits the permitted content-coding in the response.

HTTP body

The body of the request is the final component. The requests that fetch the resources, such as **GET**, **HEAD**, **DELETE**, or **OPTIONS**, often do not require one. Some requests, such as **POST** requests, transmit the data to the server in order to update it. The two headers, Content-Type and Content-Length, describe the single-resource bodies, which are made up of a single file. Multiple-resource bodies are made up of several parts, each of which contains a distinct piece of information. The HTML Forms are commonly connected with this.

Connection reachability

When we are required to establish a connection with a server with RESTful APIs for handling and managing the user information, the mobile devices must work properly with the Internet connection. The connections lost in between or before the API calls may cause several issues to your app. For this, we need to check for the Internet connection reachability as well as our server reachability. There might be cases where the Internet connection would work perfectly but the server might be down. To check the Internet and the server connection, we will write a class named Reachability, which is as follows:

```
import Foundation
import SystemConfiguration


open class Reachability {

    class func isConnectedToNetwork() -> Bool {

        var zeroAddress = sockaddr_in()
        zeroAddress.sin_len = UInt8(MemoryLayout<sockaddr_in>.size)
        zeroAddress.sin_family = sa_family_t(AF_INET)

        guard let defaultRouteReachability = withUnsafePointer(to:
&zeroAddress, {
            $0.withMemoryRebound(to: sockaddr.self, capacity: 1) {
                SCNetworkReachabilityCreateWithAddress(nil, $0)
            }
        }) else {
            return false
        }
```

```
      var flags: SCNetworkReachabilityFlags = []
      if !SCNetworkReachabilityGetFlags(defaultRouteReachability,
&flags) {
          return false
      }

      let isReachable = flags.contains(.reachable)
      let needsConnection = flags.contains(.connectionRequired)

      return (isReachable && !needsConnection)


   }
}
```

The reachability class can have a class function which will check for the connection to the Internet reach with respect to the socket flags status. Let's understand the given example in detail, as follows:

- With the use of the **SystemConfiguration** framework, we will first create a socket address which contains the IP information while connecting to the network.

- Further, **SCNetworkReachabilityCreateWithAddress** returns an object which creates a network establishment. If these operations failed to create a network reachability object, then we can return, as there is no network available.

- In some cases, we even get that object, but we need to ensure with appropriate flags whether the correct Internet connection is established or not.

- In such cases, we check on **SCNetworkReachabilityGetFlags** to get the network status flags. If we get the reachable flag as true and the connection required flag as false, then we can confirm that an Internet connection is available.

Fast and reliable network connection makes your app efficient and fast to communicate with the server. But sometimes, there is a possibility of a down server; in such cases, we must communicate to the user with a proper server down message, so that the users do not get confused when the API starts to fail. Now, we will write another class function which checks for the establishment of the connection to your API server, as follows:

```
class func isServerConnect(webSiteToPing: String?, completionHandler: @
escaping (Bool) -> Void) {

        // 1. Check the Internet Connection
        guard isConnectedToNetwork() else {
            completionHandler(false)
            return
        }

        // 2. Check the Server Connection
        var webAddress = "https://www.xyz.com" // Your Server base URL
        if let _ = webSiteToPing {
            webAddress = webSiteToPing!
        }

        guard let url = URL(string: webAddress) else {
            completionHandler(false)
            print("could not create url from: \(webAddress)")
            return
        }

        let urlRequest = URLRequest(url: url)
        let session = URLSession.shared
        let task = session.dataTask(with: urlRequest, completionHandler:
{ (data, response, error) in
            if error != nil || response == nil { .
                completionHandler(false)
            } else {
                completionHandler(true)
            }
        })

        task.resume()
    }
```

In this class function, before making a request to the server, we will first check for a successful Internet connection. Let's understand the given example in detail, as follows:

- After checking for the network connection, we can perform a check on whether the server is up or down and available for making the server-side requests.

- Further, the URL request object is passed to the **URLsession** singleton which makes a data task request. (We will discuss **URLsession** in detail in the latter part of this chapter.)

- When a data task request returns an error as nil with a properly handled response, the server connection is reachable.

Alamofire

Alamofire provides an attractive and reusable HTTP network request interface. It doesn't have its own HTTP networking implementation. Instead, it uses the Foundation framework's URL Loading System, which is provided by Apple. The **URLSession** and **URLSessionTask** subclasses are at the heart of the system. Alamofire covers these APIs, as well as many others, in a more user-friendly interface and provides a wide range of capabilities for the contemporary HTTP networking application development. It's vital to understand where many of Alamofire's basic behaviors come from; therefore, you should be familiar with the URL Loading System. The Alamofire Software Foundation has produced additional component libraries to offer extra functionality to the Alamofire ecosystem in order to keep Alamofire focused exclusively on the fundamental networking solutions. There are two such libraries, which are as follows.

- **Alamofire Image**: Image response serializers, **UIImage** and **UIImageView** extensions, custom image filters, an auto-purging in-memory cache, and a priority-based picture downloading mechanism are all included in this image library.

- **Alamofire Network Activity Indicator**: Alamofire is used to control the appearance of the network activity indicator on iOS. It has delay timers that may be configured to assist reduced flicker, and it can handle the **URLSession** instances that aren't controlled by Alamofire.

API encoding

API encoding refers to the accepted encoding format for the data in request. Encoding API allows the developers to encode and decode the strings using a wide range of character encodings. If your app supports multi language features, then you must use UTF8 encoding and decoding for proper handling of the texts in their provided languages. In general, you may use JSON encoding for APIs.

URL encoding

URL encoding is the process of converting the characters into a format that can be sent over the Internet. Only the ASCII character set may be used to send the URLs over the Internet. Because the URLs frequently contain characters that are not part of the ASCII set, they must be transformed to a valid ASCII format. Safe ASCII characters are replaced by a *percent* (%) followed by two hexadecimal numbers in the URL encoding. Spaces are not allowed in URLs.

Alamofire headers

Alamofire has its own **HTTPHeaders** type, which is a case-insensitive and order-preserving representation of the HTTP header name value pairs. The **HTTPHeader** classes encapsulate a single name value combination and give a range of static header values, as shown as follows:

```
let headers: HTTPHeaders = [
      "Authorization": "Basic VXNlcm5hbWU6UGFzc3dvcmQ=",
      "Accept": "application/json"
    ]
```

For every request, the default Alamofire session gives a default set of headers which includes accept encoding, accept language, user agent, etc.

Alamofire request

Alamofire allows you to send any Encodable type as a request parameter. These parameters are then appended to the **URLRequest**, which is subsequently transmitted across the network, using a type that follows the **ParameterEncoder** protocol. **JSONParameterEncoder** and **URLEncodedFormParameterEncoder** are two types of **parameterEncoder** that Alamofire supports. The most popular encodings used by contemporary services are covered by these kinds, as shown as follows:

```
struct Login: Encodable {
      let email: String
      let password: String
    }

    let login = Login(email: "test@test.test", password: "Password")

    AF.request("https://samplesiteurl.org/post",
            method: .post,
```

```
            parameters: login,
            encoder: JSONParameterEncoder.default
            headers: headers).response { response in
        debugPrint(response)
    }
```

In the given code, you can see the request parameters as method type, login parameters, encoder, and headers etc. All these parameters are optional and one or more of them can be removed from the request, if required.

Alamofire response handling

Regardless of the content of the answer, Alamofire considers any completed request to be successful. If the response has an unsatisfactory status code or MIME type, using **validate()** before a response handler causes an error to be produced. Also, you may manually validate, as shown as follows:

```
AF.request("https://samplesiteurl.org/get")
        .validate(statusCode: 200..<300)
        .validate(contentType: ["application/json"])
        .responseData { response in
            switch response.result {
            case .success:
                print("Validation Successful")
            case let .failure(error):
                print(error)
            }
        }
```

Alamofire image

Before the first download request is completed, the application logic may attempt to download an image multiple time. The image is frequently downloaded multiple times as a result of this. **AFImage** gracefully handles this situation by combining the duplicate downloads. **AFImage** may combine the duplicate image filters in addition to the duplicate downloads. When two image filters with the same identifier are connected to the same download, the image filter is only run once, and both the completion handlers receive the same image. For a variety of reasons, it may be essential to cancel an image download. Using the **RequestReceipt** type and the **cancelRequestForRequestReceipt** function, **AFImage** can intelligently manage the cancellation logic in the **ImageDownloader**. Each request for a download generates a **RequestReceipt**, which can be used to cancel the request later. The **UIImage** extensions, image filters, image cache, and image downloader were all created to be versatile and stand-alone while still serving as the backbone of the **UIImageView** extension. The **UIImageView** APIs are succinct, easy to use, and offer a lot of capability, thanks to the robust support of the various classes, protocols, and extensions. We can use the **UIImage** extension for the image download, as shown as follows:

```
let imageView = UIImageView(frame: frame)
let url = URL(string: "https://sampleImagesite.org/image/png")!
imageView.af.setImage(withURL: url)
```

In case you want to show a default placeholder image, you can use the image view extension, as shown as follows:

```
let pImage = UIImage(named: "placeholder.png")
imageView.af.setImage(withURL: url, placeholderImage: pImage)
```

Image downloader

We may leverage the image downloader features which are also part of **AlamofireImage** to adjust the cache capacities, download priority, request cache rules, timeout durations, and so on. The **ImageDownloader** class is in charge of downloading the images in a prioritized queue in parallel. All of the downloading and response image serializations are handled by an internal Alamofire **SessionManager** object. An **ImageDownloader**'s startup utilizes a default **URLSessionConfiguration** with the most common parameter values by default. We can set the parameters of the image downloader, as shown as follows:

```
let imageDownloader = ImageDownloader(
        configuration: ImageDownloader.defaultURLSessionConfiguration(),
        downloadPrioritization: .fifo,
        maximumActiveDownloads: 4,
        imageCache: AutoPurgingImageCache()
    )
```

After the initialization of the image downloader, the URL with the URL request needs to be set in the same object to perform the custom image downloading, as shown as follows:

```
 let downloader = ImageDownloader()
    let urlRequest = URLRequest(url: URL(string: "https://
sampleImagesite.org/image/jpeg")!)
```

```
downloader.download(urlRequest) { response in
    print(response.request)
    print(response.response)
    debugPrint(response.result)

    if case .success(let image) = response.result {
        print(image)
    }
}
```

Alamofire Network Activity Indicator

In iOS, you may control the activity indicator using the non-safe app extension APIs. This logic could not be included in the Alamofire framework in order for Alamofire to continue to be utilized in App Extensions. It will show a spinner in the status bar when an API call is there. You can just set it to enable, as shown as follows:

```
NetworkActivityIndicatorManager.shared.isEnabled = true
```

To minimize flickering, starting, and stopping the delays must be introduced to make the activity indicator experience as pleasant as possible for the user. In the shared manager, there are two such delay timers. The start delay is a time interval that specifies the minimum amount of networking activity that should take place before the activity indicator appears. The completion delay is a time interval that specifies how long no networking activity should be monitored before the activity indication is dismissed. This permits the activity indicator to remain visible while several network requests are being processed, as shown as follows:

```
NetworkActivityIndicatorManager.shared.completionDelay = 0.2
NetworkActivityIndicatorManager.shared.startDelay = 1.0
```

URLSession

The **URLSession** class and its subclasses offer an API for receiving and uploading the data to the URL-based destinations. This API may also be used by your program to execute the background downloads when it isn't operating or, in the case of iOS, when it is suspended. To handle the authentication and to receive events like redirection and task completion, use the associated **URLSessionDelegate** and **URLSessionTaskDelegate**. One or more **URLSession** instances are created by your program, each of which coordinates a collection of linked data-transfer activities. If you're making a web browser, for example, your program may establish one session for every session or window, or one for interactive usage and another for background downloads. Your program adds a series of tasks to each session, each of which represents a request for a certain URL.

Operation queue

Based on their priority and readiness, an operation queue calls its queued Operation objects. When you add an operation to a queue, it will stay in the queue until it completes its duty. You can't delete an operation from a queue once it's been added. **Key-value coding (KVC)** and **key-value observing (KVO)** are supported by the `OperationQueue` class. These attributes can be used to control the other sections of your program. The Dispatch framework is used by the operation queues to start the execution of their operations. As a result, regardless of whether the operation is synchronous or asynchronous, the queues always invoke it on a different thread. Let's create an operation queue with its configurations, as follows:

```
fileprivate var operations = [Int: DownloadOperation]()
private let queue: OperationQueue = {
        let _queue = OperationQueue()
        _queue.name = "download"
        _queue.maxConcurrentOperationCount = 1
        return _queue
    }()
```

Add operation in operation queue

At any given moment, an operation object may only be in one operation queue, and it cannot be added if it is actively executing or completed. If any of the error conditions are true for any of the operations in the **ops** parameter, this function raises an **NSInvalidArgumentException** exception. The requested operation is added to the queue and remains there until it is completed with the completed method returning true, as shown as follows:

```
func addDownload(_ url: URL) -> DownloadOperation
{
    let operation = DownloadOperation(session: session, url: url)
    operations[operation.task.taskIdentifier] = operation
    queue.addOperation(operation)
    return operation
}

func cancelAll()
```

```
{
    queue.cancelAllOperations()
}
```

Types of URL sessions

For the simple requests, **URLSession** has a singleton shared session (which does not contain a configuration object). It's not as flexible as the sessions you design, but it's the right place to start if you only have a few needs. The shared class function is used to access this session. Create a **URLSession** with one of the three settings for the different types of sessions, shown as follows:

- A default session is similar to a shared session, but it allows you to customize it. You may also delegate the default session to a delegate to get the data progressively.

- Ephemeral sessions are identical to the shared sessions except that they don't save caches, cookies, or credentials to the memory.

- While your program isn't operating, the background sessions allow you to execute the content uploads and downloads in the background.

URLSessionConfiguration

When establishing a **URLSession** object to upload and download the data, a **URLSessionConfiguration** object sets the behavior and policies to employ. When uploading or downloading the data, the initial step is always to create a configuration object. This object is used to set the timeout settings, caching rules, connection requirements, and other information that will be used with the **URLSession** object. The type of configuration used to generate a URL session has a significant impact on the behavior and capabilities of the session. The default sessions function similarly to the shared sessions (until further customized), except that they allow you to access the data progressively via a delegate. The default method on the **URLSessionConfiguration** class may be used to establish a default session setup, as shown as follows:

```
lazy var session: URLSession = {
        let config = URLSessionConfiguration.default
        return URLSession(configuration: config, delegate: self,
delegateQueue: nil)
}()
```

The Ephemeral sessions are identical to the regular sessions, except that they don't save caches, cookies, or credentials to the disc. The ephemeral method on the

URLSessionConfiguration class may be used to generate an ephemeral session configuration.

Types of URL session tasks

You may build the tasks within a session that upload the data to a server and then receive the data from the server as a file on the storage memory or one or more **NSData** objects in the memory. There are four kinds of tasks available in the **URLSession** API, which are as follows:

- **NSData** objects are used by the data activities to deliver and receive the data. The data tasks are designed for brief, interactive server queries.

- The upload tasks are similar to the data tasks, in that they deliver the data and allow for the background uploads even when the app isn't open.

- While the program isn't operating, the download tasks retrieve the data in the form of a file and allow the background downloads and uploads.

- The WebSocket tasks use the RFC 6455 defined WebSocket protocol to send and receive the messages via TCP and TLS.

URLSession delegate

A common delegate object is shared by all the tasks in a session. This delegate is used to offer and collect the information when certain events occur, such as the following:

- When the authentication fails.

- When the data arrives from the server.

- When the data becomes available for caching.

Using the methods described in **URLSessionTaskDelegate**, each task you create using the session calls back to the session's delegate. By writing a separate task-specific delegate, you may intercept these callbacks before they reach the session delegate, as shown as follows:

```
extension Download: URLSessionDownloadDelegate
{


func urlSession(_ session: URLSession, downloadTask:
URLSessionDownloadTask, didFinishDownloadingTo location: URL)
{
    operations[downloadTask.taskId]?.urlSession(session, downloadTask:
downloadTask, didFinishDownloadingTo: location)
```

```
}


func urlSession(_ session: URLSession, downloadTask:
URLSessionDownloadTask, didWriteData bytesWritten: Int64,
totalBytesWritten: Int64, totalBytesExpectedToWrite: Int64)
{
    operations[downloadTask.taskIdentifier]?.urlSession(session,
downloadTask: downloadTask, didWriteData: bytesWritten,
totalBytesWritten: totalBytesWritten, totalBytesExpectedToWrite:
totalBytesExpectedToWrite)
 }
}


// MARK: URLSessionTaskDelegate methods
extension Download: URLSessionTaskDelegate {


func urlSession(_ session: URLSession, task: URLSessionTask,
didCompleteWithError error: Error?)
{
    let key = task.taskIdentifier
            operations[key]?.urlSession(session, task: task,
didCompleteWithError: error)
            operations.removeValue(forKey: key)

}
```

When your app wants to upload large files to the server destination, there is a need for the output stream and the input stream with a buffer to upload the file's byte data with the help of the **URLSession** upload task, as shown in *figure 13.2*, as follows:

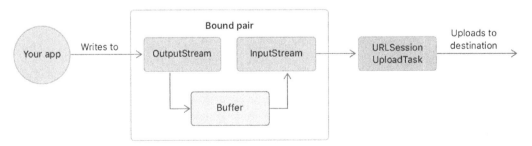

Figure 13.2: URLSession Upload Task

App transport security

App Transport Security (ATS) is a networking feature on the Apple platforms that enhances the privacy and data integrity for all the applications and app extensions. All HTTP connections established with the URL Loading System — typically using the **URLSession** class — must use HTTPS, according to ATS. It also applies additional security tests on top of the **Transport Layer Security (TLS)** protocol's default server trust evaluation. The connections that do not satisfy the minimum-security requirements are blocked by ATS.

Conclusion

The communication of the app clients from the server with the help of REST APIs gives enhanced capabilities to the app developers to sync with the other client's data, and stream the data from the devices to the server backend. Sometimes, you may need to implement a third-party library and its data to showcase on your app after the authentication, would also require similar capabilities which we discussed in this chapter in detail. Alamofire is an advanced level library that hides all the difficult steps for you and gives advanced performance with cache handling, proper data handling, image downloading, error handling, file data management, etc.

Although Alamofire takes care of the no Internet and server not responding issue, it's good to handle it separately, as we discussed initially in this chapter. In case you want more configuration and deep level integration for making the REST API requests, you may use **URLSession** provided by Apple in its Network framework.

In the next chapter, we will discuss in detail the best App Architecture practices and design patterns to enhance your coding level and make scalable mobile apps.

Multiple choice questions

1. **Which of the following is NOT the request method type in HTTP?**
    a. GET
    b. POST
    c. DELETE
    d. IDENTITY

2. **Reachability is used for _____.**
    a. Internet Connectivity
    b. Making Request
    c. Downloading Image
    d. Calling API

3. **AlamofireImage used for** _____.
   a. Making API Request
   b. Image Downloading
   c. Canceling Request
   d. Cache Handling

4. **URL Encoding is required to** _____.
   a. Remove unsupported characters
   b. Apply API encoding
   c. Apply Cache
   d. Handle File download

5. **Operation Queue is used for** _____.
   a. Adding task/operations in a queue
   b. Downloading Images
   c. Cache Handling
   d. None of the Above

6. **Image Downloader is part of** _____.
   a. Alamofire
   b. AlamofireImage
   c. AlamofireActivityIndicator
   d. None of the Above

Answers

1. d
2. a
3. b
4. a
5. a
6. b

CHAPTER 14

Mobile App Patterns and Architectures

Introduction

When an application scales up in size and features, there might be architectural design issues or loopholes. This needs to be addressed carefully with respect to code reusability, clean code, and correct use of the object-oriented programming and the protocol-oriented programming. Many of the Cocoa environment's structures and processes make good use of the design patterns, such as abstract designs that tackle recurrent issues in a specific context. This chapter covers the key design patterns implemented in Cocoa, with an emphasis on Model View Controller and MVVM. The major goal of this chapter is to raise your knowledge of Cocoa and the mobile application design patterns that may be utilized in the iOS application development and to urge you to apply these patterns in your own iOS applications. Further, we will discuss the redux architecture in iOS which gained popularity after the React native app development was introduced as well as the three main core architectures with the mobile app development perspective.

Structure

In this chapter, we will cover the following topics:

- Design patterns in iOS

- Architecture case studies
- Mobile app architectures
- Redux architecture in iOS

Objective

After studying this chapter, you will be able to develop a complete commercial iOS application with clean, reusable, structured architecture designs, such that if that application scales to a large size, it should not impact the overall quality of the application.

Design patterns in iOS

Design patterns have always aided in the development of the software that is controllable, tested, reusable, and optimized. It aids in the modularization of the apps, ensuring that each component is distinct and responsible for a particular task. They significantly enhance the readability of the code, which is critical for conveying the software code. Furthermore, using well-proven design principles, the software development process is dramatically accelerated. The mobile apps are becoming larger and virtually identical in terms of functionality to their desktop and web counterparts, necessitating the consideration of the design patterns prior to going into the development mode. There are three types of Design Patterns category which consists of many popular design patterns used in Swift iOS, as follows:

- Creational patterns
- Structural patterns
- Behavioral patterns

Let's discuss these patterns in detail for the understanding of better code reusability and architecture.

Creational patterns

The object generation processes are addressed in the design patterns, with the goal of creating things that are appropriate for the context. The most basic type of object generation may cause the design issues or contribute to the design's complexity. This challenge is solved by creational design patterns, which regulate the creation of objects in some way. There are mainly five design patterns that come in the Creational patterns, which are as follows:

- Prototype pattern

- Factory pattern
- Abstract Factory Pattern
- Builder pattern
- Singleton Design pattern

Prototype pattern

This design pattern is used to create a new item by cloning an existing object known as a prototype. When you clone an item, all of its attributes are transferred to another object. This design pattern should be utilized when you need to construct an object but don't know the class hierarchy, shown as follows:

```
protocol Fruit {
    func set(price: String?)
    func clone() -> Fruit
}


class Orange: Fruit {
    var count: Int
    var price: String?

    init(count: Int) {
        self.count = count
    }

    func set(price: String?) {
        self.price = price
    }

    // function definition for cloning the object
    func clone() -> Fruit {
        return Orange(count: self.count)
    }
}


let prototype = Orange(count: 6)
let redOrange: Orange = prototype.clone() as! Orange
```

```
print(redOrange.count) // 6
redOrange.set(price: "$4")
print(redOrange.price!) // $4
```

Factory pattern

It is the most popular design pattern. It essentially abstracts the construction of an item. Any instance returned by the factory would be of the type **Interface** (in Swift protocol), which every factory candidate class must implement. At runtime, the type of object created is determined. This design approach makes it easier to add or delete new kinds from the codebase, shown as follows:

```
protocol Fruit {
    func getPrice() -> String
    func getCount() -> Int
}


class Orange: Fruit {
    func getPrice() -> String {return "$5"}
    func getCount() -> Int {return 2}
}


class Banana: Fruit {
    func getPrice() -> String {return "$2"}
    func getCount() -> Int {return 5}
}


class Grapes: Fruit {
    func getPrice() -> String {return "$3.5"}
    func getCount() -> Int {return 1}
}
```

Here, we made three different types of fruit classes which are actually of class **Fruit**. In this case, the superclass methods are overridden in the other **fruit** child classes that can be differentiated via a simple **enum**, as shown in the following code:

```
// Enum of Fruit Type
enum FruitType {
    case orange, banana, grapes
}
```

```
// A factory class with static method
class FruitFactory {
    // Return object of class that implements Fruit protocol
    static func getFruit(forType type: FruitType) -> Fruit? {
        switch type {
        case .orange:
            return Orange()
        case .banana:
            return Banana()
        case .grapes:
            return Grapes()
        }
    }
}

let orange = FruitFactory.getFruit(forType: .orange)
orange?.getPrice() // "$5
orange?.getCount() // 2
```

Abstract Factory pattern

This design pattern provides an interface for building the families of related items without naming their concrete classes. They are frequently built using the Factory Method pattern. It shows the interface rather than the implementation. Abstract Factory is similar to a procedure that we will use to build the objects on a concrete class. Refer to the following code example:

```
protocol ApplianceFactory {
    static func createTable() -> Table
    static func createChair() -> Chair
}
protocol Table {
    func count() -> Int
}

protocol Chair {
    func count() -> Int
```

```
}
class Factory: ApplianceFactory {
    static func createChair() -> Chair {return MyChair()}
    static func createTable() -> Table {return MyTable()}
}
private class MyChair: Chair {
    func count() -> Int {return 4}
}
private class MyTable: Table {
    func count() -> Int {return 1}
}
let chair = Factory.createChair()
chair.count() // 4
```

Builder pattern

This design pattern separates the process of creating the items from the actual use of the products. Because it does not expose the implementation details, you may use the Builder approach for creating the public APIs. It has the ability to conceal complexity. It hides a complicated operation behind a simple API. Refer to the following code example:

```
protocol ShoeShop {
    func produceShoe()
}
// class that conforms to Shoe Shop protocol
class Nike: ShoeShop {
    func produceShoe() {
        print("Shoe Produce")
    }
}
class Director {
    let shoeShop: ShoeShop

    init(shoeShop: ShoeShop) {
        self.shoeShop = shoeShop
    }
    func produce() {
```

```
        shoeShop.produceShoe()
    }
}
let nike = Nike()
let director = Director(shoeShop: nike)
print(director.produce())
```

Singleton Design pattern

The static keyword is used in Swift to define the Singleton classes. It implies that the object will only be instantiated once. The static properties are lazily initialized, which means, they will not be created until they are invoked. This object has a single copy and is shared by all the other objects. Singletons assure that there is only one object of its kind and offers a single point of access to it for any other code. Singletons have nearly the same advantages and disadvantages as the global variables. They're useful, yet they destroy the modularity of your code. Refer to the following code example:

```
class Automobile {
    static let sharedInstance = Automobile()
    // private initialization
    private init() {}

    func getName() -> String {
        return "Car"
    }
    func getModel() -> String {
        return "Honda Amaze"
    }
}
```

Each time when we want to access the class **Automobile**, we will not create any factory object of this class; rather, we will access via a static initialization shared instance that will restrict the developers to use multiple instances of the class. Refer to the following example:

```
print(Automobile.sharedInstance.getName()) // Car
print(Automobile.sharedInstance.getModel()) // Honda Amaze
```

Structural patterns

The goal of streamlining the app design process while identifying the simplest technique for linking the objects and classes is known as structural. By identifying the linkages, the structural design patterns simplify the structure. These patterns are concerned with how the classes inherit from one another and how they are made up of the other classes. There are mainly four design patterns that come in the structural patterns, which are as follows:

- Facade Design

- Adapter

- Bridge

- Decorator

Facade Design

When working with a large number of classes, especially those that are difficult to use or comprehend, this approach is perfect. Facade Designs gives complicated systems a single interface. You just offer one basic unified API to the user, rather than a variety of classes and their APIs. If the classes beneath the facade are expected to change, this is also beneficial since the facade class may keep the same API while the things change behind the scenes. Refer to the following code example:

```
import XCTest
class Facade {

    private var subsystem1: Subsystem1
    private var subsystem2: Subsystem2

    init(subsystem1: Subsystem1 = Subsystem1(),
         subsystem2: Subsystem2 = Subsystem2()) {
        self.subsystem1 = subsystem1
        self.subsystem2 = subsystem2
    }

    func operation() -> String {

        var result = "Facade - Sub Systems:"
        result += " " + subsystem1.operation1()
        result += " " + subsystem2.operation1()
```

```
        result += "\n" + "Facade orders Sub Systems to perform the
Action:\n"
        result += " " + subsystem1.operationN()
        result += " " + subsystem2.operationZ()
        return result
    }
}
class Subsystem1 {
    func operation1() -> String {
        return "Subsystem ONE: Ready!\n"
    }
    func operationN() -> String {
        return "Subsystem ONE: Go!\n"
    }
}
class Subsystem2 {
    func operation1() -> String {
        return "Subsystem TWO: Get ready!\n"
    }
    func operationZ() -> String {
        return "Subsystem TWO: Fire!\n"
    }
}


class Client {
    static func clientCode(facade: Facade) {
        print(facade.operation())
    }
}
```

Here, the **Facade** class uses the other subsystem classes in it, and when we want to use its internal operations, we can just pass the facade instance to the **Client** class, so that it will never know what happens in the complexity of the facade operations. Refer to the following code example:

```
// Let's see how it all works together -
class FacadeConceptual: XCTestCase {
    func testFacadeConceptual() {
```

```
        let subsystem1 = Subsystem1()
        let subsystem2 = Subsystem2()
        let facade = Facade(subsystem1: subsystem1, subsystem2:
subsystem2)
        Client.clientCode(facade: facade)
    }
}


let concept = FacadeConceptual()
concept.testFacadeConceptual()
```

Adapter

The Adapter design pattern transforms a class's interface into a client-facing interface. The adapter allows the classes that would not otherwise be able to operate together due to the conflicting interfaces. It separates the client from the targeted object's class. You'll need to incorporate the **EventKit** framework and change the **Event** model from the model framework in your iOS app if you want to include a calendar and event management feature. An adapter wraps the framework and makes it compatible with the model of your project. Refer to the following code example:

```
import Foundation
import EventKit


// Event protocol
protocol Event {
    var title: String { get }
    var startDate: String { get }
    var endDate: String { get }
}


// Adapter Wrapper Class
class EventAdapter {
    private lazy var dateFormatter: DateFormatter = {
        let dateFormatter = DateFormatter()
        dateFormatter.dateFormat = "yyyy. MM. dd. HH:mm"
        return dateFormatter
```

```
    }()
    private var event: EKEvent

    init(event: EKEvent) {
        self.event = event
    }
}


// Adapter Implementation
extension EventAdapter: Event {
    var title: String {
        return self.event.title
    }
    var startDate: String {
        return self.dateFormatter.string(from: event.startDate)
    }
    var endDate: String {
        return self.dateFormatter.string(from: event.endDate)
    }
}
```

An event protocol is implemented in the event adapter class such that, if required, the other fields and values can be adapted by the class at a later point in time. We can set those parameters while implementing and testing that adapter, as shown in the following code:

```
// Test Adapter Implementation
let dateFormatter = DateFormatter()
dateFormatter.dateFormat = "MM/dd/yyyy HH:mm"

let calendarEvent = EKEvent(eventStore: EKEventStore())
calendarEvent.title = "iOS Class Deadline"
calendarEvent.startDate = dateFormatter.date(from: "09/30/2021 10:00")
calendarEvent.endDate = dateFormatter.date(from: "09/30/2021 11:00")

// Use Adapter class as an Event protocol
let adapter = EventAdapter(event: calendarEvent)
adapter.title
```

```
adapter.startDate
adapter.endDate
```

Bridge

The Bridge Pattern separates an abstraction from its implementation, allowing the two to change independently. It is quite useful when you don't know the specific business logic to implement but need to develop your abstraction due to a project deadline. When the business logic is derived from a client's request, only the business logic must be coded. Refer to the following code example:

```swift
protocol Switch {
    var appliance: Appliance { get set }
    func turnOn()
}


protocol Appliance {
    func run()
}


final class RemoteControl: Switch {
    var appliance: Appliance

    func turnOn() {
        self.appliance.run()
    }

    init(appliance: Appliance) {
        self.appliance = appliance
    }
}


final class TV: Appliance {
    func run() {
        print("Television Turned ON");
    }
}
```

```
final class VacuumCleaner: Appliance {
    func run() {
        print("Vacuum Cleaner Turned ON")
    }
}


let tvRemoteControl = RemoteControl(appliance: TV())
tvRemoteControl.turnOn()

let remoteControlVC = RemoteControl(appliance: VacuumCleaner())
remoteControlVC.turnOn()
```

Decorator

A decorator is a structural design pattern that enables you to wrap new functions in the helpful wrappers to dynamically fix them to an object. The Decorator design pattern is also known as the Wrapper design pattern. The basic concept behind this pattern is that you may nest a target object within a wrapper object, which then activates the target item's behavior and adds it to the result. You may mix the behavior of several wrappers by using them all at the same time. It's an alternative to subclassing, in which you change the functionality of a class by wrapping it in another object. In Objective C, we can achieve this pattern by Category implementation, and in Swift, we can make Extensions to the class to achieve this pattern. Refer to the following code example:

```
protocol Transporting {
    func getSpeed() -> Double
    func getTraction() -> Double
}

final class RaceCar: Transporting {
    private let speed = 10.0
    private let traction = 10.0

    func getSpeed() -> Double {return speed}
    func getTraction() -> Double {return traction}
}

let raceCar = RaceCar()
let defaultSpeed = raceCar.getSpeed()
```

```
let defaultTraction = raceCar.getTraction()

class TireDecorator: Transporting {
    private let transportable: Transporting
    init(transportable: Transporting) {
        self.transportable = transportable
    }
    func getSpeed() -> Double {
        return transportable.getSpeed()
    }


    func getTraction() -> Double {
        return transportable.getTraction()
    }
}

class OffRoadTireDecorator: Transporting {
    private let transportable: Transporting

    init(transportable: Transporting) {
        self.transportable = transportable
    }

    func getSpeed() -> Double {
        return transportable.getSpeed() - 3.0
    }

    func getTraction() -> Double {
        return transportable.getTraction() + 3.0
    }
}

class ChainedTireDecorator: Transporting {
    private let transportable: Transporting

    init(transportable: Transporting) {
        self.transportable = transportable
    }

    func getSpeed() -> Double {
```

```
        return transportable.getSpeed() - 1.0
    }


    func getTraction() -> Double {
        return transportable.getTraction() * 1.1
    }
}

// Create Race Car
let defaultRaceCar = RaceCar()
defaultRaceCar.getSpeed() // 10
defaultRaceCar.getTraction() // 10

// Modify Race Car
let offRoadRaceCar = OffRoadTireDecorator(transportable: defaultRaceCar)
offRoadRaceCar.getSpeed() // 7
offRoadRaceCar.getTraction() // 13
```

Behavioral patterns

The behavioral design pattern is involved with how the items interact with one another. It defines how the objects communicate with one another and how the phases of a task are split up across multiple objects to increase flexibility and testability. There are many design patterns that come in the behavioral patterns, but due to the limitation of this book, we will discuss only the important patterns which are used most of the time in the best architecture, which are listed as follows:

- Template pattern
- State pattern
- Observer pattern
- Mediator pattern
- Iterator pattern

Template pattern

The purpose of this Swift design pattern for the iOS apps is to keep the implementation-specific behavior out of the generic class. Only the base classes that implement the algorithm steps are used to communicate across the classes. We will utilize the interface delegation in Swift to do this. The base class defines the template of an algorithm and lets the subclass implement these abstract methods in the same way they are defined in the base class without changing the overall structure. Refer to the following code example:

```
protocol Office {
    func officeSchedule()
}
protocol Employee {
    func work()
    func getPaid()
}
class MyOffice: Office {
    var delegate: Employee

    init(employee: Employee) {
        self.delegate = employee
    }
    func officeSchedule() {
        delegate.work()
        delegate.getPaid()
    }
}
class Developer: Employee {

    func work() {
        print("Developer has worked 60 hours per week this month")
    }
    func getPaid() {
        print("Developer has earned Rs 80,000 this month")
    }
}

class ProjectManager: Employee {
    func work() {
        print("Project Manager has worked 55 hours per week this month")
    }
    func getPaid(){
        print("Project Manager has earned Rs 100,000 this month")
    }
```

```
}

let xyzOfficeDev = MyOffice(employee: Developer())
let xyzOfficeManager = MyOffice(employee: ProjectManager())
xyzOfficeDev.officeSchedule()
xyzOfficeManager.officeSchedule()
```

State pattern

Each application state passes through a funnel defined by ReSwift until one reducer responds to it and executes the desired behavior. The user interface would then reflect each new state. Refer to the following code example:

```
protocol Human {
    func getState() -> ManState
    func set(state: ManState)
}

protocol ManState {
    func stand()
    func walk()
    func toString() -> String
}

extension ManState {
    func stand() {}
    func walk() {}
}

class Man: Human {
    var state: ManState?
    init() {state = nil}
    func set(state: ManState) {
        self.state = state
    }
    func getState() -> ManState {
        return state!
    }
}
```

```swift
class StandingState: ManState {
    var human: Human
    init(_ human: Human) {
        self.human = human
    }
    func stand() {
        print("The Man State is - Standing Position")
        human.set(state: self)
    }

    func toString() -> String {
        return "Standing State"
    }
}

class WalkingState: ManState {

    var human: Human
    init(_ human: Human) {
        self.human = human
    }
    func walk() {
        print("The Man State is - Walking Position")
        human.set(state: self)
    }
    func toString() -> String {
        return "Walking State"
    }
}

let man = Man()
let standingState = StandingState(man)
standingState.stand()
print(man.getState().toString())

let walkingState = WalkingState(man)
walkingState.walk()
print(man.getState().toString())
```

Observer pattern

In this design, one object notifies the other objects when its state changes, that is, when one object's state changes, the other objects that are subscribed to it are alerted. As a result, the connection is one-to-many. The observable or subject is the entity whose state changes, and the observers are the objects that subscribe to the changes in the observable. Refer to the following code example:

```swift
protocol Observable {
    func add(customer: Observer)
    func remove(customer : Observer)
    func notify()
}

protocol Observer {
    var id: Int { get set }
    func update()
}

class  OrangeSeller: Observable {
    private var observers: [Observer] = []
    private var count: Int = 0
    var fruitCount: Int {
        set {
            count = newValue
            notify()
        }
        get {return count}
    }
    func add(customer: Observer) {
        observers.append(customer)
    }
    func remove(customer : Observer) {
        observers = observers.filter{ $0.id != customer.id }
    }
    func notify() {
        for observer in observers {
            observer.update()
        }
```

```
    }
}

class Customer: Observer {
    var id: Int
    var observable:  OrangeSeller
    var name: String
    init(name: String, observable:  OrangeSeller, customerId: Int) {
        self.name = name
        self.observable = observable
        self.id = customerId
        self.observable.add(customer: self)
    }
    func update() {
        print("Wait, \(name)! \(observable.fruitCount) Oranges arrived
at shop.")
    }
}

let seller = OrangeSeller()
let james = Customer(name: "James", observable: seller, customerId: 101)
let david = Customer(name: "David", observable: seller, customerId: 102)
seller.fruitCount = 10
seller.remove(customer: james)
seller.fruitCount = 20
```

Mediator pattern

Consider a situation in which two or more classes must interact with one another. Instead of interacting directly with one another and learning about their implementation, they can communicate through a **Mediator**. In this case, two teams are competing against one another for a spot in the game's finals. The Avatar is on **TeamA**, and the Bengaluru Techriders are on **TeamB**. Instead of conversing directly with one another, they register with the mediator object and then use the **Mediator** to deliver the messages to one another, shown as follows:

```
protocol Receiver {
    var name: String { get }
    func receive(message: String)
}
```

```swift
protocol Sender {
    var teams: [Receiver] { get set }
    func send(message: String, sender: Receiver)
}

class Mediator: Sender {
    var teams: [Receiver] = []

    func register(candidate: Receiver) {
        teams.append(candidate)
    }

    func send(message: String, sender: Receiver) {
        for team in teams {
            if team.name != sender.name {
                team.receive(message: message)
            }
        }
    }
}
struct TeamA: Receiver {
    var name: String
    init(name: String) {
        self.name = name
    }
    func receive(message: String) {
        print("\(name) Received: \(message)")
    }
}

struct TeamB: Receiver {
    var name: String
    init(name: String) {
        self.name = name
    }
    func receive(message: String) {
        print("\(name) Received: \(message)")
```

```
        }
    }

    let mediator = Mediator()
    let teamA = TeamA(name: "The Roadies")
    let teamB = TeamB(name: "The League of Extraordinary Gentlemen")
    mediator.register(candidate: teamA)
    mediator.register(candidate: teamB)
    mediator.send(message: "Selected for final! from \(teamA.name)", sender:
    teamA)
    mediator.send(message: "Not selected for final! from \(teamB.name)",
    sender: teamB)
```

Iterator pattern

This pattern is used to repeatedly iterate over a set of items. It provides an interface that iterates through the collection of components without disclosing the underlying representation, rather than exposing the data structure used to implement it. Have you ever wondered how Swift's for-in loop works? Swift has a **Sequence** protocol that aids in the creation of iterators. By constructing an iterator, the **Sequence** protocol provides the sequential access to its items, as follows:

```
struct GreatFilms: Sequence {
    let films: [String]

    func makeIterator() -> GreatFilmsIterator {
        return GreatFilmsIterator(films)
    }
}

struct GreatFilmsIterator: IteratorProtocol {

    var films: [String]
    var cursor: Int = 0

    init(_ films: [String]) {
        self.films = films
    }

    mutating func next() -> String? {
        defer { cursor += 1 }
```

```
        return films.count > cursor ? films[cursor] : nil
    }
}

let myFilms = GreatFilms(films: ["3 Idiots", "The Great Gatsby",
"Godfather Trilogy"])
for film in myFilms {
    print(film)
}
```

Here, with the help of the iterator protocol, you can iterate on the list of text, name, or any kind of serial data which can help you present the data in a better format in a structured way.

Mobile app architecture case studies

The App architecture case studies are real time architectural issues that you may come across while designing and implementing a consumer end product. Although there is no limit to discussing such cases, we will take two problems that can be resolved with the correct architectural decision making.

CASE - 1

There are requirements of the iOS Project, where every text of the label, content color, font name, and label size should be configurable from the Server side at any point in time, even after the app is uploaded to the Apple Store. Some features of this app could be offline too, and the others are heavily dependent upon the server API data. What architectural approach will you take to fulfil these criteria?

Case 1: Solution discussion

In the given requirements, we have a specific problem, which is that every design text label configuration should be dynamically changed from the server side. From the start of the native app development, this was a really challenging task, because once we upload an app on the app store, all the design interfaces kept inside that package can be changed once we upload a new version of the app with those changes, due to this nature of the native design developers that prefers the cross-platform hybrid development with HTML CSS. But this problem can be easily maintained by the native elements too. We have to develop a framework that takes every design component from a specific file. Let's consider a **plist** file (this could be an XML or JSON too). We have to keep this file in the document directory initially which will be bundled in the app package, and when the first-time code gets initialized, we can put those files into the document directory. Now, whenever a page design will load, it will refer to those files for size, color, and default text of the labels.

The framework of the design labels should be configured in such a way that we can keep those files on the backend side and keep track of the changes. When a regular API notifies that those files have some change, only those changes can be sent to the client app via the API request in XML or JSON and the app will update those files and the app designs will continue as usual, following the flow.

CASE - 2

There is an ecommerce iOS Application, where the users can browse the app even without the login. Requirements contain – category, subcategory, and featured items, and every subcategory should be configured from the server and dynamic (does not change frequently but may change in 15 days). There should be some featured items in each category/subcategory which should show as fast as possible; even in a low network, there should be no delay due to any circumstances. The server team comes up with 14 API to call for all such data (category, subcategory, and featured items with images), and the data could be changed in the future. During testing, the Product Owner of the app observed that after the App Download, sometimes the server fails, and no data (category, subcategory, and featured items) is there, only blank screens. The Product Owner thinks it would give a very bad impression if after downloading, there are blank screens even if it is due to a reason such as no Internet or server failure. So, the users should be able to see at least the category, subcategory, and featured items with the images in any condition.

Case 2: Solution discussion

In the given case, there might be multiple solutions that can be implemented as per the development cost and time. If you have less time, then you can simply put all the 14 APIs JSON responses in the files, and further, you can put those files in the app bundle; and when an app is installed for the first time, all the file responses can be provided to those development modules that expected the response from the server, which due to either no Internet and low Internet, failed to receive that data. In the long-term solution, a local database can be maintained which will already keep some data that will be initially shown irrespective of the Internet or no Internet. Later, that database can be synced to the server-side data, if required.

Mobile app architectures

The mobile app architecture refers to a collection of structural components and their interfaces that make up the system, as well as their behavior within the context of all the structural elements. This may be considered the skeleton of a program, and its quality determines the entire work of the mobile application. You risk the success of your project by overlooking a crucial component when designing a mobile app architecture. The difficulty of creating high-quality architecture is proportional to the application's size. In the future, appropriate architecture will allow for a significant time, energy, and cost savings. In the mobile client applications, whenever the user interacts with the app, the first presentation layer comes across which have the UI components. The presentation layer further interacts with the business layer which has the actual logic of the tasks and processes that uses the data models which might be interacting with the local database in some cases, as shown in *figure 14.1* as follows:

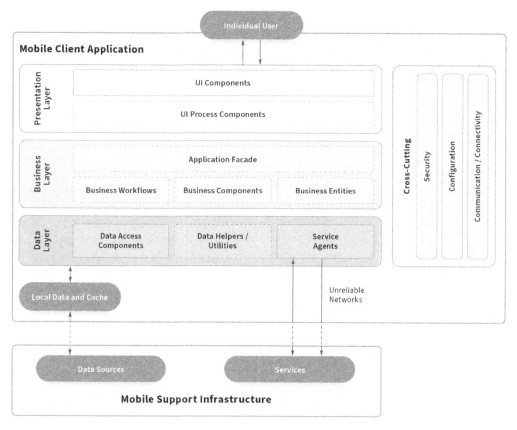

Figure 14.1: *Mobile Client Application Layer Architecture*

All the successful projects with the best architecture approaches that are now operating on iOS were built entirely by hand, without the assistance of frameworks or other comparable tools. The existence of any library should not be relied upon the architecture. As a result, you may utilize the frameworks as tools rather than trying to force your system to conform to their constraints. A good architecture is, first and foremost, a lucrative design that simplifies and streamlines the process of building and maintaining a program. A well-architected software is easier to grow and alter, as well as to test, debug, and comprehend. The basic building blocks of architecture start with the fundamental layers, which are as follows:

- Data layer

- Business layer

- Presentation layer

Data layer

All the data utilities, service agents, and data access components are part of the data layer. This layer is dedicated to the data maintenance security, which includes access, utilities, and service tools. It's the foundation on which you may build your business logic and presentation features. Your app's behavior is determined by the patterns you pick for the main functions.

Business layer

All the different processes and business entities, as well as the business components themselves, are included in the business layer. This platform hides all the management efforts involved in developing the app, such as logging, caching, verifying, and other technological activities, that will be divided into distinct tasks. This is also where you'll find the complicated company procedures and corporate policies. To put it in another way, you have an application facade with processes, components, and entities behind.

Presentation layer

The most essential step here is to create the customer profile, so that your users are satisfied with the visuals on the screen and the layout of the items. Now, your consumer is always right – even when it comes to the data format decisions. This layer isn't about picking the perfect data; it's about creating a format that prohibits the incorrect data from being entered.

Types of mobile app architectures

The evaluation of architecture can be done on multiple parameters such as distribution, testability, and ease of use, where the ease of use is given less priority in large scalable projects. A defined and structured architecture is required for a balanced distribution of responsibilities among every entity of a project. While we strive to figure out how things operate, the distribution puts a considerable amount of strain on our brains. You are correct if you believe that the more you develop, the better your brain will adapt to grasping the complexity. However, this talent does not scale linearly and rapidly approaches its limit. Further, testability comes even with the first feature which is not an issue for those who are writing the unit test cases while developing the new features.

Writing a test unit can save time for those developers who might take weeks to fix the bugs to deliver at the user end. However, it is worth mentioning that the finest code is that which has never been written. As a result, the less code you have, the fewer problems you will encounter. This implies that a developer's desire to write less code should never be attributed entirely to laziness, and you should never choose a better solution without considering its maintenance costs. Writing a lesser code architecture gives ease of use with good maintenance of the overall code. When it comes to the architecture design patterns, we can divide this into the following four categories:

- Model View Controller (MVC)

- Model View Presenter (MVP)

- Model View View-Model (MVVM)

- Clean Architecture (VIPER)

Model View Controller

The Controller in Apple's MVC architecture acts as a mediator between the View and the Model, ensuring that they are unaware of one another. Cocoa MVC is so closely involved in the life cycle of the views that it is difficult to say that they are independent. Although you can still offload some of the business logic and data processing to the Model and you don't have much option when it comes to offloading the work to the View, the View's primary duty is to transmit the actions to the Controller in most cases. Apple MVC performs the view and controller related task in one module, which we called ViewController, and which can handle the view as well as the other task handling and processing which further updates the data models whenever required, as shown in *figure 14.2* as follows:

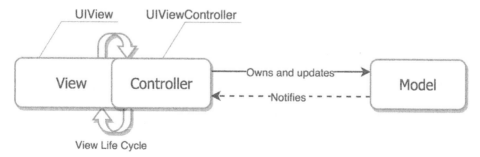

Figure 14.2: Model View Controller

Model View Presenter

The UIViewController subclasses are the Views, not the Presenters, according to the MVP. This difference provides excellent testability at the cost of the development speed, since the manual data and event binding is required. The View's UI business logic is defined in the Presenter. The Presenter is the recipient of all the invocations from the View. The Presenter is also separated from the View and communicates with it via an interface. This is because the View may be mocked in a unit test. In MVP, the presenter plays a major role which communicates to the model, as shown in *figure 14.3* as follows:

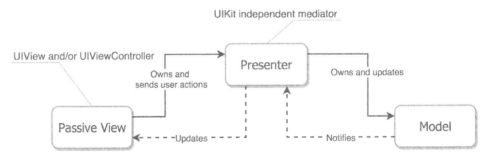

Figure 14.3: Model View Presenter

Model View View-Model

In MVVM, the view controller is treated as the View, and the View and the Model are not tightly coupled. It binds in the same way as the Supervising version of the MVP does, except, this time between the View and the View Model, rather than the View and the Model. The View in MVVM has additional responsibilities than the View in MVP, as the first one sets up bindings to update its state from the View Model, whilst the second one just sends all the events to the Presenter and does not update itself. When a user interacts with the UI components, the architecture flow starts from the View which further calls the View model for processing and task handling, while doing this, if there is any need to update the model then we can further call associated models, as shown *figure 14.4* as follows:

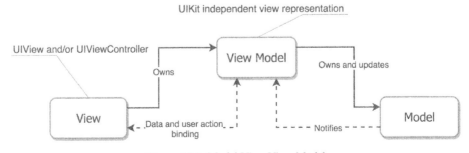

Figure 14.4: Model View View-Model

VIPER Clean architecture

VIPER iterates on the concept of dividing the responsibilities yet again, this time with five levels. For clarity and testability, the Clean Swift design pattern separates the responsibilities of distinct entities. These elements come together to make the settings. Each scene may run on its own, utilizing only the components included in that scene. All the five components play their responsibility and communicate with each other, as shown in *figure 14.5* as follows:

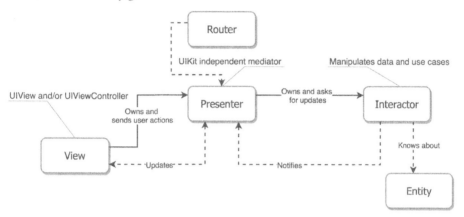

Figure 14.5: *VIPER Clean Architecture*

The VIPER architecture can be formed with five distinct responsible components, which are discussed in detail as follows:

- **View Controller**: XCode interface or XIB controlled by the view controller.

- **Interactor**: It includes the data entity or networking business logic, such as generating new instances of entities or retrieving them from the server. You'll need some Services and Managers for those reasons, which aren't considered a part of the VIPER module but rather of the external dependencies.

- **Presenter:** The Presenter is the class that is in charge of displaying the object that the Interactor generates. The Presenter will convert the data object into a ViewModel object and return it to the ViewController to be displayed.

- **Model or Entities**: When requesting an action from the other classes in the VIPER cycle, each class will contribute a data object. When the ViewController instructs the Interactor to perform an action, the ViewController creates a 'Request' object. This object includes all the information required by the interactor to complete the business logic.

- **Router**: A Router is used to navigate between the ViewControllers in Clean Swift. A Router class is added to the ViewController, if the navigation options are provided for the ViewController. The Router class includes all the navigation options available to that particular ViewController.

Redux architecture in iOS

Redux has a particular location for the state (the store) and where the state is updated (the reducers). The flow of the data is unidirectional. This implies that your data is only handled in one direction. The idea is that your subscribers (for example, ViewController) just listen for the updates and do not alter the data they get. Your app's current state is represented by the state. The substates in the states can include the navigation state and one for each view of your app. The store keeps track of the full App State, and when a request to alter it comes in, it calls the reducer to make the change. It alerts the subscriber connected with the state with the new data when a change occurs.

The state changes are triggered by actions, when a user begins a timer, for example. The store, where the state resides, will dispatch actions. When the store receives an action, it will notify the Reducer. The reducers are in charge of carrying out the action and changing the state. The subscribers choose a certain state for which they will get the notifications later. My timer-view, for example, will only subscribe to the timer state. The subscriber will not be notified if a state change happens that does not affect the timer-state.

ReSwift in iOS

Swift's ReSwift is a small redux-like implementation. It includes a store and procedures to help you get started with redux quickly. You may use your preferred package management to integrate it into your projects. Each application state passes through a funnel defined by ReSwift until one reducer responds to it and executes the desired behavior. The user interface would then reflect each new state. In Redux Architecture, when a user initiates the interaction, the flow of the process starts from the View which triggers the actions and the actions might change the state of the variables, which is managed by the Store globally in the whole project, as shown in *figure 14.6* as follows:

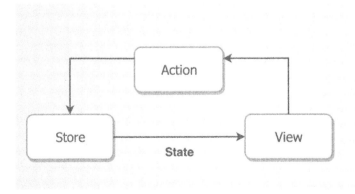

Figure 14.6: *Redux like Architecture in iOS*

Now, we will understand the concept of redux with a simple implementation of the counter features. Store implementation must be kept in AppDelegate, so that it can be started with the app start if it is not there. The Reducer functionality could be triggered from the view controller which will change the app state in real time, shown as follows:

```
import ReSwift

let mainStore = Store<AppState>(
    reducer: counterReducer,
    state: nil
)

func counterReducer(action: Action, state: AppState?) -> AppState {
    var state = state ?? AppState()

    switch action {
    case _ as CounterActionIncrease:
        state.counter += 1
    case _ as CounterActionDecrease:
        state.counter -= 1
    default:
        break
    }

    return state
}

struct AppState: StateType {
    var counter: Int = 0
}
```

The counter reducer method is designed to take the actions that have the instance of the app state and make the decision on the basis of the action type. Further, the view controllers subscribed to the main store updates it on each state change, shown as follows:

```
struct CounterActionIncrease: Action {}
struct CounterActionDecrease: Action {}

class ViewController: UIViewController, StoreSubscriber {
```

```
    typealias StoreSubscriberStateType = AppState


    @IBOutlet weak var counterLabel: UILabel!


    Override func viewDidLoad() {
        super.viewDidLoad()
        mainStore.subscribe(self)
    }


    func newState(state: AppState) {
        counterLabel.text = "\(mainStore.state.counter)"
    }


    @IBAction func downTouch(_ sender: AnyObject) {
        mainStore.dispatch(CounterActionDecrease());
    }
    @IBAction func upTouch(_ sender: AnyObject) {
        mainStore.dispatch(CounterActionIncrease());
    }
}
```

Whenever the user increases or decreases the counter, it dispatches the action to the main store, and when it actually changes the counter value in the app state which reflects via the new state function, you can use this function to the view controller UI component updates.

Conclusion

Clean Architecture, MVVM, and Redux are the most popular architectures in mobile programming. MVVM and Clean Architecture may both be used independently; however, MVVM only offers the separation of concerns inside the Presentation Layer, whereas Clean Architecture divides your code into the modular levels that are easy to test, reuse, and understand. Clean architecture pairs well with Test Driven Development because it makes the project testable and allows for an easy layer replacement. It's critical not to omit creating a Use Case, even if the Use Case only calls Repository. When a fresh developer looks at your use cases, your architecture will be self-explanatory. Creational and Structural app patterns help the developers design and make better reusable code modules. In this chapter, we also studied two problem cases which gave you an idea about what type of problems can come at your end that can be solved with the use of either the patterns or the architectural approaches.

In the next chapter, we will discuss the process of publishing apps on the Apple App Store as well as an analysis of the Apple design guidelines and App Store Review Guidelines.

Multiple choice questions

1. **Traditionally, Apple supports which Architecture Implementation?**
    a. MVP
    b. MVC
    c. MVVM
    d. Clean

2. **App state and Reducer are used in _____.**
    a. Redux
    b. MVC
    c. MVP
    d. Clean

3. **Which patterns notify the object when its state changes?**
    a. Observer pattern
    b. State pattern
    c. Mediator pattern
    d. Template pattern

4. **How many layers are contained in VIPER Architecture?**
    a. 4
    b. 5
    c. 6
    d. 8

5. **Which architecture is used mostly in mobile app programming?**
    a. MVP
    b. MVC
    c. MVVM
    d. None of the above

Answers

1. b
2. a
3. a
4. b
5. c

CHAPTER 15

Publish iOS App on the App Store

Introduction

When your app is completely ready with all the required features, the next most important step is to publish the app on the App store so that everyone can download your app from the app store. But Apple has some guidelines and restrictions to enhance the user experience. In this chapter, we will discuss those guidelines and learn the step-by-step process to upload your app. Uploading an app to the Apple app store will cost you a yearly fee for an Apple developer account.

Structure

In this chapter, we will cover the following topics:

- Prepare app for App Store upload
- Prepare App Store Connect for app submission
- TestFlight
- XCode Cloud
- Manage Apple review rejections

Objectives

After studying this chapter, you will be able to upload the apps on the app store and communicate to the Apple team for the app rejections and handle the Apple developer account and App Store Connect as per user access basis.

Prepare app for App Store Upload

There is some compliance that needs to be updated in the app with the help of IDE XCode. If you complete the following steps, there will be no issue at the time of app submissions:

1. **Launch image:**

   You can use the **LaunchScreen.storyboard** file for the **Launch** screen and design for your app branding as per your requirements. Here, you can experiment with your app logo, app name, or some tag line for branding and communication which will be the first impression for your app users, as shown in *figure 15.1* as follows:

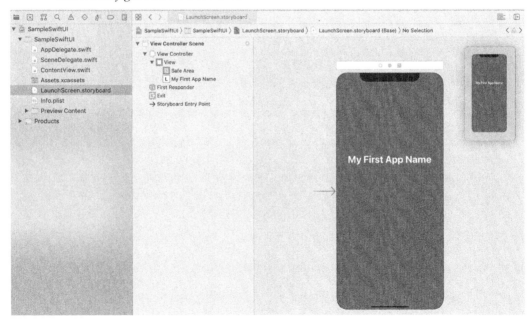

Figure 15.1: Launch Image

Also, you need to add this screen name in the app target settings, as shown in *figure 15.2*, as follows:

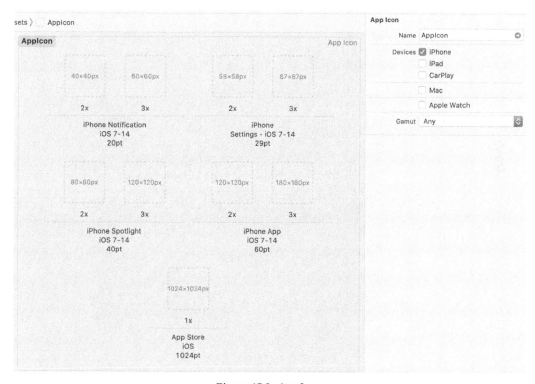

Figure 15.2: *App Icon and Launch Image Settings*

2. **App icons:**

First, you must take a decision on an app that is for an iPhone only or will support the iPad responsive designs too. You may use a Mac software **Prepo** (which can be installed from the Mac app store), which will help you generate all the app icons for your app. In **image.assets**, the **AppIcons** image set is already there to fill with the different sizes of icons, as shown in *figure 15.3* as follows:

Figure 15.3: *App Icons*

After that, you can check the other app information, like whether the version number is synced with the app store, build number, portrait, and landscape modes, etc.

Prepare build for App Store

If you want to submit your apps to the Apple App Store, you must be enrolled in the Apple Developer Program which costs you around 99$ for one year of access. After successfully joining this program, you can log into your Apple developer account via developer.apple.com/account. Now, you will be able to access the section **Certificates, Identifier, and Profiles**.

Create distribution certificate

We need to generate an app store certificate from the developer which requires a private key certificate from your Mac system as the input. To create, you need to open a Mac system software keychain access and request a certificate from a certificate authority from the certificate assistant, as shown in *figure 15.4*, as follows:

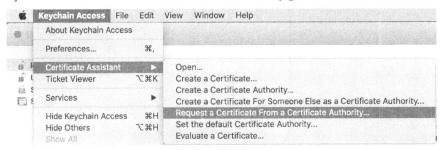

Figure 15.4: *Request a Certificate from Certificate Authority*

Requesting a certificate from Keychain Access will open up a window for the certificate information such as email and common name. After completing these details, you should select the **Save To Disk** option which will save a certificate on your local computer in the certificate (with file extension **cer**) format, as shown in *figure 15.5*, as follows:

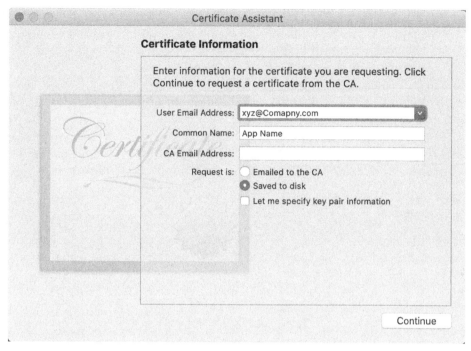

Figure 15.5: Certificate Assistant

We can proceed now to create a new certificate via selecting the certificate type App Store Distribution, as well as by selecting the private keychain certificate which we generated earlier. This will generate your App Store Distribution Certificate which can be used for any App Store Signed app required to be uploaded on your developer account. After successful creation of the distribution certificate, you will be able to view, edit, and delete it from the certificate list, as shown in *figure 15.6* as follows:

 Developer

Certificates, Identifiers & Profiles

Certificates

Identifiers

Devices

Profiles

Certificates ⊕

NAME ∧	TYPE	PLATFORM
~~	Distribution	All

Figure 15.6: App Distribution Certificate

Register an app identifier

Next, you will create an identifier that must be unique for every new app on the App Store. When you create a new identifier in the Identifiers section of the developer portal, this will open up a window to further select the option of App ID. To enable your app to use accessible services and identify your app in a provisioning profile, you must first register an App ID. When you establish an App ID, you have the option of enabling the app services or changing these settings afterwards. When you move forward and continue, in the final section, you will get the option for **Description** and **App ID Prefix**, as shown in *figure 15.7*, as follows:

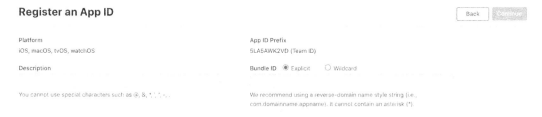

Figure 15.7: Register an App ID

In the description, you cannot use special characters, such as @, &, *, ', ", -, . For App ID, Apple suggests that you use a reverse-domain name style string like, **com. domain name.appname**. It cannot have an asterisk (*) in it, although you are free to use any unique combination.

Create distribution profile

Apple Distribution Profile is a signed document specific to a single app that can be used to make the signed app builds for the app store deployments. You can select the Profile section on the developer account and start creating a new profile for your app, as shown in *figure 15.8*, as follows:

Figure 15.8: App Store Distribution Profile

In the first step of the profile creation, you can select the App Store and proceed further for the app ID selection for this profile. You can select the app ID which we created earlier. In the final step of this process, there will be a list of distribution certificates and you can select one which you created from your own Mac system. This will finally create your app distribution profile.

Create app build for App Store

When the whole process of creating a certificate and profile gets completed, you need to download both the files and install them via double clicking. For the confirmation, you can check Keychain Access to know whether the certificate and profile get installed or not. To create app build, open your iOS app in XCode and select the section **Signing and Capabilities** from the application configurations, as shown in *figure 15.9*, as follows:

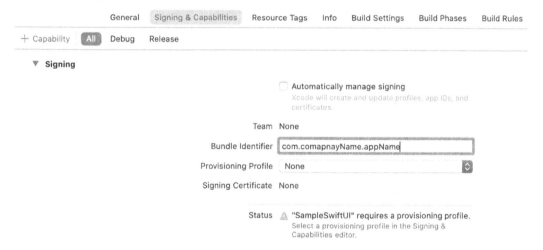

Figure 15.9: XCode Build Signing

The app identifier, which we made on the developer account, must be the same as the bundle identifier of the app; then you can select the installed Provisioning Profile from the drop-down list provided, which will auto select the distribution certificate. These actions will remove the warning related to the provisioning profile. Sometimes, there might be issues in selecting the correct profile; in such cases, you must open the signing configuration in the build setting section to select those certificates in the release and debug fields. In the XCode, select the device field; you need to select **Any iOS Device** to generate a generic iOS build that can run on all types of iOS devices.

Further, from the product menu option, select **Archive**, which will start the process of making the app build, as shown in *figure 15.10* as follows:

Figure 15.10: XCode Build Archiving

After successfully building an app, XCode will open App Organizer and there you can locate the app build. After the selection of the build, app distribution can be started. Either you can upload that build directly from XCode or you can just export that build and upload from the Transporter Mac app provided by Apple specifically for the app upload. Both the options will require the Apple developer login credentials from which you joined the Apple Developer Program to proceed further. Now, you can see the app processing in the **TestFlight** section of the App Store Connect.

Prepare App Store connect for app submission

To upload an app on the Apple app store, you must enroll in Apple Developer Program either as an individual or as an organization. If you don't have the necessary documents required for the organization account program, you can continue as an individual developer program. When you log in with the admin role in the developer account, you will see multiple options, such as my apps, app analytics, sales and trends, payments and financial reports, user and access, agreements, tax, and banking, as shown in *figure 15.11* as follows:

App Store Connect

News

Tax Category Setting Now Available in App Store Connect

You can now assign tax categories to your apps and in-app purchases to be used in all territories where Apple administers tax on behalf of developers. If you choose not to make any changes, the App Store software category will be assigned at the same tax rate used today. **Learn More**

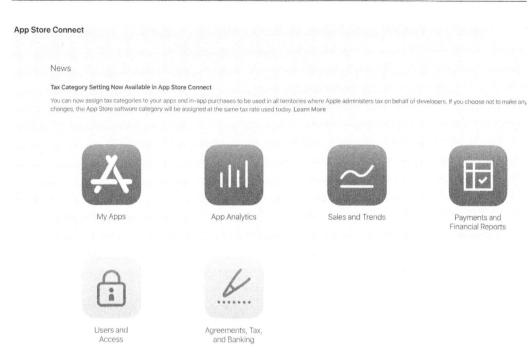

My Apps   App Analytics   Sales and Trends   Payments and Financial Reports

Users and Access   Agreements, Tax, and Banking

Figure 15.11: *App Store Connect Dashboard*

Further, you need to add a new app in the section My Apps which will show a detailed form to fill with some initial details of your app, as shown in *figure 15.12* as follows:

Figure 15.12: *New App Create on App Store Connect*

The new application registration asks for several information regarding the app, which you are publishing on the Apple store; these are discussed in detail as follows:

- **Add Platform**: Apple provides mainly three platform options of apps while creating a new app. In our case, we want to upload a mobile iOS app, so we will select the iOS option.

- **Primary Language**: Select your preferred language from the list. If you are not sure, you can select English as the default language.

- **Bundle ID**: First you need to create a new identifier for your app on the developer account section of Certificates, Identifiers, and Profiles. We will check and learn this section in the upcoming part of this chapter. If you already have a bundle ID, then you can select that.

- **SKU**: This is just a unique identifier used for your app and will not be shown in the app store. So, you can provide as you like.

- **User Access**: Mostly, every app is built and uploaded on the App store targeting full access to the users and not limited to specific users.

Users and access

When you join the Apple Developer Program, you are automatically assigned as the Account Holder for your membership. When you're enrolled as an organization, you may expand your team by adding more members with different roles, as shown in *figure 15.13*, as follows:

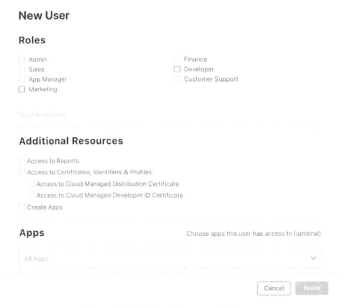

Figure 15.13: App Users and Access

Across the Apple Developer website and App Store Connect, each company has a single team with a single set of roles. App Store Connect is where the users and roles are managed. An App Store Connect user is represented by the user's resource. The users can be changed or deleted, but they cannot be added directly. Create a user invitation to add the users. When the user accepts the invitation, App Store Connect adds them to your team.

My Apps

In 40 languages, you may add your app's name, subtitle, keywords, description, and more. For each supported language, you may upload up to 10 screenshots and three optional app samples, and pick the order in which they display, as shown in *figure 15.14*, as follows:

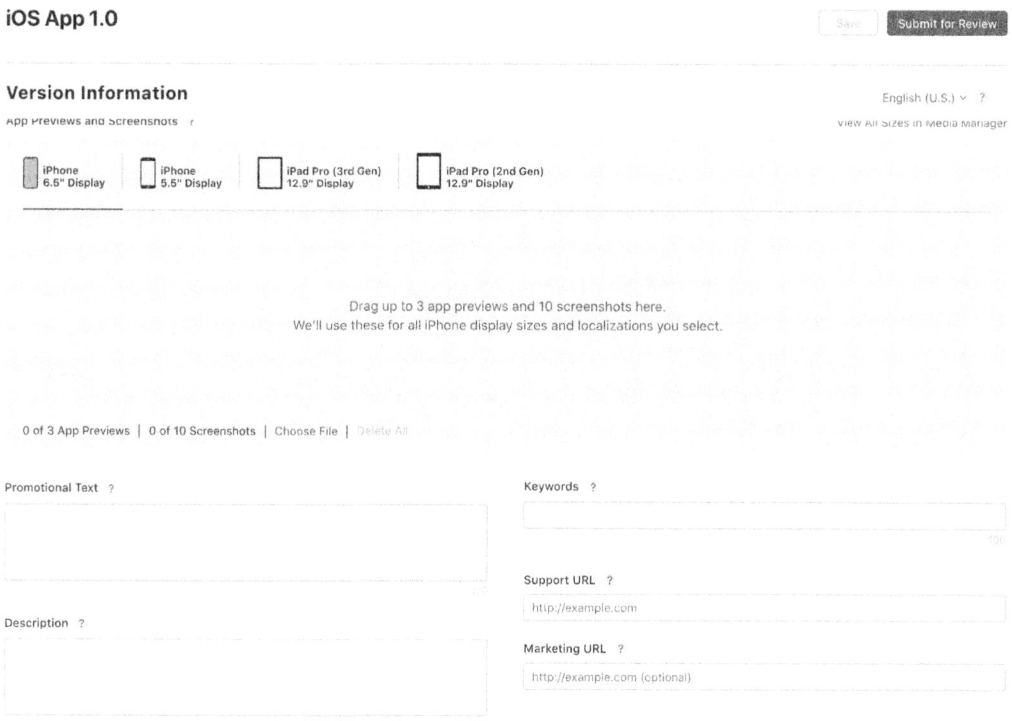

Figure 15.14: App Product Page

In case your app requires login credentials, that also needs to be provided with proper details in the notes section. When you finish updating all the information required in the app dashboard, you can select the Build section to select build, which you uploaded earlier for the app store (the one which is the latest and most stable), as shown in *figure 15.15*, as follows:

Figure 15.15: *App Product Build Section*

Other than the general app information and marketing policy links in the **Pricing and Availability** section of the app, the pricing needs to be updated, which can be either free or can be selected in terms of US dollar unit pricing. Further, for the location availability of the app, you may choose to select some specific country or continue with all the countries, as shown in *figure 15.16*, as follows:

Pricing and Availability   Save

Price Schedule ⊕   All Prices and Currencies

PRICE ?   START DATE ?   END DATE ?

| USD 0.0 (Free)   ˅ | Other Currencies   Sep 29, 2021   No End Date

Tax Category ? Edit

Category: **App Store software**

Pre-Orders

Pre-orders allow customers to order your app before its release date. Once your app is released for download, customers will be notified and your app will automatically download to their device. For paid apps, customers will be charged before download. Any app that hasn't been published to the App Store can be made available for pre-order. Learn More

    Make available for pre-order

Availability

◉ All countries or regions selected   Edit

○ Remove from sale

Figure 15.16: *App Product Pricing and Availability*

Now you can submit for review which will change the status of the app to **Waiting for Review**. Once the app is approved via Apple, the app will show the status as pending developer release (in case of manual release selection) or **Ready for Sale** (if you selected **Automatic Release**).

Update a new version of app

Once you are live on the App store, you might need to release new versions of the app due to either bug fixes or major feature releases. On the App Store Connect portal, you can add a new version of the live app under the section iOS App which will prompt you to enter a new version which you will submit. This will create a new version of the app prefilled with all the old details such as app description and links; you may update that if you want to, otherwise, leave it as it is. Similar to the earlier build section, you can select the build which must be properly tested before submitting it to the App store. There will be one new section called **What's New in this Version**, as shown in *figure 15.17*, as follows:

Figure 15.17: New Version Information

In the version information, you may describe the new feature implementation or bug fixes and performance improvements details, so that, before updating to the app, the users would be aware of what new features they will get with this version update. To better display, specific features, or content within your app, create many versions of your product page with varied promotional language, images, and app samples. Use a unique URL to direct the targeted viewers to a specific page and track the performance in App Analytics. Improve the app discovery on the App Store and offer high-quality app and in-app purchase experiences by leveraging the newest features.

TestFlight

Before publishing your apps on the App Store, TestFlight makes it simple to invite the consumers to test your apps and App Clips and get vital feedback. You may invite up to 10,000 testers by simply sending them an email or posting a public link. TestFlight supports iOS, iPad OS, tvOS, watchOS, and iMessage applications, as well as the automated upgrades to guarantee that the testers are constantly testing the most recent release available. Internally or externally, up to 100 applications may be evaluated at once, and several builds can be checked at the same time. After being uploaded, the builds are active for 90 days.

On the other side, in case you want to test an app, you first need to install the TestFlight App from the Apple App Store and then login with the Apple ID (in case you don't have one, you need to create it first; it's as simple as setting up of the Google or Yahoo mail accounts). Now you can share your Apple ID with whom you will be getting an invite for testing the apps. Once you receive an invite, you can open that invite link in the mobile mail client, so it will automatically be redirected to TestFlight App. Once you accept the invite and agree to the terms and conditions, you can install that app and give the feedback from the same `testflight` app. When you open the app details, you will find a section of the previous build with their version number that will help you compare or find the bugs, if it occurs in some specific version of the app.

Internal and external tester groups

Up to 100 people of your team with the roles of Account Holder, Admin, App Manager, Developer, or Marketing can be designated as beta testers. You may even make several groups and assign various builds to each one, depending on the aspects that each one should emphasize.

Invite up to 10,000 external testers through email or by activating and publishing a public link, which invites anybody to test your app. You can create a group of testers and assign them to the builds you want them to test. You may even make many groups and assign various builds to each one, based on the qualities you wish to emphasize. The initial build of your app of each version must be authorized by TestFlight App Review before the testing can begin. When you add a build to a group, it is automatically forwarded for review.

Invite testers

If you have a tester's email address, you can send them an invitation along with a link to download and test your app. An email may be an efficient approach to distribute the beta versions of your application with an existing group of external testers or specific persons you would like to ask to test. When you want to invite a tester to an external group, first select that external group from the menu of TestFlight Dashboard; then you can add the tester either via import of CSV, which would have all the tester's information or you can add via the **Add New Testers** section, as shown in *figure 15.18*, as follows:

Testers (0) ⊕

Add New Testers

Add Existing Testers

Import from CSV

Testers in this group will be notified when a new build is available and will have access to all builds added to this group.

Figure 15.18: Add New Testers

This selection will open up a form that will ask for First Name, Last Name, and Email ID of the invitee tester. You may even continue to add multiple testers at the same time, as shown in *figure 15.19*, as follows:

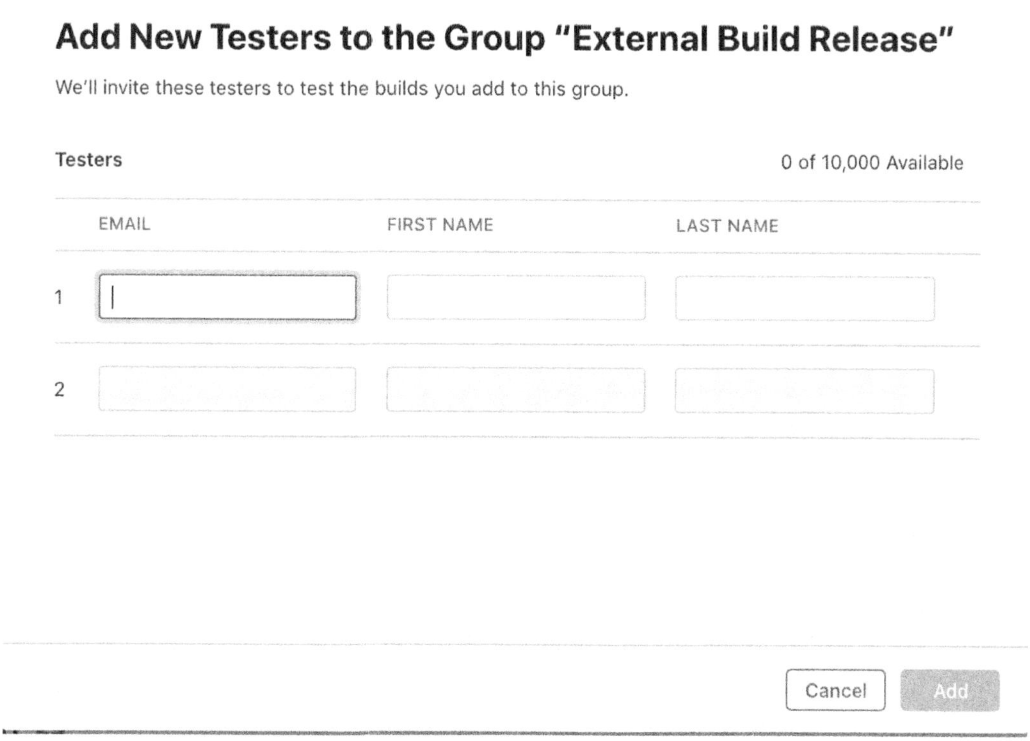

Add New Testers to the Group "External Build Release"

We'll invite these testers to test the builds you add to this group.

Testers   0 of 10,000 Available

	EMAIL	FIRST NAME	LAST NAME
1			
2			

Cancel   Add

Figure 15.19: Invite New Testers with Email

If you don't have an established network of testers, the public links are an efficient approach to connect with people who can test your app. There is no need to provide any contact information. Simply go to the TestFlight page for your app, choose an existing group, and select `Enable Public Link`, as shown in *figure 15.20*, as follows:

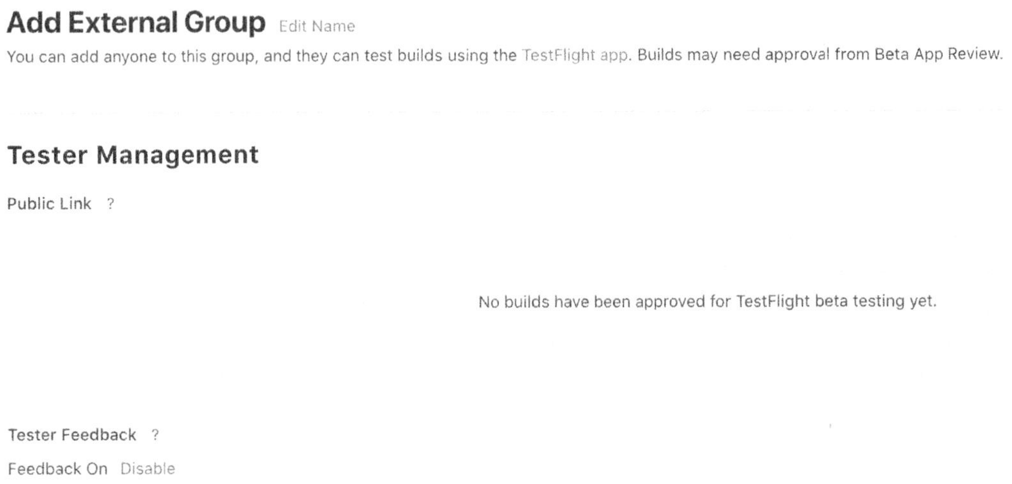

Add External Group Edit Name

You can add anyone to this group, and they can test builds using the TestFlight app. Builds may need approval from Beta App Review.

Tester Management

Public Link   ?

No builds have been approved for TestFlight beta testing yet.

Tester Feedback   ?

Feedback On   Disable

Figure 15.20: App Public Link for Testing

The URL may then be copied and shared on social media, messaging platforms, email campaigns, and other platforms. You may also use the public link to limit the number of testers who can join. If the group limit is reached or your public link is disabled, anybody trying to join your beta will receive a notice stating that your beta is no longer accepting new testers. Consider where you distribute your public link and when it would be appropriate to delete it to provide a positive user experience.

Test information

You will need to tell the testers what to test as well as any other pertinent information when sharing your app with the external testers. In App Store Connect, add these details to your app's Test Information page. You should also include an email address that you can check often, so that you can receive and respond to the tester comments. When sending your software to the internal testers, the test information is optional.

Beta app feedback

The testers may provide comments straight from your app using the TestFlight app for iOS and iPadOS by capturing a snapshot. They can also give more information about an app crash right after it happens. Go to your app's TestFlight page in App Store Connect and select `Crashes or Screenshots` in the **Feedback** section to see this feedback. The email address you specify in Test Information will get the feedback from the testers using iOS 12 or earlier, tvOS, or watchOS.

XCode Cloud

XCode Cloud is a continuous integration and delivery tool for the Apple developers that is incorporated into XCode. It brings together the cloud-based technologies that let you design the applications, run automated tests in parallel, distribute the apps to the testers, and see and manage the user feedback to speed up the creation and delivery of high-quality apps. Using the XCode Cloud workflows, you can develop your app on the cloud without the requirement for a separate build environment. Configure the workflows to fit your development process, or start with the built-in workflow and tweak it as your process progresses, as shown in *figure 15.21*, as follows:

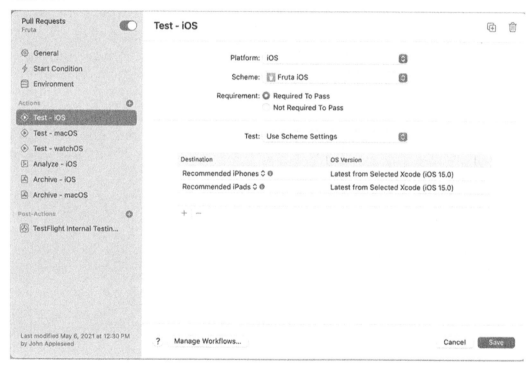

Figure 15.21: XCode Cloud

You may build every committed code change, and your entire team will be notified immediately if the change causes any problems, possibly saving days of lost effort before the fault is discovered by the end users. Configure XCode Cloud to test one or two device types for a rapid check on the health of your project or test a wider variety of device configurations for the edge situations less often. While you and your Mac continue to code, XCode Cloud allocates the resources in parallel to complete the testing work swiftly.

Manage Apple review rejections

All applications and app updates submitted to the App Store are reviewed by Apple to see if they are trustworthy, function as anticipated, respect user privacy, and include no objectionable content. Use the iOS app design standards while you develop and construct your app to make the approval process go as smoothly as possible.

iOS human interface design guidelines

A native iOS app has the best opportunity to deliver the content and design rich features to enable a better user experience. Here, we will discuss the design's expectations by Apple for quality and functionality, as follows:

- The text should be legible at all sizes, the icons must be precise and clear, the adornments should be modest and suitable, and the design must be driven by a firm focus on utility.

- People can comprehend and interact with content with the fluid motion and a clear, attractive interface that never competes with it. Translucency and blurring frequently hint at more, whereas the content generally cover the full screen.

- Different graphic layers and realistic motion help express hierarchy, energy, and comprehension. Touch and discoverability contribute to the enjoyment by allowing access to more functionality and material without losing context. As you move through the material, the transitions give you a sense of depth.

- By employing modest, unobtrusive visuals, conventional controls, and predictable behaviors, an app that assists the individuals with serious work may keep them focused. An immersive app, such as a game, on the other hand, might have a fascinating look that promises fun and excitement while promoting exploration.

- A consistent app uses the system-provided interface components, well-known iconography, standard text styles, and standardized language to adopt the recognized standards and conventions. The software includes the features and behaviors in ways that the users are accustomed to.

- To keep the individuals informed, the feedback recognizes the activities and displays the results. Every user action is accompanied by audible feedback from the built-in iOS applications. When tapped, the interactive components are temporarily illuminated, the progress indicators indicate the state of the long-running processes, and the animation and music assist in clarifying the outcomes of the actions.

- By keeping the interaction components familiar and predictable, confirming harmful acts, and making it easy to abort activities, even while they're already underway, an app may make the consumers feel in control.

- When an app's virtual items and actions are metaphors for familiar experiences, whether in the real or digital world, people learn faster. The metaphors function effectively in iOS because the users interact with the screen physically. They shift the views out of the way, so that the material beneath may be seen. They move the material around by dragging and swiping. The switches are toggled, the sliders are moved, and the picker values are scrolled through.

- Direct manipulation of the onscreen material fascinates viewers and aids comprehension. When the users spin the device or utilize the motions to change the display content, they are directly manipulating it. They can see the immediate, tangible effects of their activities when they use direct manipulation.

Avoid common app rejection

Before you submit your app, educate yourself with the technical, content, and design criteria used by Apple to assess all the apps listed in the App Store Review Guidelines. The scope of this chapter does not allow for a comprehensive discussion of all the guidelines. To assist you in properly preparing your applications before submitting them for review, let's see a compiled list of the most frequent concerns that lead the apps to be rejected.

Not enough features

It's possible that your app won't be accepted by the app store if it doesn't have much functionality or content, or if it only pertains to a tiny niche market. Take a look at the applications in your category on the App Store before you start developing your app and think about how you can improve the user experience.

Incomplete information

In the App Evaluate Information area of App Store Connect, fill in all the information needed to review your app. Provide a valid demo account username and password if some functions require it. Include the specifications if there are any unique configurations to be made. Prepare to offer a demo video or the hardware if the features need a difficult-to-replicate setting or specialized gear. Please double-check that your contact information is accurate and up to date.

Requesting permissions

You should clearly and thoroughly state how your app will utilize the users or use the data when asking for permission to access it. The users will understand why your app is asking for access to their personal information. Let us take an example – if your app's code calls one or more APIs that access the sensitive user data, the app's **Info.plist** file should include an **infoPlistKey** with a user facing purpose string that explains why the data is needed. A purpose string is required for all the apps submitted to the App Store that access user data.

Crashes and bugs

You should only submit your app for evaluation after it is finished and ready to go live. Before submitting your app, be sure to properly test it on the devices running the most recent version and solve any issues. Bug fixes for the applications that are currently on the App Store but have minor guideline problems can be accepted as long as there are no legal issues.

Broken links and placeholder contents

All the links in your app must work. All apps must have a link to the user support with up-to-date contact information as well as a link to your privacy policy. Before sending your app in for evaluation, make sure that all the pictures and text are in place. Apps that are still in development and include placeholder content cannot be approved since they are not ready to be released.

Conclusion

Make sure that your app is ready for public release and your product page is optimized before submitting it for review. The App Store evaluates all the apps based on a set of technical, content, and design criteria. Get important input from the beta testers before completing your app for release. Use TestFlight to test your app on a smartphone and simply invite additional testers after uploading it to App Store Connect. In this chapter, we discussed the step-by-step processes of building an App Store app build with Certificates and profiles and the app product page process of submissions. Apple reviews every app very carefully, so the developers need to follow all the app store review and design guidelines very adequately such that there is no chance of rejection.

To ensure that your app looks excellent, you must identify and fix the UI issues before testing on a device. To offer the app's launch screen, the updates must use an XCode storyboard. The new apps for the iPhone must also support all the iPhone displays, and the new apps for the iPad must support all the iPad screens. The App Store is intended to provide the consumers with programs that operate in combination with the capabilities of their devices. When submitting a new app that uses cutting-edge technology, make sure that your information property list (**info. plist**) is compliant with any device requirements. In every technology, learning never ends and you always have an opportunity to learn advanced topics. You may continue to learn from the Apple WWDC sessions as well as from their developer documentation of iOS technologies.

Multiple choice questions

1. **When do we use What's New in this Version?**
   a. New App Upload
   b. New Version Upload
   c. When creating App Product Page for the first time
   d. None of the above

2. **The internal tester's limit in App Store Connect is _____.**
   a. 10
   b. 20
   c. 30
   d. 40

3. **The external tester's limit in App Store Connect is _____.**
   a. 1000
   b. 5000
   c. 10000
   d. 12000

4. **XCode Cloud is used for _____.**
   a. Making build in the cloud
   b. Uploading New Builds
   c. Managing Rejections of the App
   d. None of the above

5. **Transporter Mac App is used for _____.**
   a. Making build in the cloud
   b. Uploading New Builds
   c. Managing Rejections of the App
   d. None of the above

Answers

1. b
2. c
3. c
4. a
5. b

Index

Symbols

3D touch interactions 192

  UIPreviewInteraction 192, 193

A

actions, simulator

  device rotation 12

  device shake 12

  GPS, simulating 12

Alamofire 252

  Alamofire headers 253

  Alamofire Image 252, 254, 255

  Alamofire Network Activity
    Indicator 252, 256

  Alamofire request 253, 254

  Alamofire response handling 254

  API encoding 252

  ImageDownloader class 255

  URL encoding 253

animation views 123

API encoding 252

app build, preparing for App Store

  app build, creating 303, 304

  app identifier, registering 302

  distribution certificate, creating 300,
    301

  distribution profile, creating 302, 303

app bundle container 157

App file manager 159

  AppFileManipulation protocol 162-
    165

  AppFileStatusChecking protocol 159-
    161

  AppFileSystemMetaData protocol 161

  using 172

AppFileManipulation protocol

file, copying 165

file, deleting 170

file extension, changing 169, 170

file list, getting 171, 172

file, saving 170

file, writing 165

AppFileSystemMetaData protocol

file attributes, obtaining at given
path 161, 162

files, listing from directory 161

Apple review rejections

iOS human interface design guidelines
314, 315

managing 314

Application Programming Interface
(API) 246

App life cycle 82, 83

UIApplicationDelegate, launching
with 83

UISceneDelegate, launching with 84

App Location Manager 197

activity type 198

allow background location 199, 200

current user location, obtaining 202

delegate methods 203

desired accuracy 198

distance filter 198

location enabled, checking 200, 201

location tracking, starting 201

location tracking, stopping 202

push location updates 198

setting up 197

significant location change 204

App media permissions 214, 215

editing, enabling 217

option for selecting camera and
gallery, adding 215-217

source types 218

app, preparing for App Store upload

app icons 299

image launch 298

App Store Connect, for app submission

beta app feedback 312

internal and external tester groups 310

My Apps 307, 308

preparing 304, 305

testers, inviting 310-312

TestFlight 309, 310

test information 312

users and access, configuring 306, 307

version update 309

App Transport Security (ATS) 261

architecture views 124

arithmetic operators 22

array, Swift 31, 32

assignment operators 22

Assistant editor 10

Automatic retain Count (ARC) 87

B

basic type annotations, Swift 5.5

Bool 21

Character 21

Double 21

Float 21

Int Or UInt 21

String 21

Tuples 21

Behavioral design patterns 277
  Iterator pattern 284, 285
  Mediator pattern 282
  Observer pattern 281
  State pattern 279
  Template pattern 277, 278
Binary 22

C
Camera app
  camera preview, displaying 222
  capture session, configuring 221
  features, implementing 221
  photo, capturing 223-225
  rear and front cameras, switching 222
Characters 30
  concating strings 30
  String interpolation 30
classes
  features 50
  identity operator 50, 51
  reference type 50
  versus structures 49
CLLocationManager 196
  location permissions, adding 196
closed range operators 25
closure expression 42
closures 41
  autoclosures 43
  trailing closures 42
collection types, Swift 31
  arrays 31, 32
  dictionaries 33
  mutability of collections 31

  sets 32
common app rejection
  preventing 315
common app rejection, frequent
    concerns
  broken links 316
  crashes and bug fixes 316
  incomplete information 315
  not enough features 315
  permission request 316
  placeholder contents 316
comparison operators 23
compound assignment operator 22
conditional statements
  if:else 36, 37
  switch statements 37
connection reachability 249-252
container views
  group 114
  GroupBox 114
  list 113
  section 115
Content Types, RESTful APIs
  Binary file 246
  JSON 246
  Plain text 246
  XML/XSLT 246
control flow statements, Swift
  for-in loops 34
  while loops 35
control transfer statements 37, 38
  break 38
  continue 38
  early exit 39

fallthrough 39

CoreData 145

versus SQLite 146

CoreData schema

creating 146-149

data, deleting 151

data, inserting 149, 150

data, retrieving 150

Core Location Errors

types 208

Core ML 228

converters 228

Create ML 230, 231

MLActionClassifier 232

MLActivityClassifier 232

MLImageClassifier 231

MLSoundClassifier 232

MLTextClassifier 231, 232

model accuracy, improving 232, 233

model file, updating to model
packages 229, 230

model packages, saving 229

Create ML 230, 231

Creational design patterns 264

Abstract Factory pattern 267

Builder pattern 268

Factory pattern 266

Prototype pattern 265

Singleton Design pattern 269

current location, on map

core location errors 208

displaying 204

location, converting into place
mark address 206

location with Apple Maps 205, 206

location with Google Maps 204, 205

place address, converting to location
coordinates 207

region monitoring 209

region notification, handling 209, 210

custom gesture recognizer

cancellation, handling 187

gesture recognizer state machine 187

implementing 187

D

data container 157

document directory 157

file sharing, enabling in document
directory 157, 158

library, application support directory
158

library, cache 158

temp directory 159

default project setup

AppDelegate 8

Assets 9

Info.plist 9

Main.storyboard 9

SceneDelegate 8

ViewController 9

Deinitializers 60

delegate 74

delegate methods, Location Manager

didchangeAuthorization 203

didFailWithError 203

didUpdateLocations 203

delegate methods,
UIVideoEditorController
  didFailWithError 220
  didSaveEditedVideoToPath 220
design patterns, iOS
  Behavioral patterns 277
  Creational patterns 264
  Structural patterns 270
dictionary, Swift 33
discrete gesture recognizers
  implementing 188, 189
  touch events 189-192

E
enumerations 48
  recursive enumeration 49
error handling 65
  do-catch using 66
  error propagation, disabling 67
  errors, throwing 65
  optional values, converting to 66, 67
  throwing function, using 66
extensions 69, 70
  computed properties 70
  initializers 70, 71
  methods 71
  subscripts 71

F
file systems in iOS 156
  app bundle container 157
  data container 157
  iCloud container 159
for-in loop 34
functions, Swift 39

  calling 40
  defining 40
  function parameters 40
  nested functions 41
  return values 40

G
geofencing 209

H
half-open range operator 25
Hover gesture recognizer 186
HStacks 110
HTTP methods
  CONNECT 247
  DELETE 247
  GET 247
  HEAD 247
  OPTIONS 247
  POST 247
  PUT 247
  TRACE 247
HTTP structure, REST 246, 247
  HTTP body 249
  HTTP headers 248
  request methods 247

I
iCloud container 159
inheritance 57
  base class 57
  overriding 58, 59
  subclassing 57, 58
initialization 59
  customizing 60

initializers 59

Interface Builder (IB) 80

  app-based life-cycle events,
    responding
    to 85, 86

  App life cycle 82, 83

  Segue, using 82

  Storyboard 80, 81

iOS

  design patterns 264

  file systems 156

  human interface design
    guidelines 314, 315

  Redux architecture 292

  ReSwift 292-294

K

key features, SwiftUI

  accessibility 106

  dark mode 106

  declarative syntax 106

  design tools 106

  dynamic type 106

  localization 106

  native 106

key-value coding (KVC) 257

key-value observing (KVO) 257

L

Live Photos 221

location permissions,
    CLLocationManager

  always use 197

  when using app 196

logical operators 26

  combining 28

logical AND operator 27

logical NOT operator 26

logical OR operator 27

Long-press gesture recognizer 183, 184

M

methods

  instance methods 56

  type methods 56, 57

MLActionClassifier 232

MLActivityClassifier 232

MLImageClassifier 231

MLSoundClassifier 232

MLTextClassifier 231, 232

mobile app architectures 286, 287

  business layer 288

  case studies 285, 286

  data layer 288

  presentation layer 288

  types 288, 289

mobile app architectures, types

  Model View Controller 289

  Model View Presenter 290

  Model View View-Model 290

  VIPER Clean architecture 291

Model View Controller 289

Model View Presenter 290

Model View View-Model 290

N

Natural Language (NL) framework 235

  language identification in text 236

  named identity recognition 238

  parts of speech tagging 237

  text tokenizing 236, 237

Nested Types 69

Nil:Coalescing operator 24

O

Object Relational Mapping (ORM) 146

one-sided range operator 26

optional chaining 64

  importance 64

override keyword 88

P

Pan gesture recognizer 181-183

Pinch gesture recognizer 179, 180

Playground functions, in Xcode

  console 14

  editor 14

  output 14

  status bar 14

presentation views 127

  ActionSheet view 128-130

  action view 128

  Action view 127

press-and-hold gestures 184

properties 51

  computed properties 51

  global variables 54

  local variables 54

  read-only computed property 51

  stored properties 51

  type properties 54, 55

Property list (plist) 135, 136

  data, writing to 137

  reading, with Swift 136, 137

property observers 52

property wrappers 53

protocols 72

  as types 74

  class only protocols 75

  delegations 74, 75

  inheritance 75

  initializer requirements 73

  method requirement 72, 73

  property requirement 72

R

range operators 25, 26

  closed range operators 25

  half-open range operator 25

Redux architecture, in iOS 292

REST architecture 246

  HTTP structure 246, 247

  information content type 246

RESTful APIs

  Content Types 246

REST (REpresentational State Transfer) 246

ReSwift, in iOS 292-294

Rotation gesture recognizer 185

S

self keyword

  versus super keyword 88

sets, Swift 32

short-circuit evaluation 24

simulator 11

  actions, on real devices 12

sound analysis 241

  audio file sound classification 241, 242

Speech framework 239

  live audio speech recognition 240, 241

speech recognition permissions 239

split view 125-127

SQLite

  database, connecting to 139

  database, creating 139

  features 138

  table, creating 139-141

  versus CoreData 146

  working with, in Swift 138, 139

standard gestures 176

Storyboard 80

  View Controller Scene 81, 82

string literals 28

  empty strings 29

  special characters 29

  string mutability 29

Structural design patterns 270

  Adapter 272, 273

  Bridge 274

  Decorator 275

  Facade Design 270, 271

Swift 19

  conditional statements 36

  constant 20, 21

  control flow statements 34

  features 20

  functions 39

  methods 56

  syntax 20

  type inference 20

  types 20, 21

  type-safe language 20

  variable 20, 21

Swift 5.5

  basic type annotations 21

Swift Generics 75, 76

  generic type, extending 76, 77

  type parameters 76

  type parameters, naming 76

Swift operators 22

  arithmetic operator 22

  assignment operator 22

  comparison operator 23

  compound assignment operator 22

  logical operator 26

  Nil:Coalescing operator 24

  range operator 25

  ternary conditional operator 23, 24

SwiftUI

  container views 113

  declarative framework 107

  features 106

  form and navigation, working with 116-118

  getting started with 108

  Grids, with ScrollView 111-113

  View protocol 107

SwiftUI drawing and animations 118, 119

  curved shapes, drawing 121-123

  custom shapes, drawing with path 120, 121

SwiftUI elements 109

  PreviewProvider protocol 109

  views, combining with stacks 109

Swipe gesture recognizer 180, 181

T

table, in SQLite

creating 139-141

data, deleting 144

data, inserting 141, 142

data, reading 142-144

data, retrieving 142-144

tab view 124, 125

Tap gesture recognizer 178, 179

ternary conditional operator 23, 24

TestFlight app 309, 310

Tinary 22

Transport Layer Security (TLS) 261

type casting 67

Any 69

Any object 69

downcasting 68

type checker operator, using 68

type properties 54

querying 55

setting 55

U

UIButton 91

UICollectionView 98

cell 98

data source 99

delegate 99

UI components 88

window object 89

UI control 90

adding, on Storyboard View
Controller 89

first responder 90

UIDatePicker 94, 95

UI element

connecting, to Swift code 90

UIIMagePickerController 218, 219

live photos, working with 219

movies, working with 219

UIImageView 95

UIKit gesture

handling 176-178

Hover gesture recognizer 186

Long-press gesture recognizer 183, 184

Pan gesture recognizer 181-183

Pinch gesture recognizer 179, 180

Rotation gesture recognizer 185

Swipe gesture recognizer 180, 181

Tap gesture recognizer 178

UILabel 91

UINavigationBar 102

UINavigationController 101

UIPageControl 94

UIPickerView 94

UIProgressView 94

UISegmentController 94

UISlider 93

UIStepper 93, 94

UISwitch 93

UITabBar 95

UITableView 96, 97

UITextField 92

UITextView 92

UIVideoEditorController 219

delegate methods 220

Unary 22

URL encoding 253

URLSession 256

App Transport Security (ATS) 261

operation, adding in operation queue
    257

operation queue 257

tasks, types 259

types 258

URLSessionConfiguration 258

URLSessionTaskDelegate 259, 260

UserDefaults 134, 135

Utility area

    Attribute Inspector 10

    File Inspector 10

    Quick Help Inspector 10

    Size Inspector 10

V

View controller 86

View controller life cycle 86

    deinit 87

    didReceiveMemoryWarning 87

    init 86

    loadView 86

    viewDidAppear 87

    viewDidDisappear 87

    viewDidLayoutSubviews 87

    viewDidLoad 86

    viewWillAppear 86

    viewWillDisappear 87

    viewWillLayoutSubviews 87

    viewWillTransition 87

VIPER Clean architecture 291

    Interactor 291

    Model or Entities 291

    Presenter 291

    Router 291

View Controller 291

Vision framework 233

    object detection, in still images 233

    object detection results 235

    using 235

    vision request, creating 234

VStacks 109

W

while loop 35

    repeat:while 35

    while 35

X

xcarchives 15

Xcode 2

    downloading 2

    installing 3, 4

XCode Cloud 313

Xcode IDE 2

    requisites 2

Xcode iOS project

    building 10

    running 10

    running, in simulator 11, 12

    running, on device 12, 13

Xcode Organizer

    Archives section 15

    Crashes 15

    energy 15

    metrics 15

Xcode Playground

    coding, with 13, 14

Xcode project

    Bundle Identifier 5

Checkboxes 6
Language 5
Life Cycle 5
Organization Identifier 5
Organization Name 5
Product Name 4
Team 4
User Interface 5
Xcode project configuration
Assistant editor 10
default project setup 8
file, adding 9
file, creating 9
performing 7, 8

Storyboard UI, building 10
Utility area 10
Xcode user interface 6
Debug area 6
Editor area 6
Inspector area 6
Navigation area 6
ToolBar 6
Windows pan bar 6
Xcode issue navigator 7
Xcode search navigator 6, 7

Z
ZStack 110

Printed in Great Britain
by Amazon

78471456R00203